UDDI, SOAP, and WSDL:

The Web Services Specification Reference Book

AARON E. WALSH, EDITOR

Prentice Hall PTR
Upper Saddle River, NJ 07458
www.phptr.com

ISBN 0-13-085726-2

Library of Congress Cataloging-in-Publication Data

UDDI, SOAP, and WSDL : the Web services specification reference book / Aaron E. Walsh, editor.
    p. cm.
  ISBN 0-13-085726-2
  1. Web site development--Handbooks, manuals, etc. 2. Internet
Programming--Handbooks, manuals, etc. 3. Object oriented
Programming--Handbooks, manuals, etc. I. Title: Universal description,
discovery, and integration, Simple object oriented protocol, and Web
services description language. II. Walsh, Aaron E.
  TK5105.888.U33 2002
  005.2'76--dc21   2002020196

Production Supervision: *Donna Cullen-Dolce*
Acquisitions Editor: *Tim Moore*
Editorial Assistant: *Allyson Kloss*
Manufacturing Buyer: *Maura Zaldivar*
Cover Design: *Talar Boorujy*
Cover Design Director: *Jerry Votta*
Marketing Manager: *Debby van Dijk*

 Preface and Introduction © 2002 by Prentice Hall PTR
A division of Pearson Education, Inc.
Upper Saddle River, NJ 07458

Universal Description, Discovery and Integration (UDDI) 1.0:

Copyright © 2000 by Ariba, Inc., International Business Machines Corporation, and Microsoft Corporation. All Rights Reserved.

These documents are provided by the companies named above ("Licensors") under the following license. By using and/or copying this document, or the document from which this statement is linked, you (the licensee) agree that you have read, understood, and will comply with the following terms and conditions:

Permission to use, copy, and distribute the contents of this document, or the document from which this statement is linked, in any medium for any purpose and without fee or royalty under copyrights is hereby granted, provided that you include the following on ALL copies of the document, or portions thereof, that you use:

1. A link to the original document.
2. An attribution statement : "Copyright © 2000 by Ariba, Inc., International Business Machines Corporation, and Microsoft Corporation. All Rights Reserved."

If the Licensors own any patents or patent applications which that may be required for implementing and using the specifications contained in the document in products that comply with the specifications, upon written request, a non-exclusive license under such patents shall be granted on reasonable and non-discriminatory terms.

THIS DOCUMENT IS PROVIDED "AS IS," AND LICENSORS MAKE NO REPRESENTATIONS OR WARRANTIES, EXPRESS OR IMPLIED, INCLUDING, BUT NOT LIMITED TO, WARRANTIES OF MERCHANTABILITY, FITNESS FOR A PARTICULAR PURPOSE, NON-INFRINGEMENT, OR TITLE; THAT THE CONTENTS OF THE DOCUMENT ARE SUITABLE FOR ANY PURPOSE; NOR THAT THE IMPLEMENTATION OF SUCH CONTENTS WILL NOT INFRINGE ANY THIRD PARTY PATENTS, COPYRIGHTS, TRADEMARKS OR OTHER RIGHTS.

LICENSORS WILL NOT BE LIABLE FOR ANY DIRECT, INDIRECT, SPECIAL OR CONSEQUENTIAL DAMAGES ARISING OUT OF ANY USE OF THE DOCUMENT OR THE PERFORMANCE OR IMPLEMENTATION OF THE CONTENTS THEREOF.

(Copyright continues on next page)

Simple Object Access Protocol (SOAP) 1.1:
Copyright © 2000 by DevelopMentor, International Business Machines Corporation, Lotus Development Corporation, Microsoft, UserLand Software.
All Rights Reserved.

Web Services Description Language (WSDL) 1.1:
Copyright © 2001 by Ariba, International Business Machines Corporation, Microsoft. All rights reserved.

THESE DOCUMENTS ARE PROVIDED "AS IS," AND COPYRIGHT HOLDERS MAKE NO REPRE-
SENTATIONS OR WARRANTIES, EXPRESS OR IMPLIED, INCLUDING, BUT NOT LIMITED TO,
WARRANTIES OF THE MERCHANTABILITY, FITNESS FOR A PARTICUALR PURPOSE, NON-
INFRINGEMENT, OR TITLE; THAT THE CONTENTS OF THE DOCUMENT ARE SUITABLE FOR
ANY PURPOSE; NOR THAT THE IMPLEMENTATION OF SUCH CONTENTS WILL NOT IN-
FRINGE ANY THIRD PARTY PATENTS, COPYRIGHTS, TRADEMARKS OR OTHER RIGHTS.

COPYRIGHT HOLDERS WILL NOT BE LIABLE FOR ANY DIRECT, INDIRECT, SPECIAL OR CON-
SEQUENTIAL DAMAGES ARISING OUT OF ANY USE OF THE DOCUMENT OR THE PERFOR-
MANCE OR IMPLEMENTATION OF THE CONTENTS THEREOF.

The name and trademarks of copyright holders may NOT be used in advertising or publicity pertaining to this document or its contents without specific, written prior permission. Title to copyright in
this document will at all times remain with copyright holders.

UDDI logo used by permission.

Prentice Hall books are widely used by corporations and government agencies for training, marketing, and resale.

The publisher offers discounts on this book when ordered in bulk quantities.
For more information, contact: Corporate Sales Department, Phone: 800-382-3419; Fax: 201-236-7141;
E-mail: corpsales@prenhall.com; or write: Prentice Hall PTR, Corp. Sales Dept., One Lake Street,
Upper Saddle River, NJ 07458.

Printed in the United States of America

ISBN 0-13-085726-2

Pearson Education LTD.
Pearson Education Australia PTY, Limited
Pearson Education Singapore, Pte. Ltd.
Pearson Education North Asia Ltd.
Pearson Education Canada, Ltd.
Pearson Educación de Mexico, S.A. de C.V.
Pearson Education—Japan
Pearson Education Malaysia, Pte. Ltd.

Contents

v

CHAPTER 5
UDDI XML Schema 1.0 (1999)

CHAPTER 6
UDDI XML Schema 1.0 (2001)

Part 2 Simple Object Access
Protocol (SOAP) 1.1

CHAPTER 7
W3C Simple Object Access Protocol (SOAP) 1.1

CHAPTER 12
WSDL 1.1   External Hyperlinks   **303**

Preface

.

Welcome to the future of Internet-based application development and deployment. This book contains the official technical specifications for a promising triumvirate of technologies that enable Web services. Herein you'll find technical specifications for Universal Description, Discovery and Integration (UDDI) 1.0, Simple Object Access Protocol (SOAP) 1.1, and Web Services Description Language (WSDL) 1.1.

The UDDI documents in this book appear courtesy of the UDDI Community (UDDI.org), with thanks in particular to Tom Glover. As UDDI.org Program Manager, Tom helped guide the UDDI portion of this book through the publication production on behalf of the UDDI Community, an effort for which I am grateful. The SOAP and WSDL specifications, meanwhile, are taken directly from corresponding World Wide Web (W3C) Notes. Thanks to Janet Daly and Joseph M. Reagle, the W3C's SOAP and WSDL Notes appear alongside UDDI, which together comprise the three Web services technologies detailed in this book.

As this book went to print, the term "Web services" was sweeping through the Internet and Web development communities, carrying with it the promise of a new and improved way of conducting business over public and private communications networks. Generally speaking, *Web services* refer to loosely coupled software applications distributed across the Internet and/or World Wide Web. Unlike traditional distributed software applications, for which the distributed components are tightly bound to the application using them, Web services are entirely self-contained and self-describing. As such, a Web service is a fully encapsulated, modular unit of application logic that can be found and used by other applications without requiring an intimate knowledge of the inner working of the service.

Based on well-known open standards such as Extensible Markup Language (XML) and Hypertext Transfer Protocol (HTTP), Web services can be mixed and matched with other Web services as needed. This enables applications that use Web services to orchestrate them into a series of rich and increasingly complex transactions. A long-promised but only recently realized Holy Grail of computing, Web services usher in an era of truly componentized, reusable, and distributed software on a grand scale that we've not seen before today.

UDDI, SOAP, and WSDL are central to the emerging Web services paradigm. They are independent, yet inter-related technologies that are typically used together. UDDI provides an open, platform-independent framework for describing services, discovering businesses, and integrating services over the Internet. In addition, UDDI is an operational registry of available services that can be thought of as a modern-day "yellow pages" directory specifically for Web services.

Access to and from the UDDI registry typically takes place with SOAP, which is a lightweight XML-based protocol used to exchange information in a decentralized, distributed environment. WSDL, meanwhile, is an XML-based service description language that complements UDDI by providing a uniform mechanism for describing services and network protocol bindings.

Taken together, the UDDI, SOAP, and WSDL specifications detailed in this book provide a solid foundation upon which many legacy applications will be rebuilt, and countless new and as-of-yet unimagined software products will be built from the ground up. I hope that you find them as invaluable in your own Web services development efforts as I imagine they will be.

Aaron E. Walsh

Introduction

The Web services specifications in this book are organized into three distinct parts, one each for UDDI, SOAP, and WSDL. Following is a brief description of each part and the chapters they contain.

Part 1: Universal Description, Discovery and Integration (UDDI) 1.0

Part 1 covers UDDI version 1.0. UDDI is a platform-independent, open framework for describing services, discovering businesses, and integrating business services using the Internet, as well as an operational registry.

The first two chapters in this section are informational white papers produced by the UDDI Community, the organization responsible for the design and development of official UDDI specifications. Following these white papers are four chapters dedicated to the official UDDI 1.0 specification.

Chapter 1: UDDI Executive White Paper

As a high-level overview of UDDI, this chapter explains that UDDI is focused on sharing business information, making it easier for you to publish your preferred means of conducting business, find trading partners and have them find you, and interoperate with these trading partners over the Internet.

Note: This chapter is a white paper, not a formal part of the UDDI specification.

Chapter 2: UDDI Technical White Paper

Building on the high-level overview presented in Chapter 1, this chapter digs deeper into UDDI and its capabilities. Starting with the concept that UDDI is a specification for distributed Web-based information registries of Web services, and also a publicly accessible set of implementations of the specification that allow businesses to register information about the Web services they offer so that other businesses can find them, this chapter explains that Web services are the next step in the evolution of the Web itself. This chapter explains how UDDI registries are used to promote and discover distributed Web services, thereby allowing programmable elements to be placed on Web sites where others can access distributed behaviors.

Note: This chapter is a white paper, not a formal part of the UDDI specification.

Chapter 3: UDDI Programmer's API 1.0

This chapter describes the programming interface that is exposed by all instances of the UDDI registry. The programmatic interface provided for interacting with systems that follow the UDDI specifications makes use of XML and SOAP (a specification for using XML in simple message-based exchanges). The UDDI Programmer's API Specification defines approximately 30 SOAP messages that are used to perform inquiry and publishing functions against any UDDI-compliant business registry.

Chapter 4: UDDI Data Structure Reference 1.0

This document outlines the details of each XML structure associated with the approximately 30 SOAP messages described in Chapter 3 that are used to perform inquiry and publishing functions against any UDDI-compliant business registry. This chapter is co-requisite to the UDDI XML schema documents described in Chapters 5 and 6.

Chapter 5: UDDI XML Schema 1.0 (1999)

This chapter lists the complete UDDI XML Schema version 1.0 released in 1999. This schema complements the UDDI Data Structure Reference described in Chapter 4.

Chapter 6: UDDI XML Schema 1.0 (2001)

This chapter lists the complete UDDI XML Schema version 1.0 released in 2001. This schema complements the UDDI Data Structure Reference described in Chapter 4.

Part 2: Simple Object Access Protocol (SOAP) 1.1

Part 2 covers SOAP 1.1. SOAP is a lightweight protocol for exchanging information in a decentralized, distributed environment. It is an XML-based protocol that consists of three parts: an envelope that defines a framework for describing what is in a message and how to process it, a set of encoding rules for expressing instances of application-defined data types, and a convention for representing remote procedure calls and responses.

The first chapter (Chapter 7) is the SOAP 1.1 specification; the second chapter (Chapter 8) lists all external hyperlinks that appear in the SOAP 1.1 specification; the third chapter (Chapter 9) details the current SOAP 1.1 envelope schema; and the final chapter in this section (Chapter 10) details the current SOAP 1.1 envelope schema encoding.

Note: The SOAP schemas that appear in these chapters are based on schemas originally submitted to the World Wide Web Consortium (W3C) by the same companies that submitted the SOAP 1.1 specification; see http://www.w3.org/Submission/2000/05/ for the original schemas.

Chapter 7: SOAP 1.1 Specification (W3C Note 08 May 2000)

This chapter details the SOAP 1.1 specification in the form of a W3C Note that documents this submission by W3C members Ariba, Inc., Commerce One, Inc., Compaq Computer Corporation, DevelopMentor, Inc., Hewlett-Packard Company, International Business Machines Corporation, IONA Technologies, Lotus Development Corporation, Microsoft Corporation, SAP AG, and UserLand Software Inc.

Chapter 8: SOAP 1.1 External Hyperlinks

This chapter contains the external hyperlinks that appear in the text of the SOAP 1.1 specification in Chapter 7.

Chapter 9: SOAP 1.1 Envelope Schema

This chapter lists the SOAP 1.1 envelope schema referenced by the SOAP 1.1 specification in Chapter 7.

Note: The schema in this chapter is based on the schema submission found at http://www.w3.org/Submission/2000/05/.

Chapter 10: SOAP 1.1 Encoding Schema

This chapter lists the SOAP 1.1 encoding schema referenced by the SOAP 1.1 specification in Chapter 7.

Note: The schema in this chapter is based on the schema submission found at http://www.w3.org/Submission/2000/05/.

Part 3: Web Services Description Language (WSDL) 1.1

Part 3 covers WSDL 1.1. WSDL is an XML format for describing network services as a set of endpoints operating on messages containing either document-oriented or procedure-oriented information. The operations and messages are described abstractly, and then bound to a concrete network protocol and message format to define an endpoint. Related concrete endpoints are combined into abstract endpoints (services).

The first chapter in this section (Chapter 11) is the WSDL 1.1 specification, while the second chapter (Chapter 12) lists all external hyperlinks that appear in the WSDL 1.1 specification.

Chapter 11: WSDL 1.1 Specification (W3C Note 15 March 2001)

This chapter details the WSDL 1.1 specification in the form of a W3C Note that documents this submission by W3C members International Business Machines Corporation, Microsoft Corporation, Allaire, Ariba, Inc., BEA, Bowstreet, Commerce One, Compaq Computer Corporation, DataChannel, Epicentric, Fujitsu Limited, Hewlett-Packard Company, Intel, IONA Technologies, Jamcracker, Lotus Development Corporation, Oracle, Rogue Wave, SAP, TIBCO, VeriSign, Vitria, webMethods, XML Global Technologies, and XMLSolutions.

Chapter 12: WSDL 1.1 External Hyperlinks

This chapter contains the external hyperlinks that appear in the text of the WSDL 1.1 specification in Chapter 11.

PART
1

Universal Description, Discovery and Integration (UDDI) 1.0

CHAPTER
1

UDDI Executive White Paper
September 6, 2000

The New Trading Environment

With the explosive growth of B2B eCommerce, the Internet presents incredible value and reach for businesses of all sizes, providing opportunities to find new customers, streamline supply chains, provide new services, and secure unprecedented financial gain.

Organizations that have decisively moved their business online are already realizing significant economic and competitive gains: increased revenue, lowered costs, new customer relationships, innovative branding opportunities, and the creation of new lines of customer service.

Despite the outstanding growth of B2B eCommerce in the last few years, a major impediment has held back its enormous potential to open up trade worldwide not only to those already conducting B2B eCommerce, but also to businesses that are not yet players in the digital economy.

Most eCommerce-enabling applications and Web services currently in place take divergent paths to connecting buyers, suppliers, marketplaces, and service providers. Without large investments in technology infrastructure, businesses from a semiconductor manufacturer in Taiwan to a cabinetmaker in Athens to a specialized industrial engineering firm in New Delhi can transact Internet-based business only with the global trading partners they have discovered and, of those, only the ones using the same applications and Web services.

In order to fully open the doors to these existing and potential B2B players, truly successful eCommerce requires that businesses be able to discover each other, make their needs and capabilities known, and integrate services using each businesses' preferred technology, Web services, and commerce processes.

Challenges

Supply and demand alone does not control the flow of business when buyers and sellers are not connected. With all the myriad ways businesses use to reach their customers and partners with information about their products and Web services, and because global eCommerce participants have not yet agreed on one standard or backbone on which to communicate their services, finding and working with potential trading partners is severely limited.

Until now, there has been no central way to easily get information about what standards different companies support and no single point of access to all markets of opportunity, allowing them to easily connect with all possible target trading partners. Successful B2B eCommerce requires seamless access to information about trading partners and the ability to integrate with them.

This basic fundamental challenge is limiting the promise of business to business collaboration on the web, making it harder for buyers to get return on their eCommerce investment and for all B2B participants to easily add trading partners and services.

A supplier of ball bearings to large industrial customers—perhaps all of which are already online—can take its business to the Internet but not be able to transact with more than half of its current customer base because they're all using different applications and services to conduct Web-enabled business. Without major investments in technology infrastructure, the supplier may not be able to offer— even to its current customers—all the advantages of B2B eCommerce and may lose them to suppliers who can.

Solutions

Marketplaces, businesses, and directory providers are all attempting to solve these communication and transaction problems, and all are adopting distinct and divergent approaches centered on their own requirements. The result is a staggering diversity in approach, content, and architecture that is preventing the optimum utilization of B2B eCommerce by businesses of all sizes around the world.

The last few years have seen remarkable evolution in Web-based B2B eCommerce, electronic sales, online auctions, dynamic electronic marketplaces, and applications that process and route information. These comprise the essential foundation of B2B eCommerce infrastructure, ensuring an organization's ability to establish connectivity, put product or service information online, access and interact with a broad range of customers, process transactions, and fill orders.

Thus, the model of the business Internet must change, to move forward in ways that enable businesses to connect, to discover and reach each other, to learn what kinds of capabilities their potential trading partners have, and to continuously discover new potential trading partners, understand what their capabilities are, and seamlessly conduct eCommerce with them.

To accomplish this, a comprehensive solution is needed for businesses to publish their information to any customer or business partner around the world. Just as a common method for publishing data on the web spawned the evolution of e-business, a common means to publish information about business services will make it possible for organizations to quickly discover the <u>right</u> trading partners out of the millions that are online; to define how to conduct business once preferred businesses are discovered; and to create an industry-wide approach for businesses to quickly and easily integrate with their customers and partners on the Internet with information about their products and services, and how they prefer to be integrated into each other's systems and business processes.

New Approach

Within a more distributed model of the business Internet, a flexible, open, yet comprehensive framework is required to embrace this diversity, encouraging agreement on standards, but also stimulating the innovation and differentiation that is fueling the growth of B2B eCommerce.

The framework also needs to allow businesses to describe the business services their Web sites offer, and how they can be accessed globally over the Web. A global solution needs to go beyond traditional directories, but needs to define standards for how businesses will share information, what information they need to make public, what information they choose to keep private, and how to describe their services and their business.

The solution is the creation of a service registry architecture that presents a standard way for businesses to build a registry, query other businesses, and enable those registered businesses to interoperate and share information globally in a distributed manner, just as the Internet was intended to be used.

A Web services framework and public registry will enable buyers and sellers and marketplaces around the world to share information, to connect Web services at low cost, to support multiple standards, and to prosper in the new digital economy.

UDDI Project

To address this challenge, a group of technology and business leaders have come together to develop the Universal Description, Discovery and Integration [UDDI] specification—a sweeping initiative that creates a global, platform-independent, open framework to enable businesses to (1) discover each other, (2) define how they interact over the Internet, and (3) share information in a global registry that will more rapidly accelerate the global adoption of B2B eCommerce.

Each incremental advance in Web-enabled commerce has carried deep implications for business processes and organizational culture. UDDI is a **major** advance—the first cross-industry effort driven by platform providers, software developers, marketplace operators, and eCommerce and business leaders that comprehensively addresses the problems limiting the growth of B2B eCommerce, and that will benefit businesses of *all* sizes by creating this global, platform-independent, open framework.

UDDI is a building block to enable businesses to quickly, easily and dynamically find and transact with one another via their preferred applications. Participation in UDDI can help an established B2B eCommerce player expand into new markets and services or allow any size company just entering the online space to accelerate toward a world-class business presence.

The UDDI specifications take advantage of World Wide Web Consortium (W3C) and Internet Engineering Task Force (IETF) standards such as Extensible Markup Language (XML), HTTP, and Domain Name System (DNS) protocols. Additionally, cross platform programming features are addressed by adopting early versions of the proposed Simple Object Access Protocol (SOAP) messaging specifications found at the W3C Web site.

More Than Just a Specification

UDDI differs from other standards initiatives by virtue of the substantial commitment from industry partners to use this technology and implement it in their core businesses today—ensuring the standard will truly solve the problems facing small and large businesses, marketplaces, and technology providers.

As a demonstration of this commitment, the UDDI founding companies are launching a jointly operated UDDI Business Registry on the web. The UDDI Business Registry is an implementation of the UDDI specification and will enable all businesses to leverage this effort in their eCommerce activities.

The UDDI initiative leverages industry standards such as HTTP, XML, SOAP, and other specifications, thus demonstrating the openness of the approach and platform-independent *commitment*. This foundation gives all businesses that register in the UDDI Business Registry a kind of ID card, a globally unique identifier for them as a business.

Registering with UDDI will enable a company to publicly list a definition of itself, its services, and methods for engagement. Registered companies will then be accessible in searches by potential buyers and marketplaces. As registrants, integration will be significantly easier and more dynamic for partner companies. Organizations participating in UDDI represent many industries and core competencies.

UDDI reaches far beyond today's Internet business listings and search directories that provide specific, but limited value to an organization. Major benefits have been historically derived by the use of widely adopted standards in all industries and/or initiatives. UDDI-enabled businesses will realize unprecedented value from the rapid acceleration of eCommerce as a result of this global initiative.

Using UDDI, the supplier of ball bearings will be able to continue to serve its existing online customers, to quickly and easily discover new trading partners, and to conduct B2B eCommerce with them all.

Summary

In summary, UDDI is all about sharing business information, making it easier to publish your preferred means of doing business, find trading partners and have them find you, and interoperate with these trading partners over the Internet. By automating these processes:

▼ Businesses will have a means to describe their services and business processes in a global, open environment on the Internet thus extending their reach.

▼ Potential trading partners will quickly and dynamically discover and inter-act with each other on the Internet via their preferred applications thus re-ducing time to market.

▼ The barriers to rapid participation in the global Internet economy will be re-moved for any business anywhere thus allowing them to fully participate in the new digital economy.

CHAPTER
2

UDDI Technical White Paper
September 6, 2000

Abstract

Universal Description, Discovery and Integration (UDDI) is a specification for distributed Web-based information registries of Web services. UDDI is also a publicly accessible set of implementations of the specification that allow businesses to register information about the Web services they offer so that other businesses can find them.

Web services are the next step in the evolution of the World Wide Web (WWW) and allow programmable elements to be placed on Web sites where others can access distributed behaviors. UDDI registries are used to promote and discover these distributed Web services. This paper describes the capabilities that these registries add to the World Wide Web.

The intended audience is the anyone looking for a conceptual overview of UDDI for the purpose of understanding what it is, who uses it, and how a distributed registry makes it possible for your programs to discover and interact with Web services that other companies expose on the Web

Introduction

Overview

The Universal Description, Discovery and Integration (UDDI) specifications define a way to publish and discover information about Web services. The term "Web service" describes specific business functionality exposed by a company, usually through an Internet connection, for the purpose of providing a way for another company or software program to use the service.

Web services are becoming the programmatic backbone for electronic commerce. For example, one company calls another's service to send a purchase order directly via an Internet connection. Another example is a service that calculates the cost of shipping a package of a certain size or weight, so many miles via a specific carrier.

At first glance, it would seem simple to manage the process of Web service *discovery*. After all, if a known business partner has a known electronic commerce gateway, what's left to discover? The tacit assumption, however, is that all of the information is already known. When you want to find out which business partners have which services, the ability to discover the answers can quickly become difficult. One option is to call each partner on the phone, and then try to find the right person to talk with. For a business that is exposing Web services, having to staff enough highly technical people to satisfy random discovery demand is difficult to justify.

Another way to solve this problem is through an approach that uses a Web services description file on each company's Web site. After all, Web crawlers work by accessing a registered URL and are able to discover and index text found on nests of Web pages. The "robots.txt" approach, however, is dependent on the ability for a crawler to locate each Web site and the location of the service description file on that Web site. This distributed approach is potentially scalable but lacks a mechanism to insure consistency in service description formats and for the easy tracking of changes as they occur.

UDDI takes an approach that relies upon a distributed registry of businesses and their service descriptions implemented in a common XML format.

UDDI business registrations and the UDDI business registry

The core component of the UDDI project is the UDDI business registration, an XML file used to describe a business entity and its Web services. Conceptually, the information provided in a UDDI business registration consists of three components: "white pages" including address, contact, and known identifiers; "yellow pages" including industrial categorizations based on standard taxonomies; and "green pages", the technical information about services that are exposed by the business. Green pages include references to specifications for Web services, as well as support for pointers to various file and URL based discovery mechanisms if required.

Using UDDI

UDDI includes the shared operation of a business registry on the Web. For the most part, programs and programmers use the UDDI Business Registry to locate information about services and, in the case of programmers, to prepare systems that are compatible with advertised Web services or to describe their own Web services for others to call. The UDDI Business Registry can be used at a business level to check whether a given partner has particular Web service interfaces, to find companies in a given industry with a given type of service, and to locate information about how a partner or intended partner has exposed a Web service in order to learn the technical details required to interact with that service.

After reading this paper, the reader will have a clearer understanding of the capabilities defined in the UDDI specifications and have a clearer understanding of the role of Web service registries that implement these specifications.

Background

The number of ways that companies are using the World Wide Web varies considerably. Many companies are starting to define ways to allow their internal applications to interact with the business systems at other companies using the emerging Web infrastructure. Left alone, each company invents a unique approach based on the experiences of designers, available technologies, and project budgets. The proliferation of integration approaches and unique solutions have spawned an entire sub-industry focused on bridging incompatible service layers within and across company boundaries.

Recent work within the W3C starts to raise hopes that Extensible Markup Language (XML) will play a role in simplifying the exchange of business data between companies. Further, collaboration between computer industry giants and small companies alike have outlined a framework called SOAP that allows one program to invoke service interfaces across the Internet, without the need to share a common programming language or distributed object infrastructure. All of this is good news for companies feeling the cost pressures associated with electronic commerce because the foundations for common interoperability standards are being laid. Because of these foundation technologies and emerging standards, some of the intractable problems of the past are becoming easier to approach.

From XML and SOAP, one can observe that the integration and interoperability problem has been simplified in layers. XML provides a cross-platform approach to data encoding and formatting. SOAP, which is built on XML, defines a simple way to package information for exchange across system boundaries. SOAP bindings for HTTP are built on this packaging protocol and define a way to make remote procedure calls between systems in a manner that is independent of the programming language or operating system choices made by individual companies. Prior approaches involved complex distributed object standards or technology bridging software. Neither of these approaches has proven to be cost effective in the long run. Using XML and SOAP, this cross-language, cross-platform approach simplifies the problem of making systems at two companies compatible with each other.

Even when one considers XML and SOAP, though, there are still vast gaps through which any two companies can fall in implementing a communications infrastructure. As any industry pundit will tell you: "What is required is a full end-to-end solution, based on standards that are universally supported on every computing platform." Clearly, there is more work to do to achieve this goal. The UDDI specifications borrow the lesson learned from XML and SOAP to define a next-layer-up that lets two companies share a way to query each other's capabilities and to describe their own capabilities.

The following diagram depicts this layered view:

Interop Stack	Universal Service Interop Protocols (these layers are not defined yet)
	Universal Description, Discovery Integration (UDDI)
	Simple Object Access Protocol (SOAP)
	Extensible Markup Language (XML)
	Common Internet Protocols (HTTP, TCP/IP)

UDDI is a "next layer" in an emerging stack enabling rich Web services. UDDI uses standards-based technologies such as TCP/IP, HTTP, XML and SOAP to create a uniform service description format and service discovery protocol.

FIGURE 1

UDDI – the technical discovery layer

The Universal Description, Discovery and Integration (UDDI) specification describes a conceptual cloud of Web services and a programmatic interface that define a simple framework for describing any kind of Web service. The specification consists of several related documents and an XML schema that defines a SOAP-based programming protocol for registering and discovering Web services. These specifications were defined over a series of months by technicians and managers from several leading companies. Together, these companies have undertaken the task of building the first implementation of the UDDI services and running these services as a publicly accessible, multi-site partnership that shares all registered information.

The following diagram shows the relationship between the specifications, the XML schema and the UDDI business registry cloud that provides "register once, published everywhere" access to information about Web services.

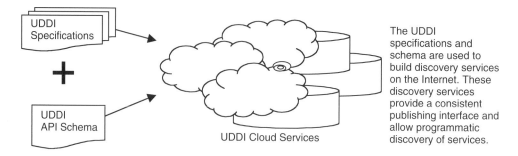

UDDI Cloud Services

The UDDI specifications and schema are used to build discovery services on the Internet. These discovery services provide a consistent publishing interface and allow programmatic discovery of services.

FIGURE 2

Using the UDDI discovery services, businesses individually register information about the Web services that they expose for use by other businesses. This information can be added to the UDDI business registry either via a Web site or by using tools that make use of the programmatic service interfaces described in the UDDI Programmer's API Specification. The UDDI business registry is a logically centralized, physically distributed service with multiple root nodes that replicate data with each other on a regular basis. Once a business registers with a single instance of the business registry service, the data is automatically shared with other UDDI root nodes and becomes freely available to anyone who needs to discover what Web services are exposed by a given business.

Next steps

As the layers in figure 1 show, it is important to note that UDDI does not form a full-featured discovery service. UDDI services are targeted at enabling technical discovery of services. With the facilities defined by UDDI, a program or programmer can locate information about services exposed by a partner, can find whether a partner has a service that is compatible with in-house technologies, and can follow links to the specifications for a Web service so that an integration layer can be constructed that will be compatible with a partners service. Businesses can also locate potential partners through UDDI directly, or more likely, from online marketplaces and search engines that use UDDI as a data source for their own value-added services. Technical compatibility can be discovered so that software companies can use the UDDI registries on the Web to automatically configure certain technical connections as software is installed or accounts are configured.

Business discovery and UDDI

UDDI is designed to complement existing online marketplaces and search engines by providing them with standardized formats for programmatic business and service discovery. The ability to locate parties that can provide a specific product or service at a given price or within a specific geographic boundary in a given timeframe is not directly covered by the UDDI specifications. These kinds of advanced discovery features require further collaboration and design work between buyer and sellers. Instead, UDDI forms the basis for defining these services in a higher layer.

In Figure 3 we can see the relationship between the technical discovery layers defined by UDDI and the role of aggregation and specialized search capabilities that address business level searches. Currently, marketplaces and search portals fill this need, and can be integrated or populated using information published in the UDDI distributed registries.

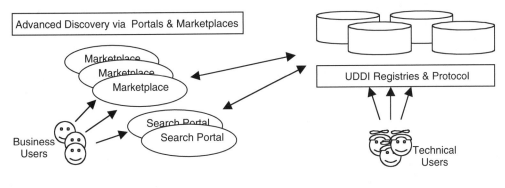

FIGURE 3

Future work

The teams working on the UDDI are planning on extending the functionality beyond what is in the Open Draft specification to address more than just technical discovery. Future features will address the ability to locate products and services, define Web service implementation conventions and provide the ability to manage hierarchical business organizations, communities and trade groups. The driving goal is to provide a public specification for Web service interoperability, whether the focus is marketplace-to-marketplace or business-to-business.

The remainder of this paper is a technical overview of the various features of the UDDI discovery service and specifications.

Technical overview

The Universal Description, Discovery and Integration (UDDI) specifications consist of an XML schema for SOAP messages, and a description of the UDDI API specification. Together, these form a base information model and interaction framework that provides the ability to publish information about a broad array of Web services.

Four information types

The core information model used by the UDDI registries is defined in an XML schema. XML was chosen because it offers a platform-neutral view of data and allows hierarchical relationships to be described in a natural way. The emerging XML schema standard was chosen because of its support for rich data types as well as its ability to easily describe and validate information based on information models represented in schemas.

The UDDI XML schema defines four core types of information that provide the kinds of information that a technical person would need to know in order to use a partners Web services. These are: business information; service information, binding information; and information about specifications for services.

The information hierarchy and the key XML element names that are used to describe and discover information about Web services are shown in figure 4[1].

Business information: the businessEntity element

Many partners will need to be able to locate information about your services and will have as starting information a small set of facts about your business. Technical staff, programmers or application programs themselves will know either your business name or perhaps your business name and some key identifiers[2], as well as optional categorization and contact information. The core XML elements for supporting publishing and discovering information about a business – the UDDI Business Registration — are contained in a structure named "businessEntity"[3].

---

[1]See appendix A for a more complete view of the UDDI information model.
[2]Business identifiers can include D&B numbers, tax numbers, or other information types via which partners will be able to identify a business uniquely.
[3]See the UDDI XML schema –http://www.uddi.org/schema/uddi_1.xsd

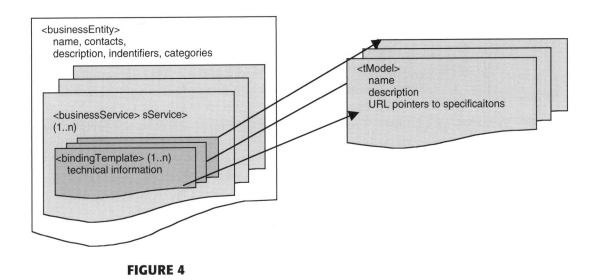

FIGURE 4

This structure serves as the top-level information manager for all of the information about a particular set of information related to a business unit[4].

The overall businessEntity information includes support for "yellow pages" taxonomies so that searches can be performed to locate businesses who service a particular industry or product category, or who are located within a specific geographic region.

Service information: the businessService and bindingTemplate elements

Technical and business descriptions of Web services – the "green pages" data — live within sub-structures of the businessEntity information. Two structures are defined: businessService and bindingTemplate. The businessService structure is a descriptive container that is used to group a series of related Web services related to either a business process or category of services. Examples of business processes that would include related Web service information include purchasing services, shipping services, and other high-level business processes.

---

[4]Complex business unit information should be registered in separate businessEntity records.

These businessService information sets can each be further categorized – allowing Web service descriptions to be segmented along combinations of industry, product and service or geographic category boundaries.

Within each businessService live one or more technical Web service descriptions. These contain the information that is relevant for application programs that need to connect to and then communicate with a remote Web service. This information includes the address to make contact with a Web service, as well as support for option information that can be used to describe both hosted services[5] and services that require additional values to be discovered prior to invoking a service[6]. Additional features are defined that allow for complex routing options such as load balancing[7].

Specification pointers and technical fingerprints

The information required to actually invoke a service is described in the information element named bindingTemplate. This was described in the previous section. However, it is not always enough to simply know where to contact a particular Web service. For instance, if I know that a business partner has a Web service that lets me send them a purchase order, knowing the URL for that service is not very useful unless I know a great deal about what format the purchase order should be sent in, what protocols are appropriate, what security required, and what form of a response will result after sending the purchase order. Integrating all parts of two systems that interact via Web services can become quite complex.

As a program or programmer interested in specific Web services, information about compatibility with a given specification is required to make sure that the right Web service is invoked for a particular need. For this reason, each bindingTemplate element contains a special element that is a list of references to information about specifications. Used as an opaque[8] set of identifiers, these

---

[5]Other companies provision hosted services, typically on a fee base. Marketplaces are good examples of hosted services.

[6]Software packages are a good example of this kind of requirement. Individual installations of a given package may have specific values that must be accommodated prior to connecting with a service.

[7]The hostingRedirector feature allows both hosting and other redirection capabilities to be deployed. See the appendix on redirection in the UDDI programmers API specification for more details.

[8]The term *opaque* in this context alludes to the fact that simply knowing a key value for a particular specification is equivalent to knowing a service is compatible with that specification.

references form a technical fingerprint that can be used to recognize a Web service that implements a particular behavior or programming interface.

In our purchase order example, the Web service that accepts the purchase order exhibits a set of well-defined behaviors if the proper document format is sent to the proper address in the right way. A UDDI registration for this service would consist of an entry for the business partner, a logical service entry that describes the purchasing service, and a bindingTemplate entry that describes the purchase order service by listing its URL and a reference to a tModel.

These references are actually the keys that can be used to access information about a specification. Called "tModels", this information is *metadata* about a specification, including its name, publishing organization, and URL pointers[9] to the actual specifications themselves. In our example, the tModel reference found in the bindingTemplate is a pointer to information about the specifics of this purchase order Web service. The reference itself is a pledge by the company that exposes the Web service that they have implemented a service that is compatible with the tModel that is referenced. In this way, many companies can provide Web services that are compatible with the same specifications.

The programmer's API

The UDDI specifications include definitions for Web service interfaces that allow programmatic access to the UDDI registry information. The full definition of the programmer's API is found in the Programmer's API Specification document. The API capabilities are briefly discussed below.

The API is divided into two logical parts. These are the Inquiry API and the Publishers' API. The Inquiry API is further divisible into two parts – one part used for constructing programs that let you search and browse information found in a UDDI registry, and another part that is useful in the event that Web service invocations experience failures. Programmers can use the Publishers API to create rich interfaces for tools that interact directly with a UDDI registry, letting a technical person manage the information published about either a businessEntity or a tModel structure.

---

[9]**Note**: Models do not actually contain the actual specifications. UDDI defines a framework for taking advantage of URLs and web servers, so that individual organizations can maintain centralized specifications. Individual implementations can then be located based on whether or not they contain references to specific specification keys.

Built on SOAP

The Simple Object Access Protocol (SOAP) is a W3C draft note describing a way to use XML and HTTP to create an information delivery and remote procedure mechanisms. Several companies, including IBM, Microsoft, DevelopMentor and Userland Software, submitted this draft note to the W3C for the purpose of, among other things, standardizing RPC (simple messaging) conventions on the World Wide Web. In its current state, the draft note describes a specification that is useful for describing a Web service. The companies that collaborated on UDDI decided to base the UDDI APIs on this SOAP specification. The specifics of how SOAP and XML are used by UDDI registry *Operators* are defined in the appendices in the API specification itself.

All of the API calls defined by the UDDI Programmer's API Specification behave synchronously – and all of the distributed UDDI registry *Operator Sites* support all of the calls described in the Programmer's API Specification.

The Inquiry API

The Inquiry API consists of two types of calls that let a program quickly locate candidate businesses, Web services and specifications, and then drill into specifics based on overview information provided in initial calls. The APIs named *find_xx* provide the caller with a broad overview of registration data based on a variety of search criteria. Alternately, if the actual keys of specific data are known ahead of time, up to date copies of a particular structure (e.g. businessEntity, businessService, bindingTemplate, tModel) can be retrieved in full via a direct call. These direct calls are called the *get_xx* APIs.

The UDDI invocation model

Each individual advertised Web service is modeled in a bindingTemplate structure. Invocation of a Web service is typically performed based on cached bindingTemplate data. With this in mind, the general scenario for using UDDI becomes clear when you consider the preparation required to write a program that uses a specific Web service. The following recipe outlines these steps

1. The programmer, chartered to write a program that uses a remote Web service, uses the UDDI business registry (either via a Web interface or other tool that uses the Inquiry API) to locate the businessEntity information registered by or for the appropriate business partner that is advertising the Web service.

2. The programmer either drills down for more detail about a business-Service or requests a full businessEntity structure. Since businessEntity structures contain all information about advertised Web services, the programmer selects a particular bindingTemplate[10] and saves this away for later use.

3. The programmer prepares the program based on the knowledge of the specifications for the Web service. This information may be obtained by using the tModel key information contained in the bindingTemplate for a service.

4. At runtime, the program invokes the Web service as planned using the cached bindingTemplate information (as appropriate).

In the general case, assuming the remote Web service and the calling program each accurately implement the required interface conventions (as defined in the specification referenced in the tModel information), the calls to the remote service will function successfully. The special case of failures and recovery is outlined next.

Recovery after remote Web service call failure

One of the key benefits of maintaining information about Web services in a distributed UDDI Registry is the "self service" capability provided to technical personnel. The recipe in the previous section outlined the tasks that the programmer is able to accomplish using the information found in the UDDI registry. This is all fine and well, but additional benefits are possible. These benefits of using a distributed UDDI registry with information hosted at an *Operator Site* are manifested in disaster recovery scenarios.

Web services businesses using Web services to do commerce with their partners need to be able to detect and manage communication problems or other failures. A key concern is the inability to predict, detect, or recover from failures within the systems of the remote partner. Even simple situations such as temporary outages caused by nightly maintenance or back-ups can make the decision to migrate to Web services difficult.

On the other hand, if you are the company that makes direct Web service connections possible, disaster recovery and the ability to migrate all of your business partners to a back-up system are prime concerns.

UDDI starts to address these "quality of service" issues by defining a calling convention that involves using cached bindingTemplate information, and when

---

[10]Using the find_xx inquiry API, a UDDI compatible browser can display more or less detail as someone searches through information. Once the appropriate information is located, the get_xx call returns full information about one of the four key UDDI XML structures.

failures occur, refreshing the cached information with current information from a UDDI Web registry. The recipe for this convention goes like this:

1. Prepare program for Web service, caching the required bindingTemplate data for use at run-time.

2. When calling the remote Web service, use the cached bindingTemplate data that was obtained from a UDDI Web registry.

3. If the call fails, use the bindingKey value and the get_bindingTemplate API call to get a fresh copy of a bindingTemplate for this unique Web service.

4. Compare the new information with the old – if it is different, retry the failed call. If the retry succeeds, replace the cached data with the new data.

Behind the scenes, when a business needs to redirect traffic to a new location or backup system, they only need to activate the backup system and then change the published location information for the effected bindingTemplates. This approach is called *retry on failure* – and is more efficient than getting a fresh copy of bindingTemplate data prior to each call.

The Publication API

The Publication API consists of four *save_xx* functions and four delete_xx functions, one each for the four key UDDI data structures (businessEntity, businessService, bindingTemplate, tModel). Once authorized, an individual party can register any number of businessEntity or tModel information sets, and can alter information previously published. The API design model is simple – changes to specific related information can be made and new information be saved using save. Complete structure deletion is accommodated by the delete calls. See the Programmer's API Specification for more information on this topic.

Security: Identity and authorization

The key operating principal for the UDDI Publishers' API is to only allow authorized individuals to publish or change information within the UDDI business registry. Each of the individual implementations of the distributed UDDI business registry maintains a unique list of authorized parties and tracks which businessEntity or tModel data was created by a particular individual. Changes and deletions are only allowed if a change request (via API call) is made by the same individual who created the effected information.

Each instance of a UDDI business registry, called an *Operator Site,* is allowed to define its own end user authentication mechanism[11], but all of the contracted UDDI *Operator Sites* are required to meet certain minimum criteria that provide similar security protections.

Other information

For more details on the UDDI schema or the UDDI Programmer's API Specification, consult the documents that are available on the uddi.org Web site.

These specifications are published as a set of linked HTML documents, with specific tModels defined for related sub service offerings. The individual tModel references are actually overview information with shared links to overview, API call, and appendix information within the overall specification.

Printable versions of the full specification in Microsoft Word and PDF format will also be available for download.

---

[11]Private implementations that are built using the UDDI specifications cannot be forced to implement any specific conventions or requirements. For this reason, be sure to consult with the UDDI implementer if you have questions about security or information access control policies.

Appendix A:
UDDI information model

The diagram below shows the relationships between the different core information elements that make up the UDDI information model.

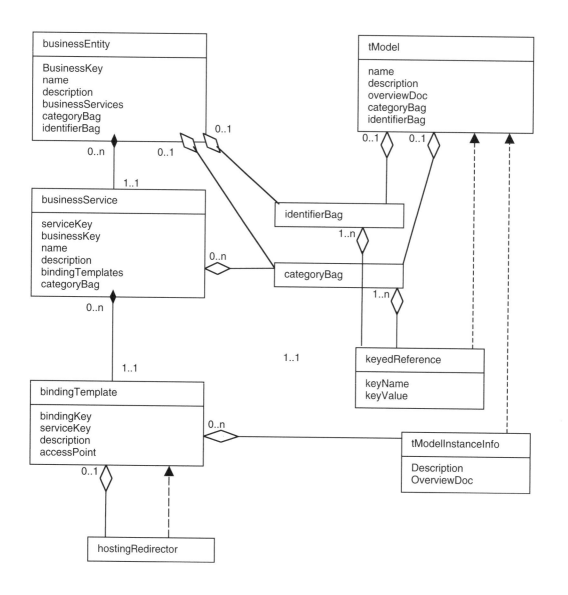

Resources

This section contains the locations of various specifications, document references and useful information where you can learn more about this subject.

▼ W3C XML and related recommendations: http://www.w3.org/TR

▼ SOAP 1.1 W3C note: http://www.w3.org/TR/#Notes

▼ UDDI Web site: http://www.uddi.org
    ▼ UDDI Programmer's API Specification:
       http://www.uddi.org/pubs/UDDI_Programmers_API_
       Specification.pdf
    ▼ UDDI Data Structure Reference:
       http://www.uddi.org/pubs/UDDI_XML_Structure_Reference.pdf
    ▼ UDDI Revision 1.0 schema: http://www.uddi.org/schema/uddi_1.xsd

CHAPTER
3

UDDI Programmer's API 1.0

UDDI Open Draft Specification 30 September 2000

This version:

http://www.uddi.org/pubs/ProgrammersAPI-V1.00-Open-20000930.html

Latest version:

http://www.uddi.org/pubs/ProgrammersAPI-V1.00-Open-20000930.html

Authors (alphabetically):

Toufic Boubez, IBM

Maryann Hondo, IBM

Chris Kurt, Microsoft

Jared Rodriguez, Ariba

Daniel Rogers, Microsoft

Contents

Introduction

Document Overview

This document describes the programming interface that is exposed by all instances of the Universal Description, Discovery & Integration (UDDI) registry. The primary audience for this document is programmers[1] that want to write software that will directly interact with a UDDI *Operator Site*[1].

What is this UDDI anyway?

UDDI is the name of a group of web-based registries that expose information about a business or other entity[2] and its technical interfaces (or API's). These registries are run by multiple *Operator Sites*, and can be used by any business that wants to make their information available, as well as anyone that wants to find that information. There is no charge for using the basic services of these operating sites.

By accessing any of the public UDDI *Operator Sites*, anyone can search for information about web services[3] that are made available by or on behalf of a business. The benefit of having access to this information is to provide a mechanism that allows others to discover what technical programming interfaces are provided for interacting with a business for such purposes as electronic commerce, etc. The benefit to the individual business is increased exposure in an electronic commerce enabled world.

The information that a business can register includes several kinds of simple data that help others determine the answers to the questions "who, what, where and how". Simple information about a business – information such as name, business identifiers (D&B D-U-N-S Number®, etc.), and contact information answers the question *"Who?"*. *"What?"* involves classification information that includes

---

[1]*Operator Site* is a term used to describe an implementation of this specification that participates in the public cloud of UDDI sites under special contract.

[2]The term *business* is used in a general sense to refer to an operating concern or any other type of organization throughout this document. This use is not intended to preclude other organizational forms.

[3]*Web Service* is a term used to describe technical services that are exposed via some public standard. Examples include purchasing services, catalog services, search services, shipping or postal services exposed over transports like HTTP or electronic mail.

industry codes and product classifications, as well as descriptive information about the services that are available for electronic interchange. Answering he question *"Where?"* involves registering information about the URL or email address (or other address) through which each type of service is accessed[4]. Finally, the question *"How?"* is answered by registering references to information about specifications that describe how a particular software package or technical interface functions. These references are called tModels in the UDDI documentation.

Compatible registries

This programmer's reference, coupled with the UDDI API schema (uddiAPI.xsd), defines a programming interface that is available for free public use. Software developers, businesses and others are encouraged to define products and tools that make use of this API and to build registries that are compatible with the API defined in this specification.

What are tModels?

In order for two or more pieces of software to be compatible with each other – that is, compatible enough to be able to exchange data for the purpose of achieving a desirable result – they must share some design goals and specifications in common. The registry information model that each UDDI site supports is based on this notion of shared specifications.

In the past, to build compatible software, two companies only had to agree to use the same specification, and then test their software. However, with UDDI, companies need a way to publish information about the specifications and versions of specifications that were used to design their advertised services. To accommodate the need to distinctly identify public specifications (or even private specifications shared only with select partners), information about the specifications themselves needs to be discoverable. This information about specifications – a classic metadata construct – is called a tModel within UDDI.

The tModel concept serves a useful purpose in discovering information about services that are exposed for broad use. To get a clearer understanding, let's consider an example.

---

[4]The information about the service point or address at which a service is exposed is sometimes referred to using the technical term *binding information.* design specs refer to this using the term *bindingTemplate.*

An example:

> Suppose your business bought a software package that let you automatically accept electronic orders via your web site. Using one of the public UDDI sites, you could advertise the availability of this electronic commerce capability.
>
> One of the reasons you chose this particular software package was its widespread popularity. In fact the salesperson that sold you the software made a point of highlighting a feature that gives your new software its broad appeal – the use and support of a widely used set of XML business documents to accommodate automatic business data interchange.
>
> As you installed and configured your new software, this software automatically consulted one of the public UDDI sites and identified compatible business partners. It did this by looking up each business you identified, and located those that had already advertised support for electronic commerce services that are compatible with your own.
>
> The configuration software accomplishes this by taking advantage of the fact that a tModel has been registered for a full specification, and in the service elements for each business, the tModel keys for this specification was referenced.

In general, it's pretty safe to think of the tModel keys within a service description as a fingerprint that can be used to trace the compatibility origins of a given service. Since many services will be constructed or programmed to be compatible with a given specification, references to information about specifications (by way of tModel entries and tModel references) don't have to be repeated with each registered electronic commerce service.

For programmers that write the software that will be used by businesses, tModels provide a common point of reference that allows compatible services to be easily identified. For businesses that use this software, the benefit is greatly reduced work in determining which particular services are compatible with the software you write. Finally, for software vendors and standards organizations, the ability to register information about a specification and then find implementations of web services that are compatible with a given tModel helps customers immediately realize the benefits of a widely used design.

Classification and Identification information

One of the immediate benefits of registering business information at one of the UDDI *Operator Instances* is the ability to specify one or more classification, or category codes for your business. Many such codes exist – NAICS, UN/SPC, SIC

Codes, etc. – and are widely used to classify businesses, industries, and product categories. Other (and there are many) classifications designate geographic information, or membership in a given organization.

Each UDDI site provides a way to add any number of classifications to a business registration. This information allows simple searching to be done on the information contained in the public registries. More important, registering information such as industry codes, product codes, geography codes and business identification codes (such as D&B D-U-N-S Numbers®) allow other search services to use this core classification information as a starting point to provide added-value indexing and classification while still referencing your UDDI information.

Design & Architecture

The UDDI programmer's API is designed to provide a simple request/response mechanism that allows discovery of businesses, services and technical service binding information.

Design Principles

The primary principal guiding the design of this programmers API was simplicity. Care has been taken to avoid complexity, overlap, and also to provide direct access to the appropriate levels of registered information with a minimum of programming overhead and round tripping.

Security

Accessing UDDI programmatically is accomplished via API calls defined in this programmer's reference. Two types of APIs are defined. A publishers API is provided for interactions between programs and the UDDI registry for the purpose of storing or changing data in the registry. An inquiry API is provided for programs that want to access the registry to read information from the registry.

Authenticated access is required to use the publishers API. Each *Operator Site* is responsible for selecting and implementing an authentication protocol that is compatible with the publishers API, as well as providing a new user sign-up mechanism. Before using any of the publisher API functions, the caller is responsible for signing up with one or more *Operator Sites* or compatible registries and establishing user credentials.

The Inquiry API functions are exposed as SOAP messages over HTTP protocol. No authentication is required to make use of the Inquiry API functions.

Versioning

In any programmers API, as well as any message set, versioning issues arise as time passes. Changes to an API over time can result in requests being misunderstood or processed incorrectly unless one can determine whether the version of the API being provided matches the version of the API used by a requesting party.

In order to facilitate a proper and controlled version match, the entire API defined by this programmer's reference is version stamped. Since the API itself is based on XML messages transmitted in SOAP envelopes over HTTP[5], this version stamp takes the form of an XML attribute.

All of the messages defined in this API must be transmitted with an accompanying application version attribute. This attribute is named *"generic*[6]*"* and is present on all messages. Each time this specification is modified, an ensuing requirement is placed on all *Operator Sites* to support generic 1.0, the current generic and at least one prior generic, if any. Compatible registries are encouraged to support at a minimum this 1.0 version.

SOAP Messaging

SOAP is a method for using Extensible Markup Language (XML) for use in message passing and remote procedure call (RPC) protocols. SOAP has been jointly defined and submitted to the World Wide Web consortium (W3C) for consideration as a standard web protocol.

SOAP is being used in conjunction with HTTP to provide a simple mechanism for passing XML messages to *Operator Sites* using a standard HTTP-POST

---

[5]HTTP is used as a general term here. HTTPS is used exclusively for all of the calls defined in the publishers API.

[6]Versioning of application behavior is accommodated via the *generic* attribute independently from the structures defined in the accompanying schema. In general, this form of versioning is preferable because it is easier to specify a new behavior against the same structures than to try and get data structure definitions to reflect business rules. Versioning the actual schema structures would present considerable technical difficulties after more than a small number of deployed applications existed.

protocol. Unless specified, all responses will be returned in the normal HTTP response document.

See the appendix on SOAP specific implementations for more information on the way that UDDI *Operator Sites* use the SOAP schema as an envelope mechanism for passing XML messages.

XML conventions

The programming interface for UDDI is based on Extensible Markup Language (XML). See the appendix (XML usage details) for more information on specific XML constructs and limitations used in the specification of the programmers interface.

Error Handling

The first line of error reporting is governed by the SOAP specification. SOAP fault reporting and fault codes will be returned for most invalid requests, or any request where the intent of the caller cannot be determined.

If any application level error occurs in processing a request message, a dispositionReport structure will be returned to the caller instead of a SOAP fault report. Disposition reports contain error information that includes descriptions and typed keys that can be used to determine the cause of the error. Refer to the appendix "Error Codes" for a general understanding of error codes. API specific interpretations of error codes are described following each API reference page.

Many of the API constructs defined in this document allow one or more of a given type of information to be passed. These API calls conceptually each represent a request on the part of the caller. The general error handling treatment is to detect errors in a request prior to processing the request. Any errors in the request detected will invalidate the entire request, and cause a dispositionReport to be generated within a SOAP Fault structure (see appendix A). In the case of an API call that involves passing multiples of a given structure, the dispositionReport will call out only the first detected error, and is not responsible for reporting multiple errors or reflecting intermediate "good" data.

White Space

Operator Sites and compatible implementations will store all data exactly as provided with one exception. Any leading or trailing white space characters will be removed from each field, element or attribute. White space characters include carriage returns, line feeds, spaces, and tabs.

XML Encoding

Despite its cross platform goals, XML still permits a broad degree of platform dependent ordering to seep into software. One of the key areas of seep has to do with the way that multiple language encoding is allowable in the XML specification. For the purpose of this specification and all UDDI *Operator Sites* consistency in handling of data is essential. For this reason, the default collation order for data registered within an *Operator Site* is binary. See appendix B for more information related to the use of byte order marks and UTF-8 and the way the SOAP listeners convert all requests to Unicode prior to processing.

API Reference

This API reference is divided into n logical sections. Each section addresses a particular programming focus. The sections are arranged in order according to the most common uses, and within each section alphabetically.

Special values within API syntax examples are shown in italics. In most cases, the following reference applies to these values:

▼ *uuid_key*: Access keys within all UDDI defined data elements are represented as universal unique identifiers (these are sometimes called a GUID). The name of the element or attribute designates the particular key type that is required. These keys are always formatted according to DCE UUID conventions with the one exception being tModelKey values, which are prefixed with a URN qualifier in the format "uuid:" followed by the UUID value.

▼ *generic*: This special attribute is a required metadata element for all messages. It is used to designate the specification version used to format the SOAP message. In the 1.0 version of the specification, this value is required to be "1.0". Any other value passed can result in an E_unsupported error.

▼ *xmlns*: This special attribute is a required metadata element for all messages. Technically, it isn't an attribute, but is formally called a namespace qualifier. It is used to designate is a universal resource name (URN) value that is reserved for all references to the UDDI schema. In the 1.0 version of the specification, this value is required to be "urn:uddi-org:api".

▼ *findQualifiers*: This special element is found in the inquiry API functions that are used to search (e.g. find_binding, find_business, find_service, find _tModel). This argument is used to signal special behaviors to be used with searching. See the Search Qualifiers appendix for more information.

▼ *maxRows*: This special qualifier is found in the inquiry API functions that are used to search (e.g. find_binding, find_business, find_service, find _tModel). This argument is used to limit the number of results re-turned from a request. When an *Operator Site* or compatible instance returns data in response to a request that contains this limiting argument, the num-ber of results will not exceed the integer value passed. If a result set is trun-cated as a result of applying this limit, the result will include the *truncated* attribute with a value of *true*.

▼ *truncated*: The truncated attribute indicates that a maximum number of pos-sible results has been returned. The actual limit set for applying this treat-ment is *Operator Site* policy specific, but in general should be a sufficiently large number so as to not normally be an issue. No behaviors such as pag-ing mechanisms are defined for retrieving more data after a truncated limit. The intent is to support the average query, but to allow *Operator Sites* the leeway required to be able to manage adequate performance.

▼ *categoryBag*: Searches can be performed based on a cross section of cate-gories. Several categories are broadly supported by all *Operator Sites* and provide three categorization dimensions. These are industry type, product and service type, and geography. Searches involving category information can be combined to cross multiple dimensions. For this reason, these searches are performed matching on ALL of the categories supplied. The net effect in generic 1 is the ability to use embedded category information as hints about how the registering party has categorized themselves, but not to provide a full third party categorization facility. This is the realm of portals and marketplaces, and may be enhanced in future generics.

▼ *identifierBag*: Searches involving identifiers are performed matching on any supplied identifier (e.g. D&B D-U-N-S Number®, etc) for any of the pri-mary elements that have identifierBag elements. These searches allow broad identity matching by returning a match when any keyedReference set used to search identifiers matches a registered identifier.

▼ *tModelBag*: Searches that match a particular technical fingerprint use UUID values to search for bindingTemplates with matching tModelKey value sets. When used to search for web services (e.g. the data described by a binding-Template structure), the concept of tModel signatures allows for highly se-lective searches for specific combinations of keys. For instance, the existence of a web service that implements all of the parts of the UDDI specifications can be accomplished by searching for a combination of tModel key values that correspond to the full set of specifications (the UDDI specification, for instance, is divided into at least 5 different, separately deployable tModels). At the same time, limiting the number of tModelKey values passed in a search can perform broader searches that look for any web service that implements a specific sub-part of the full specification. All tModelKey values are always expressed using a Universal Resource Name (URN) format that starts with the characters "uuid:" followed by a formatted Universally Unique Identifier (UUID) consisting of an octet of Hexidecimal digits arranged in the common 12-4-4-8 format pattern.

In all cases, the XML structures, attributes and element names shown in the API examples are derived from the Message API schema. For a full understanding of structure contents, refer to this schema. It is suggested that tools that understand schemas be used to generate logic that populates the structures used to make the API calls against an *Operator Site*.

Three query patterns

The Inquiry API provides three forms of query that follow broadly used conventions. These two forms match the needs of two types of software that are traditionally used with registries.

The browse pattern

Software that allows people to explore and examine data – especially hierarchical data – requires browse capabilities. The browse pattern characteristically involves starting with some broad information, performing a search, finding general result sets and then selecting more specific information for drill-down.

The UDDI API specifications accommodate the browse pattern by way of the *find_xx* API calls. These calls form the search capabilities provided by the API and are matched with summary return messages that return overview information about the registered information that match the supplied search criteria.

A typical browse sequence might involve finding whether a particular business you know about has any information registered. This sequence would start with a call to *find_business*, perhaps passing the first few characters of the businesses name that you already know. This returns a businessList result. This result is overview information (keys, names and descriptions) of the businessEntity information that matched the search results returned by find_business.

If you spot the business you are looking for, you can drill into their business-Service information, looking for particular service types (e.g. purchasing, shipping, etc) using the find_service API call. Similarly, if you know the technical fingerprint (tModel signature) of a particular product and want to see if the business you've chosen supports a compatible service interface, you can use find_binding.

The drill-down pattern

Once you have a key for one of the four main data types managed by a UDDI or compatible registry[7], you can use that key to access the full registered details for a specific data instance. The current UDDI data types are businessEntity, businessService, bindingTemplate and tModel. You can access the full registered information for any of these structures by passing a relevant key type to one of the *get_xx* API calls.

Continuing the example from the previous section on browsing, one of the data items returned by all of the *find_xx* return sets is key information. In the case of the business we were interested in, the businessKey value returned within the contents of a businessList structure can be passed as an argument to *get_business-Detail*. The successful return to this message is a *businessDetail* message containing the full registered information for the entity whose key value was passed. This will be a full *businessEntity* structure.

The invocation pattern

In order to prepare an application to take advantage of a remote web service that is registered within the UDDI registry by other businesses or entities, you need to prepare that application to use the information found in the registry for the specific service being invoked. This type of cross business service call has traditionally been a task that is undertaken at development time. This will not necessarily change completely as a result of UDDI registry entries, but one significant problem can be managed if a particular invocation pattern is employed.

Data obtained from the UDDI registry about a *bindingTemplate* information set represents the instance specifics of a given remote service. The program should

---

[7]Keys within UDDI compatible registries that are not *Operator Sites* are not synchronized with keys generated by *Operator Sites*. There is no key portability mechanism defined for crossing from a replicated operator site to a compatible registry that is not part of the replicated *Operator Cloud*.

cache this information and use it to contact the service at the registered address. Tools have automated the tasks associated with caching (or hard coding) location information in previously popular remote procedure technologies. Problems arise however when a remote service is moved without any knowledge on the part of the callers. Moves occur for a variety of reasons, including server upgrades, disaster recovery, and service acquisition and business name changes.

When a call fails using cached information obtained from a UDDI registry, the proper behavior is to query the UDDI registry where the data was obtained for fresh bindingTemplate information. The proper call is *get_bindingDetails* passing the original bindingKey value. If the data returned is different from the cached information, the service invocation should automatically retry. If the result of this retry is successful, the new information should replace the cached information.

By using this pattern with web services, a business using a UDDI *Operator Site* can automate the recovery of a large number of partners without undue communication and coordination costs. For example, if a business has activated a disaster recovery site, most of the calls from partners will fail when they try to invoke services at the failed site. By updating the UDDI information with the new address for the service, partners who use the invocation pattern will automatically locate the new service information and recover without further administrative action.

Inquiry API functions

The messages in this section represent inquiries that anyone can make of any UDDI *Operator Site* at any time. These messages all behave synchronously and are required to be exposed via HTTP-POST only. Other synchronous or asynchronous mechanisms may be provided at the discretion of the individual UDDI *Operator Site* or UDDI compatible registry.

The publicly accessible queries are:

▼ **find_binding**: Used to locate specific bindings within a registered businessService. Returns a bindingDetail message.

▼ **find_business**: Used to locate information about one or more businesses. Returns a businessList message.

▼ **find_service**: Used to locate specific services within a registered businessEntity. Returns a serviceList message.

▼ **find_tModel**: Used to locate one or more tModel information structures. Returns a tModelList structure.

▼ **get_bindingDetail**: Used to get full bindingTemplate information suitable for making one or more service requests. Returns a bindingDetail message.

▼ **get_businessDetail**: Used to get the full businessEntity information for a one or more businesses. Returns a businessDetail message.

▼ **get_businessDetailExt**: Used to get extended businessEntity information. Returns a businessDetailExt message.

▼ **get_serviceDetail**: Used to get full details for a given set of registered businessService date. Returns a serviceDetail message.

▼ **get_tModelDetail**: Used to get full details for a given set of registered tModel data. Returns a tModelDetail message.

find_binding

The find_binding message returns a bindingDetail message that contains a *bindingTemplates* structure with zero or more bindingTemplate structures matching the criteria specified in the argument list.

Syntax:

```
<find_binding serviceKey="uuid_key" generic="1.0" [ maxRows="nn" ]
    xmlns="urn:uddi-org:api" >
   [<findQualifiers/>]
   <tModelBag/>
</find_binding>
```

Arguments:

▼ *maxRows*: This optional integer value allows the requesting program to limit the number of results returned.

▼ *serviceKey*: This *uuid_key* is used to specify a particular instance of a businessService element in the registered data. Only bindings in the specific businessService data identified by the serviceKey passed will be searched.

▼ *findQualifiers*: This collection of findQualifier elements can be used to alter the default behavior of search functionality. See the Search Qualifiers appendix for more information.

▼ *tModelBag*: This is a list of tModel *uuid_key* values that represent the technical fingerprint to locate in a bindingTemplate structure contained within the businessService instance specified by the serviceKey value. If more than one tModel key is specified in this structure, only bindingTemplate information that exactly matches all of the tModel keys specified will be returned (logical AND). The order of the keys in the tModel bag is not relevant. All tModelKey values begin with a uuid URN qualifier (e.g. "uuid:" followed by a known tModel UUID value.

Returns:

This function returns a bindingDetail message on success. In the event that no matches were located for the specified criteria, the bindingDetail structure returned in the response the will be empty (e.g. contain no bindingTemplate data.)

In the even of a large number of matches, an *Operator Site* may truncate the result set. If this occurs, the response message will contain the *truncated* attribute with the value of this attribute set to *true*.

Searching using tModelBag will also return any bindingTemplate information that matches due to hostingRedirector references. The resolved bindingTemplate structure will be returned, even if that bindingTemplate is owned by a different businessService structure.

Caveats:

If any error occurs in processing this message, a dispositionReport structure will be returned to the caller in a SOAP Fault. The following error number information will be relevant:

▼ **E_invalidKeyPassed**: signifies that the *uuid_key* value passed did not match with any known serviceKey key or tModel key values. The error structure will signify which condition occurred first.

▼ **E_tooManyOptions**: signifies that more than one mutually exclusive argument was passed.

▼ **E_unsupported**: signifies that one of the findQualifier values passed was invalid.

find_business

The find_business message returns a businessList message that matches the conditions specified in the arguments.

Syntax:

```
<find_business generic="1.0" [ maxRows="nn" ] xmlns="urn:
  uddi-org:api" >
  [<findQualifiers/>]
  <name/> | <identifierBag/> | <categoryBag/> | <tModelBag/>
    | <discoveryURLs>
</find_business>
```

Arguments: All arguments to this call listed are mutually exclusive except findQualifiers

▼ *maxRows*: This optional integer value allows the requesting program to limit the number of results returned.

▼ *findQualifiers*: This collection of findQualifier elements can be used to alter the default behavior of search functionality. See the Search Qualifiers appendix for more information.

▼ *name*: This string value is a partial name. The businessList return contains businessInfo structures for businesses whose name matches the value passed (leftmost match).

▼ *identifierBag*: This is a list of business identifier references. The returned businessList contains businessInfo structures matching any of the identifiers passed (logical OR).

▼ *categoryBag*: This is a list of category references. The returned businessList contains businessInfo structures matching all of the categories passed (logical AND).

▼ *tModelBag*: The registered businessEntity data contains bindingTemplates that in turn contain specific tModel references. The tModelBag argument lets you search for businesses that have bindings that are compatible with a specific tModel pattern. The returned businessList contains businessInfo structures that match all of the tModel keys passed (logical AND). tModel-Key values must be formatted as URN qualified UUID values (e.g. prefixed with "uuid:")

▼ *discoveryURLs*: This is a list of URL's to be matched against the data associated with the discoveryURL's contents of registered businessEntity information. To search for URL without regard to useType attribute values, pass the useType component of the discoveryURL elements as empty attributes. If useType values are included, then the match will be made only on registered information that match both the useType and URL value. The returned businessList contains businessInfo structures matching any of the URL's passed (logical OR).

Returns:

This function returns a businessList on success. In the event that no matches were located for the specified criteria, a businessList structure with zero businessInfo structures is returned.

In the event of a large number of matches, an *Operator Site* may truncate the result set. If this occurs, the businessList will contain the *truncated* attribute with the value set to *true*.

Searching using tModelBag will also return any businessEntity that contains bindingTemplate information that matches due to hostingRedirector references. In other words, the businessEntity that contains a bindingTemplate with a hostingRedirector value referencing a bindingTemplate that matches the tModel search requirements will be returned.

Caveats:

If any error occurs in processing this message, a dispositionReport structure will be returned to the caller in a SOAP Fault. The following error number information will be relevant:

▼ **E_nameTooLong**: signifies that the partial name value passed exceeds the maximum name length designated by the *Operator Site*.

▼ **E_tooManyOptions**: signifies that more than one search argument was passed.

▼ **E_unsupported**: signifies that one of the findQualifier values passed was invalid.

find_service

The find_service message returns a serviceList message that matches the conditions specified in the arguments.

Syntax:

```
<find_service businessKey="uuid_key" generic="1.0" [ maxRows="nn" ]
     xmlns="urn:uddi-org:api" >
     [<findQualifiers/>]
     <name/> | <categoryBag/> | <tModelBag/>
</find_service>
```

Arguments:

The *name*, categoryBag and *tModelBag* arguments are mutually exclusive

▼ *maxRows*: This optional integer value allows the requesting program to limit the number of results returned.

▼ *businessKey*: This *uuid_key* is used to specify a particular BusinessEntity instance.

▼ *findQualifiers*: This collection of findQualifier elements can be used to alter the default behavior of search functionality. See the Search Qualifiers appendix for more information.

▼ *name*: This string value represents a partial name. Any businessService data contained in the specified businessEntity with a matching partial name value gets returned.

▼ *categoryBag*: This is a list of category references. The returned serviceList contains businessInfo structures matching all of the categories passed (logical AND).

▼ *tModelBag*: This is a list of tModel *uuid_key* values that represent the technical fingerprint to locate within a bindingTemplate structure contained within any businessService contained by the businessEntity specified. If

more than one tModel key is specified in this structure, only business-
Services that contain bindingTemplate information that matches all of the
tModel keys specified will be returned (logical AND).

Returns:

This function returns a serviceList on success. In the event that no matches were
located for the specified criteria, the serviceList structure returned will contain an
empty businessServices structure. This signifies zero matches.

In the even of a large number of matches, an *Operator Site* may truncate the result
set. If this occurs, the serviceList will contain the *truncated* attribute with the
value of this attribute set to *true*.

Searching using tModelBag will return serviceInfo structure for all qualifying
businesService data, including matches due to hostingRedirector references. In
other words, if the businessEntity whose businessKey is passed as an argument
contains a bindingTemplate with a hostingRedirector value, and that value references a bindingTemplate that matches the tModel search requirements, then the
serviceInfo for the businessService containing the hostingRedirector will be
returned.

Caveats:

If any error occurs in processing this message, a dispositionReport structure will
be returned to the caller in a SOAP Fault. The following error number information will be relevant:

▼ **E_invalidKeyPassed**: signifies that the *uuid_key* value passed did not match
with any known businessKey key or tModel key values. The error structure
will signify which condition occurred first.

▼ **E_nameTooLong**: signifies that the partial name value passed exceeds the
maximum name length designated by the *Operator Site*.

▼ **E_tooManyOptions**: signifies that more than one mutually exclusive argument was passed.

▼ **E_unsupported**: signifies that one of the findQualifier values passed was
invalid.

find_tModel

This find_tModel message is for locating a list of tModel entries that match a set
of specific criteria. The response will be a list of abbreviated information about
tModels that match the criteria (tModelList).

Syntax:

```
<find_tModel generic="1.0"  [ maxRows="nn" ]  xmlns="urn:
  uddi-org:api" >
```

```
[<findQualifiers/>]
    <name/> | <identifierBag/> | <categoryBag/>
</find_tModel>
```

Arguments:

The arguments to this call are mutually exclusive except findQualifiers

▼ *maxRows*: This optional integer value allows the requesting program to limit the number of results returned.

▼ *findQualifiers*: This collection of findQualifier elements can be used to alter the default behavior of search functionality. See the Search Qualifiers appendix for more information.

▼ *name*: This string value represents a partial name. The returned tModelList contains tModelInfo structures for businesses whose name matches the value passed (leftmost match).

▼ *IdentifierBag*: This is a list of business identifier references. The returned tModelList contains tModelInfo structures matching any of the identifiers passed (logical OR).

▼ *categoryBag*: This is a list of category references. The returned tModelList contains tModelInfo structures matching all of the categories passed (logical AND).

Returns:

This function returns a tModelList on success. In the event that no matches were located for the specified criteria, an empty tModelList structure will be returned (e.g. will contain zero tModelInfo structures). This signifies zero matches.

In the even of a large number of matches, an *Operator Site* may truncate the result set. If this occurs, the tModelList will contain the *truncated* attribute with the value of this attribute set to *true*.

Caveats:

If any error occurs in processing this message, a dispositionReport structure will be returned to the caller in a SOAP Fault. The following error number information will be relevant:

▼ **E_nameTooLong**: signifies that the partial name value passed exceeds the maximum name length designated by the *Operator Site*.

▼ **E_tooManyOptions**: signifies that more than one mutually exclusive argument was passed.

▼ **E_unsupported**: signifies that one of the findQualifier values passed was invalid.

get_bindingDetail

The get_bindingDetail message is for requesting the run-time bindingTemplate information location information for the purpose of invoking a registered business API.

Syntax:

```
<get_bindingDetail generic="1.0" xmlns="urn:uddi-org:api" >
    <bindingKey/>
    [ <bindingKey/> ...]
</get_bindingDetail>
```

Arguments:

▼ *bindingKey* : one or more *uuid_key* values that represent specific instances of known bindingTemplate data.

Behavior:

In general, it is recommended that bindingTemplate information be cached locally by applications so that repeated calls to a service described by a binding-Template can be made without having to make repeated round trips to an UDDI registry. In the event that a call made with cached data fails, the get_binding-Detail message can be used to get fresh bindingTemplate data. This is useful in cases such as a service you are using relocating to another server or being restored in a disaster recovery site.

Returns:

This function returns a bindingDetail message on successful match of one or more bindingKey values. If multiple bindingKey values were passed, the results will be returned in the same order as the keys passed.

In the event of a large number of matches, an *Operator Site* may truncate the result set. If this occurs, the bindingDetail result will contain the *truncated* attribute with the value of this attribute set to *true*.

Caveats:

If any error occurs in processing this message, a dispositionReport structure will be returned to the caller in a SOAP Fault. The following error number information will be relevant:

▼ **E_invalidKeyPassed**: signifies that one of the *uuid_key* values passed did not match with any known bindingKey key values. No partial results will be returned – if any bindingKey values passed are not valid bindingKey values, this error will be returned.

get_businessDetail

The get_businessDetail message returns complete businessEntity information for one or more specified businessEntitys.

Syntax:

```
<get_businessDetail generic="1.0" xmlns="urn:uddi-org:api" >
    <businessKey/>
    [ <businessKey/> ...]
</get_businessDetail>
```

Arguments:

▼ *businessKey* : one or more *uuid_key* values that represent specific instances of known businessEntity data.

Returns:

This function returns a businessDetail message on successful match of one or more businessKey values. If multiple businessKey values were passed, the results will be returned in the same order as the keys passed.

In the even of a large number of matches, an *Operator Site* may truncate the result set. If this occurs, the businessDetail response message will contain the *truncated* attribute with the value of this attribute set to *true*.

Caveats:

If any error occurs in processing this message, a dispositionReport structure will be returned to the caller in a SOAP Fault. The following error number information will be relevant:

▼ **E_invalidKeyPassed**: signifies that one of the *uuid_key* values passed did not match with any known businessKey values. No partial results will be returned – if any businessKey values passed are not valid, this error will be returned.

get_businessDetailExt

The get_businessDetailExt message returns extended businessEntity information for one or more specified businessEntitys. This message returns exactly the same information as the get_businessDetail message, but may contain additional attributes if the source is an external registry (not an *Operator Site*) that is compatible with this API specification.

Syntax:

```
<get_businessDetailExt generic="1.0" xmlns="urn:uddi-org:api" >
    <businessKey/>
    [ <businessKey/> ...]
</get_businessDetailExt>
```

Arguments:

▼ *businessKey* : one or more *uuid_key* values that represent specific instances of known businessEntity data.

Returns:

This function returns a businessDetailExt message on successful match of one or more businessKey values. If multiple businessKey values were passed, the results will be returned in the same order as the keys passed.

In the even of a large number of matches, an *Operator Site* may truncate the result set. If this occurs, the businessDetailExt response message will contain the *truncated* attribute with the value of this attribute set to *true*.

Caveats:

If any error occurs in processing this message, a dispositionReport structure will be returned to the caller in a SOAP Fault. The following error number information will be relevant:

▼ **E_invalidKeyPassed**: signifies that one of the *uuid_key* values passed did not match with any known businessKey values. No partial results will be returned – if any businessKey values passed are not valid, this error will be returned.

▼ **E_unsupported**: signifies that the implementation queried does not support the extended detail function. If this occurs, businessDetail information should be queried via the get_businessDetail API. *Operator Sites* will not return this code, but will instead return a businessDetailExt result with full businessDetail information embedded.

get_serviceDetail

The get_serviceDetail message is used to request full information about a known businessService structure.

Syntax:

```
<get_serviceDetail generic="1.0" xmlns="urn:uddi-org:api" >
   <serviceKey/>
   [<serviceKey/> ...]
</get_serviceDetail>
```

Arguments:

▼ *serviceKey* : one or more *uuid_key* values that represent specific instances of known businessService data.

Returns:

This function returns a serviceDetail message on successful match of one or more serviceKey values. If multiple serviceKey values were passed, the results will be returned in the same order as the keys passed.

In the even of a large number of matches, an *Operator Site* may truncate the result set. If this occurs, the response will contain a *truncated* attribute with the value of this attribute set to *true*.

Caveats:

If any error occurs in processing this message, a dispositionReport structure will be returned to the caller in a SOAP Fault. The following error number information will be relevant:

▼ **E_invalidKeyPassed**: signifies that one of the *uuid_key* values passed did not match with any known serviceKey values. No partial results will be returned – if any serviceKey values passed are not valid, this error will be returned.

get_tModelDetail

The get_tModelDetail message is used to request full information about a known tModel structure.

Syntax:

```
<get_tModelDetail generic="1.0" xmlns="urn:uddi-org:api" >
   <tModelKey/>
   [<tModelKey/> ...]
</get_tModelDetail>
```

Arguments:

▼ *tModelKey* : one or more URN qualified *uuid_key* values that represent specific instances of known tModel data. All tModelKey values begin with a uuid URN qualifier (e.g. "uuid:" followed by a known tModel UUID value.)

Returns:

This function returns a tModelDetail message on successful match of one or more tModelKey values. If multiple tModelKey values were passed, the results will be returned in the same order as the keys passed.

In the even of a large number of matches, an *Operator Site* may truncate the result set. If this occurs, the response will contain a *truncated* attribute with the value of this attribute set to *true*.

Caveats:

If any error occurs in processing this message, a dispositionReport structure will be returned to the caller in a SOAP Fault. The following error number information will be relevant:

▼ **E_invalidKeyPassed**: signifies that one of the URN qualified *uuid_key* values passed did not match with any known tModelKey values. No partial results will be returned – if any tModelKey values passed are not valid, this error will be returned. Any tModelKey values passed without a uuid URN qualifier will be considered invalid.

▼ **E_keyRetired**: signifies that the request cannot be satisfied because the owner has retired the tModel information. The tModel reference may still be valid and used as intended, but the information defining the tModel behind the key is unavailable.

Publishing API functions

The messages in this section represent inquiries that require authenticated[8] access to an UDDI *Operator Site*. Each business should initially select one *Operator Site* to host their information. Once chosen, information can only be updated at the site originally selected.

The messages defined in this section all behave synchronously and are callable via HTTP-POST only. HTTPS is used exclusively for all of the calls defined in this publishers API.

The publishing API calls are:

▼ **delete_binding**: Used to remove an existing bindingTemplate from the bindingTemplates collection that is part of a specified businessService structure.

▼ **delete_business**: Used to delete registered businessEntity information from the registry.

▼ **delete_service**: Used to delete an existing businessService from the businessServices collection that is part of a specified businessEntity.

▼ **delete_tModel**: Used to delete registered information about a tModel. If there are any references to a tModel when this call is made, the tModel will be marked deleted instead of being physically removed.

▼ **discard_authToken**: Used to inform an *Operator Site* that a previously provided authentication token is no longer valid. See get_authToken.

---

[8]Authentication is not regulated by this API specification. Individual *Operator Sites* will designate their own procedures for getting a userID and password.

▼ **get_authToken**: Used to request an authentication token from an *Operator Site*. Authentication tokens are required to use all other API's defined in the publishers API. This function serves as the programs equivalent of a login request.

▼ **get_registeredInfo**: Used to request an abbreviated synopsis of all information currently managed by a given individual.

▼ **save_binding**: Used to register new bindingTemplate information or update existing bindingTemplate information. Use this to control information about technical capabilities exposed by a registered business.

▼ **save_business**:. Used to register new businessEntity information or update existing businessEntity information. Use this to control the overall information about the entire business. Of the save_x API's this one has the broadest effect.

▼ **save_service**: Used to register or update complete information about a businessService exposed by a specified businessEntity.

▼ **save_tModel**: Used to register or update complete information about a tModel.

Special considerations around categorization

Several of the API's defined in this section allow you to save categorization information that is used to support searches that use taxonomy references. These are currently the save_business, save_service and save_tModel APIs. Categorization is specified using an optional element named categoryBag, which contains namespace-qualified references to taxonomy keys and descriptions in keyed-Reference structures.

Data contained in the keyValue attribute of each keyedReference is validated against the taxonomy referenced by the associated tModelKey. Only valid key-Values will be stored as entered. *Operator Sites* may handle invalid keyValues by either fail the request or changing the tModelKey value to reference an non-validated "etc." taxonomy which accepts all keyValues. See Appendix H for details on the validation of taxonomic information. If the *Operator Site* chooses to fail categorization mechanisms, the error codes defined in appendix H will be passed back as the error code on the relevant API calls.

delete_binding

The delete_binding message causes one or more bindingTemplate to be deleted.

Syntax:

```
<delete_binding generic="1.0" xmlns="urn:uddi-org:api" >
   <authInfo/>
   <bindingKey/>
   [<bindingKey/> ...]
</delete_binding>
```

Arguments:

▼ *authInfo*: this required argument is an element that contains an authentication token. Authentication tokens are obtained using the get_authToken API call.

▼ *bindingKey* : one or more *uuid_key* values that represent specific instances of known bindingTemplate data.

Returns:

Upon successful completion, a dispositionReport is returned with a single success indicator.

Caveats:

If any error occurs in processing this message, a dispositionReport structure will be returned to the caller in a SOAP Fault. The following error number information will be relevant:

▼ **E_invalidKeyPassed**: signifies that one of the *uuid_key* values passed did not match with any known bindingKey values. No partial results will be returned – if any bindingKey values passed are not valid, this error will be returned.

▼ **E_authTokenExpired**: signifies that the authentication token value passed in the authInfo argument is no longer valid because the token has expired.

▼ **E_authTokenRequired**: signifies that the authentication token value passed in the authInfo argument is either missing or is not valid.

▼ **E_userMismatch**: signifies that one or more of the bindingKey values passed refers to data that is not controlled by the individual who is represented by the authentication token.

▼ **E_operatorMismatch**: signifies that one or more of the bindingKey values passed refers to data that is not controlled by the *Operator Site* that received the request for processing.

delete_business

The delete_business message is used to remove one or more businessEntity structures.

Syntax:

```
<delete_business generic="1.0" xmlns="urn:uddi-org:api" >
   <authInfo/>
   <businessKey/>
   [ <businessKey/> ...]
</delete_business>
```

Arguments:

▼ *authInfo*: this required argument is an element that contains an authentication token. Authentication tokens are obtained using the get_authToken API call.

▼ *businessKey* : one or more *uuid_key* values that represent specific instances of known businessEntity data.

Returns:

Upon successful completion, a dispositionReport is returned with a single success indicator.

Caveats:

If any error occurs in processing this message, a dispositionReport structure will be returned to the caller in a SOAP Fault. The following error number information will be relevant:

▼ **E_invalidKeyPassed**: signifies that one of the *uuid_key* values passed did not match with any known businessKey values. No partial results will be returned – if any businessKey values passed are not valid, this error will be returned.

▼ **E_authTokenExpired**: signifies that the authentication token value passed in the authInfo argument is no longer valid because the token has expired.

▼ **E_authTokenRequired**: signifies that the authentication token value passed in the authInfo argument is either missing or is not valid.

▼ **E_userMismatch**: signifies that one or more of the businessKey values passed refers to data that is not controlled by the individual who is represented by the authentication token.

▼ **E_operatorMismatch**: signifies that one or more of the businessKey values passed refers to data that is not controlled by the *Operator Site* that received the request for processing.

delete_service

The delete_service message is used to remove one or more businessService structures.

Syntax:

```
<delete_service generic="1.0" xmlns="urn:uddi-org:api" >
   <authInfo/>
   <serviceKey/>
   [ <serviceKey/> ...]
</delete_service>
```

Arguments:

▼ *authInfo*: this required argument is an element that contains an authentication token. Authentication tokens are obtained using the get_authToken API call.

▼ *serviceKey* : one or more *uuid_key* values that represent specific instances of known businessService data.

Returns:

Upon successful completion, a dispositionReport is returned with a single success indicator.

Caveats:

If any error occurs in processing this message, a dispositionReport structure will be returned to the caller in a SOAP Fault. The following error number information will be relevant:

▼ **E_invalidKeyPassed**: signifies that one of the *uuid_key* values passed did not match with any known serviceKey values. No partial results will be returned – if any serviceKey values passed are not valid, this error will be returned.

▼ **E_authTokenExpired**: signifies that the authentication token value passed in the authInfo argument is no longer valid because the token has expired.

▼ **E_authTokenRequired**: signifies that the authentication token value passed in the authInfo argument is either missing or is not valid.

▼ **E_userMismatch**: signifies that one or more of the serviceKey values passed refers to data that is not controlled by the individual who is represented by the authentication token.

▼ **E_operatorMismatch**: signifies that one or more of the serviceKey values passed refers to data that is not controlled by the *Operator Site* that received the request for processing.

delete_tModel

The delete_tModel message is used to remove or retire one or more tModel structures.

Syntax:

```
<delete_tModel generic="1.0" xmlns="urn:uddi-org:api" >
   <authInfo/>
   <tModelKey/> [<tModelKey/> ...]
</delete_tModel>
```

Arguments:

▼ *authInfo*: this required argument is an element that contains an authentication token. Authentication tokens are obtained using the get_authToken API call.

▼ *tModelKey* : one or more URN qualified *uuid_key* values that represent specific instances of known tModel data. All tModelKey values begin with a uuid URN qualifier (e.g. "uuid:" followed by a known tModel UUID value.)

Returns:

Upon successful completion, a dispositionReport is returned with a single success indicator.

Behavior:

If a tModel is deleted and any other managed data references to that tModel by *uuid_key* (e.g. within a categoryBag, identifierBag or within a tModelInstanceInfo structure) it will not be physically deleted as a result of this call. Instead it will be marked as hidden. Any tModels hidden in this way are still accessible to their owner, via the get_registeredInfo, but will be omitted from any results returned by calls to find_tModel. The details associated with a hidden tModel are still available to anyone that uses the get_tModelDetail message. Publishing parties that want to remove all details about a tModel from the system should call save_tModel, passing empty values in the data fields, before calling this function. A hidden tModel can be restored and made universally visible by invoking the save_tModel API at a later time, passing the key of the hidden tModel.

Caveats:

If any error occurs in processing this message, a dispositionReport structure will be returned to the caller in a SOAP Fault. The following error number information will be relevant:

▼ **E_invalidKeyPassed**: signifies that one of the URN qualified *uuid_key* values passed did not match with any known tModelKey values. No partial results will be returned – if any tModelKey values passed are not valid, this error will be returned. Any tModelKey values passed without a uuid URN qualifier will be considered invalid.

▼ **E_authTokenExpired**: signifies that the authentication token value passed in the authInfo argument is no longer valid because the token has expired.

▼ **E_authTokenRequired**: signifies that the authentication token value passed in the authInfo argument is either missing or is not valid.

▼ **E_userMismatch**: signifies that one or more of the tModelKey values passed refers to data that is not controlled by the individual who is represented by the authentication token.

▼ **E_operatorMismatch**: signifies that one or more of the tModelKey values passed refers to data that is not controlled by the *Operator Site* that received the request for processing.

discard_authToken

The discard_authToken message is used to inform an *Operator Site* that the authentication token can be discarded. Subsequent calls that use the same auth-Token may be rejected. This message is optional for *Operator Sites* that do not manage session state or that do not support the get_authToken message.

Syntax:

```
<discard_authToken generic="1.0" xmlns="urn:uddi-org:api">
   <authInfo/>
</discard_authToken>
```

Arguments:

▼ *authInfo*: this required argument is an element that contains an authentication token. Authentication tokens are obtained using the get_authToken API call.

Returns:

Upon successful completion, a dispositionReport is returned with a single success indicator. Discarding an expired authToken will be processed and reported as a success condition.

Caveats:

If any error occurs in processing this message, a dispositionReport structure will be returned to the caller in a SOAP Fault. The following error number information will be relevant:

▼ **E_authTokenRequired**: signifies that the authentication token value passed in the authInfo argument is either missing or is not valid.

get_authToken

The get_authToken message is used to obtain an authentication token. Authentication tokens are opaque values that are required for all other publisher API calls. This message is not required for *Operator Sites* that have an external mechanism defined for users to get an authentication token. This API is provided for implementations that do not have some other method of obtaining an authentication token or certificate, or that choose to use userID and Password based authentication.

Syntax:

```
<get_authToken generic="1.0" xmlns="urn:uddi-org:api"
   userID="someLoginName"
   cred="someCredential"
</get_authToken>
```

Arguments:

▼ *userID*: this required attribute argument is the user that an individual authorized user was assigned by an *Operator Site*. *Operator Sites* will each provide a way for individuals to obtain a UserID and password that will be valid only at the given *Operator Site*.

▼ *cred*: this required attribute argument is the password or credential that is associated with the user.

Returns:

This function returns an authToken message that contains a valid authInfo element that can be used in subsequent calls to publisher API calls that require an authInfo value.

Caveats:

If any error occurs in processing this message, a dispositionReport structure will be returned to the caller in a SOAP Fault. The following error number information will be relevant:

▼ **E_unknownUser**: signifies that the Operator Site that received the request does not recognize the userID and/or pwd argument values passed as valid credentials.

get_registeredInfo

The get_registeredInfo message is used to get an abbreviated list of all businessEntity keys and tModel keys that are controlled by the individual associated the credentials passed.

Syntax:

```
<get_registeredInfo generic="1.0" xmlns="urn:uddi-org:api" >
   <authInfo/>
</get_registeredInfo>
```

Arguments:

▼ *authInfo*: this required argument is an element that contains an authentication token. Authentication tokens are obtained using the get_authToken API call.

Returns:

Upon successful completion, a registeredInfo structure will be returned, listing abbreviated business information in one or more businessInfo structures, and tModel information in one or more tModelInfo structures. This API is useful for determining the full extent of registered information controlled by a single user in a single call.

Caveats:

If any error occurs in processing this message, a dispositionReport structure will be returned to the caller in a SOAP Fault. The following error number information will be relevant:

▼ **E_authTokenExpired**: signifies that the authentication token value passed in the authInfo argument is no longer valid because the token has expired.

▼ **E_authTokenRequired**: signifies that the authentication token value passed in the authInfo argument is either missing or is not valid.

save_binding

The save_binding message is used to save or update a complete bindingTemplate structure. This message can be used to add or update one or more binding-Template structures to one or more existing businessService structures.

Syntax:

```
<save_binding generic="1.0" xmlns="urn:uddi-org:api">
   <authInfo/>
   <bindingTemplate/> [<bindingTemplate/>...]
</save_binding>
```

Arguments:

▼ *authInfo*: this required argument is an element that contains an authentication token. Authentication tokens are obtained using the get_authToken API call.

▼ *bindingTemplate*: one or more complete bindingTemplate structures. The order in which these are processed is not defined. To save a new binding-Template, pass a bindingTemplate structure with an empty bindingKey attribute value.

Behavior:

Each bindingTemplate structure passed must contain a serviceKey value that corresponds to a registered businessService controlled by the same person saving the bindingTemplate data. The net effect of this call is to establish the parent businessService relationship for each bindingTemplate affected by this call. If the same bindingTemplate (determined by matching bindingKey value) is listed more than once, any relationship to the containing businessService will be determined by processing order, which is determined by the position of the binding-Template data in first to last order.

Using this message it is possible to move an existing bindingTemplate structure from one businessService structure to another by simply specifying a different parent businessService relationship. Changing a parent relationship in this way will cause two businessService structures to be affected.

If a bindingTemplate being saved contains a hostingRedirector element, and that element references a bindingTemplate that itself contains a hostingRedirector element, an error condition (E_invalidKeyPassed) will be generated.

Returns:

This API returns a bindingDetail message containing the final results of the call that reflects the newly registered information for the effected bindingTemplate structures.

Caveats:

If any error occurs in processing this message, a dispositionReport structure will be returned to the caller in a SOAP Fault. The following error number information will be relevant:

▼ **E_authTokenExpired**: signifies that the authentication token value passed in the authInfo argument is no longer valid because the token has expired.

▼ **E_authTokenRequired**: signifies that the authentication token value passed in the authInfo argument is either missing or is not valid.

▼ **E_keyRetired**: signifies that the request cannot be satisfied because one or more *uuid_key* values specified has previously been hidden or removed by the requester. This specifically applies to the tModelKey values passed.

▼ **E_invalidKeyPassed**: signifies that the request cannot be satisfied because one or more *uuid*_key values specified is not a valid key value, or that a hostingRedirector value references a bindingTemplate that itself contains a hostingRedirector value.

▼ **E_userMismatch**: signifies that one or more of the *uuid_key* values passed refers to data that is not controlled by the individual who is represented by the authentication token.

▼ **E_operatorMismatch**: signifies that one or more of the *uuid_key* values passed refers to data that is not controlled by the *Operator Site* that received the request for processing.

▼ **E_accountLimitExceeded**: signifies that user account limits have been exceeded.

save_business

The save_business message is used to save or update information about a complete businessEntity structure. This API has the broadest scope of all of the save_x API calls in the publisher API, and can be used to make sweeping changes to the published information for one or more businessEntity structures controlled by an individual.

Syntax:

```
<save_business generic="1.0" xmlns="urn:uddi-org:api">
   <authInfo/>
   <businessEntity/> [<businessEntity/>. . .] | <uploadRegister/>
    [<uploadRegister/>...]
</save_business>
```

Arguments:

Only one type of businessEntity or uploadRegister arguments may be passed in a given save_business message. Any number of businessEntity or uploadRegister values can be passed in a single save (up to an *Operator Site* imposed policy limit), but the two types of parameters should not be mixed.

▼ *authInfo*: this required argument is an element that contains an authentication token. Authentication tokens are obtained using the get_authToken API call.

▼ *businessEntity*: one or more complete businessEntity structures can be passed. These structures can be obtained in advance by using the get_businessDetail API call or by any other means.

▼ *uploadRegister*: one or more resolvable HTTP URL addresses that each point to a single and valid businessEntity or businessEntityExt structure. This variant argument allows a registry to be updated to reflect the contents of an XML document that is URL addressable. The URL must return a pure XML document that only contains a businessEntity structure as its top-level element, and be accessible using the standard HTTP-GET protocol.

Behavior:

If any of the *uuid_key* values within in a businessEntity structure (e.g. any data with a key value regulated by a businessKey, serviceKey, bindingKey, or tModelKey) is passed with a blank value, this is a signal that the data that is so keyed is being inserted. This does not apply to structures that reference other keyed data, such as tModelKey references within bindingTemplate or keyed-Reference structures, since these are references.

To make this function perform an update to existing registered data, the keyed entities (businessEntity, businessService, bindingTemplate or tModel) should have *uuid_key* values that correspond to the registered data.

Data can be deleted with this function when registered information is different than the new information provided. One or more businessService and binding Template structures that are found in the controlling *Operator Site* but are missing from the businessEntity information provided in or referenced by this call will be deleted from the registry after processing this call.

Data that is contained within one or more businessEntity can be rearranged with this function when data passed to this function redefines parent container relationships for other registered information. For instance, if a new businessEntity is saved with information about a businessService that is registered already as part of a separate businessEntity, this will result in the businessService being moved from its current container to the new businessEntity. This only applies if the same party controls the data referenced.

If the uploadRegister URL method is used to save data, the *Operator Site* is required to make sure that the URL used is included in the discoveryURLs collection within the businessEntity structure. If the URL passed to do the upload is not contained in this collection, it will be added automatically with a useType value set to the type of structure (either businessEntity or businessEntityExt) found in the file used to perform the upload.

If the file located by the uploadRegister URL value is an extended business entity (businessEntityExt) structure, only the businessEntity data found within that structure will be registered.

If the businessEntity method is used to save data (e.g not via an uploadRegister URL reference), then the *Operator Site* will create a URL that is specific to the *Operator Site* that can be used to get (via HTTP-GET) the businessEntity structure being registered. This information will be added to (if not present already) the discoveryURLs collection automatically with a useType value of "business-Entity".

Returns:

This API returns a businessDetail message containing the final results of the call that reflects the new registered information for the businessEntity information provided.

Caveats:

If any error occurs in processing this message, a dispositionReport structure will be returned to the caller in a SOAP Fault. The following error number information will be relevant:

▼ **E_authTokenExpired**: signifies that the authentication token value passed in the authInfo argument is no longer valid because the token has expired.

▼ **E_authTokenRequired**: signifies that the authentication token value passed in the authInfo argument is either missing or is not valid.

▼ **E_keyRetired**: signifies that the request cannot be satisfied because one or more *uuid_key* values specified has previously been hidden or removed by the requester. This specifically applies to the tModelKey values passed.

▼ **E_invalidKeyPassed**: signifies that the request cannot be satisfied because one or more *uuid*_key values specified is not a valid key value. This includes any tModelKey references that are unknown.

▼ **E_invalidURLPassed**: signifies that an error occurred with one of the uploadRegister URL values.

▼ **E_userMismatch**: signifies that one or more of the *uuid_key* values passed refers to data that is not controlled by the individual who is represented by the authentication token.

▼ **E_operatorMismatch**: signifies that one or more of the businessKey values passed refers to data that is not controlled by the *Operator Site* that received the request for processing.

▼ **E_invalidCategory (20000)**: signifies that the given keyValue did not correspond to a category within the taxonomy identified by a tModelKey value within one of the categoryBag elements provided.

▼ **E_categorizationNotAllowed (20100:** Restrictions have been placed by the taxonomy provider on the types of information that should be included at that location within a specific taxonomy. The validation routine chosen by the *Operator Site* has rejected this businessEntity for at least one specified category.

▼ **E_accountLimitExceeded**: signifies that user account limits have been exceeded.

save_service

The save_service message adds or updates one or more businessService structures.

Syntax:

```
<save_service generic="1.0" xmlns="urn:uddi-org:api" >
   <authInfo/>
   <businessService/> [<businessService/>...]
</save_service>
```

Arguments:

▼ *authInfo*: this required argument is an element that contains an authentication token. Authentication tokens are obtained using the get_authToken API call.

▼ *businessService*: one or more complete businessService structures can be passed. These structures can be obtained in advance by using the get_serviceDetail API call or by any other means.

Behavior:

Each businessService structure passed must contain a businessKey value that corresponds to a registered businessEntity controlled by the same making the save_service request.. If the same businessService, or within these, binding-Template (determined by matching businessService or bindingKey value) is contained in more than one businessService argument, any relationship to the containing businessEntity will be determined by processing order – which is determined by first to last order of the information passed in the request. Using this message it is possible to move an existing bindingTemplate structure from one businessService structure to another, or move an existing businessService structure from one businessEntity to another by simply specifying a different parent businessEntity relationship. Changing a parent relationship in this way will cause two businessEntity structures to be affected.

Returns:

This API returns a serviceDetail message containing the final results of the call that reflects the newly registered information for the effected businessService structures.

Caveats:

If any error occurs in processing this message, a dispositionReport structure will be returned to the caller in a SOAP Fault. The following error number information will be relevant:

▼ **E_authTokenExpired**: signifies that the authentication token value passed in the authInfo argument is no longer valid because the token has expired.

▼ **E_authTokenRequired**: signifies that the authentication token value passed in the authInfo argument is either missing or is not valid.

▼ **E_keyRetired**: signifies that the request cannot be satisfied because one or more *uuid_key* values specified has previously been hidden or removed by the requester. This specifically applies to the tModelKey values passed.

▼ **E_invalidKeyPassed**: signifies that the request cannot be satisfied because one or more *uuid*_key values specified is not a valid key value. This includes any tModelKey references that are unknown.

▼ **E_userMismatch**: signifies that one or more of the *uuid_key* values passed refers to data that is not controlled by the individual who is represented by the authentication token.

▼ **E_operatorMismatch**: signifies that one or more of the *uuid_key* values passed refers to data that is not controlled by the *Operator Site* that received the request for processing.

▼ **E_invalidCategory (20000)**: signifies that a keyValue did not correspond to a category within the taxonomy identified by the tModelKey in the categoryBag data provided.

▼ **E_categorizationNotAllowed (20100:** The taxonomy validation routine chosen by the *Operator Site* has rejected the businessService data provided.

▼ **E_accountLimitExceeded**: signifies that user account limits have been exceeded.

save_tModel

The save_tModel message adds or updates one or more tModel structures.

Syntax:

```
<save_tModel generic="1.0" xmlns="urn:uddi-org:api">
  <authInfo/>
  <tModel/> [<tModel/>...] |<uploadRegister/> [<upload
    Register/>...]
</save_tModel>
```

Arguments:

▼ *authInfo*: this required argument is an element that contains an authentication token. Authentication tokens are obtained using the get_authToken API call.

▼ *tModel*: one or more complete tModel structures can be passed. If adding a new tModel, the tModelKey value should be passed as an empty element.

▼ *uploadRegister*: one or more resolvable HTTP URL addresses that each point to a single and valid tModel structure. This variant argument allows a registry to be updated to reflect the contents of an XML document that is URL addressable. The URL must return a pure XML document that only contains a tModel structure as its top-level element, and be accessible using the standard HTTP-GET protocol.

Behavior:

If any of the *uuid_key* values within in a tModel structure (e.g. tModelKey) is passed with a blank value, this is a signal that the data is being inserted.

To make this function perform an update to existing registered data, the tModel Key values should have *uuid_key* values that correspond to the registered data. All tModelKey values that are non-blank are formatted as urn values (e.g. the characters "uuid:" precede all UUID values for tModelKey values)

If a tModelKey value is passed that corresponds to a tModel that was previously hidden via the delete_tModel message, the result will be the restoration of the tModel to full visibility (e.g. available for return in find_tModel results again).

Returns:

This API returns a tModelDetail message containing the final results of the call that reflects the new registered information for the effected tModel structures.

Caveats:

If any error occurs in processing this message, a dispositionReport structure will be returned to the caller in a SOAP Fault. The following error number information will be relevant:

▼ **E_authTokenExpired**: signifies that the authentication token value passed in the authInfo argument is no longer valid because the token has expired.

▼ **E_authTokenRequired**: signifies that the authentication token value passed in the authInfo argument is either missing or is not valid.

▼ **E_keyRetired**: signifies that the request cannot be satisfied because one or more *uuid_key* values specified has previously been hidden or removed by the requester. This specifically applies to the tModelKey values passed.

▼ **E_invalidKeyPassed**: signifies that the request cannot be satisfied because one or more *uuid*_key values specified is not a valid key value. This will occur if a *uuid_key* value is passed in a tModel that does not match with any known tModel key.

▼ **E_invalidURLPassed**: an error occurred with one of the uploadRegister URL values.

▼ **E_userMismatch**: signifies that one or more of the *uuid_key* values passed refers to data that is not controlled by the individual who is represented by the authentication token.

▼ **E_operatorMismatch**: signifies that one or more of the *uuid_key* values passed refers to data that is not controlled by the *Operator Site* that received the request for processing.

▼ **E_invalidCategory**: signifies that the given keyValue did not correspond to a category within the taxonomy identified by a tModelKey value within one of the categoryBag elements provided.

▼ **E_categorizationNotAllowed**: Restrictions have been placed by the taxonomy provider on the types of information that should be included at that location within a specific taxonomy. The validation routine chosen by the *Operator Site* has rejected this tModel for at least one specified category.

▼ **E_accountLimitExceeded**: signifies that user account limits have been exceeded.

Appendix A: Error code reference

Error Codes

The following list of error codes can be returned in the errno values within a dispositionReport response to the API calls defined in this programmer's reference. The descriptions in this section are general and when used with the specific return information defined in the individual API call descriptions are useful for determining the reason for failures.

▼ **E_authTokenExpired**: (10110) signifies that the authentication token information has timed out.

▼ **E_authTokenRequired**: (10120) signifies that an invalid authentication token was passed to an API call that requires authentication.

▼ **E_accountLimitExceeded**: (10160) signifies that a save request exceeded the quantity limits for a given structure type. See "Structure Limits" in Appendix D for details.

▼ **E_busy**: (10400) signifies that the request cannot be processed at the current time.

▼ **E_categorizationNotAllowed**: (20100) Restrictions have been placed by the on the types of information that can categorized within a specific taxonomy. The data provided does not conform to the restrictions placed on the category used. Used with categorization only.

▼ **E_fatalError**: (10500) signifies that a serious technical error has occurred while processing the request.

▼ **E_invalidKeyPassed**: (10210) signifies that the uuid_key value passed did not match with any known key values. The details on the invalid key will be included in the dispositionReport structure.

▼ **E_invalidCategory** (20000): signifies that the given keyValue did not correspond to a category within the taxonomy identified by the tModelKey. Used with categorization only.

▼ **E_invalidURLPassed**: (10220) signifies that an error occurred during processing of a save function involving accessing data from a remote URL. The details of the HTTP Get report will be included in the dispositionReport structure.

▼ **E_keyRetired**: (10310) signifies that a *uuid_key* value passed has been removed from the registry. While the key was once valid as an accessor, and is still possibly valid, the publisher has removed the information referenced by the *uuid_key* passed.

▼ **E_languageError**: (10060) signifies that an error was detected while processing elements that were annotated with xml:lang qualifiers. Presently, only the description element supports xml:lang qualifiacations.

▼ **E_nameTooLong**: (10020) signifies that the partial name value passed exceeds the maximum name length designated by the policy of an implementation or *Operator Site*.

▼ **E_operatorMismatch**: (10130) signifies that an attempt was made to use the publishing API to change data that is mastered at another *Operator Site*. This error is only relevant to the public *Operator Sites* and does not apply to other UDDI compatible registries.

▼ **E_success**: (0) Signifies no failure occurred. This return code is used with the dispositionReport for reporting results from requests with no natural response document.

▼ **E_tooManyOptions**: (10030) signifies that incompatible arguments were passed.

▼ **E_unrecognizedVersion**: (10040) signifies that the value of the *generic* attribute passed is unsupported by the *Operator Instance* being queried.

▼ **E_unknownUser**: (10150) signifies that the user ID and password pair passed in a get_authToken message is not known to the *Operator Site* or is not valid.

▼ **E_unsupported**: (10050) signifies that the implementer does not support a feature or API.

▼ **E_userMismatch**: (10140) signifies that an attempt was made to use the publishing API to change data that is controlled by another party. In certain cases, E_operatorMismatch takes precedence in reporting an error.

dispositionReport overview

Errors that are not reported by way of SOAP Faults are reported using the dispositionReport structure. This structure can be used to signal success for asynchronous requests as well.

Success Reporting with the dispositionReport structure

The general form of a success report is:

```
<?xml version="1.0" encoding="UTF-8" ?>
<Envelope xmlns="http://schemas.xmlsoaporg.org/soap/envelope/">
<Body>
   <dispositionReport generic="1.0" operator="OperatorUrl"
        xmlns="urn:uddi-org:api" >
    <result errno="0" >
     <errInfo errCode="E_success" />
    </result>
   </dispositionReport>
</Body>
</Envelope>
```

Error reporting with the dispositionReport structure

All application errors are communicated via the use of the SOAP FAULT structure. The general form of an error report is:

```
<?xml version="1.0" encoding="UTF-8" ?>
<Envelope xmlns="http://schemas.xmlsoaporg.org/soap/envelope/">
<Body>
  <Fault>
        <faultcode>Client</faultcode>
        <faultstring>Client Error</faultstring>
        <detail>
          <dispositionReport generic="1.0" operator="OperatorUrl"
               xmlns="urn:uddi-org:api" >
           <result errno="10050" >
            <errInfo errCode="E_notSupported">
               The findQualifier value passed is unrecognized.
            </errInfo>
           </result>
          </dispositionReport>
        </detail>
     </Fault>
</Body>
</Envelope>
```

Multiple *result* elements may be present within the dispositionReport structure, and can be used to provide very detailed error reports for multiple error conditions. The number of *result* elements returned within a disposition report is implementation specific. In general it is permissible to return an error response as soon as the first error in a request is detected.

Appendix B: SOAP usage details

This appendix covers the SOAP specific conventions and requirements for *Operator Sites*.

Support for SOAPAction

In version 1, the SOAPAction HTTP Header is required. The value passed in this HTTP Header must be an empty string that is surrounded by double quotes. Example:

```
POST /get_BindingDetail HTTP/1.1
Host: www.someOperator.com
Content-Type: text/xml; charset="utf-8"
Content-Length: nnnn
SOAPAction: ""
```

Support for SOAP Actor

In version 1 of the UDDI specification, the SOAP Actor feature is not supported. *Operator Sites* will reject any request that arrives with a SOAP Actor attribute.

Support for SOAP encoding

In version 1 of the UDDI specification, the SOAP encoding feature (section 5) is not supported. *Operator Sites* will reject any request that arrives with a SOAP encoding attribute.

Support for SOAP Fault

SOAP Fault applies when unknown API references invoked, etc. Applegate specific errors will be handled via the dispositionReport API within SOAP Fault structures (see appendix A). The following SOAP fault codes are used:

▼ **VersionMismatch**: An invalid namespace reference for the SOAP envelope element was passed. The valid namespace value is "http://www.xmlsoap.org/soap/envelope/".

▼ **MustUnderstand**: A SOAP header element was passed to an *Operator Site*. *Operator Sites* do not support any SOAP headers, and will return this error whenever a SOAP request is received that contains any Headers element.

▼ **Client**: A message was incorrectly formed or did not contain enough information to perform more exhaustive error reporting.

Support for SOAP Headers

In version 1 of the UDDI specification, SOAP Headers are not supported. *Operator Sites* are permitted to ignore any headers received. SOAP headers that have the must_understand attribute set to true will be rejected with a SOAP fault—MustUnderstand.

Document encoding conventions – default namespace support

Operator Sites are required to support the use of the default namespaces in SOAP request and response documents as shown in the following HTTP example:

```
POST /get_bindingDetail HTTP/1.1
Host: www.someoperator.org
Content-Type: text/xml; charset="utf-8"
Content-Length: nnnn
SOAPAction: ""

<?xml version="1.0" encoding="UTF-8" ?>
<Envelope xmlns="http://schemas.xmlsoap.org/soap/envelope/">
    <Body>
       <get_bindingDetail generic="1.0"
           xmlns="urn:uddi-org:api">
...
```

UTF-8 to Unicode: SOAP listener behavior

The decision to use the UTF-8 encoding in all requests simplified the number of encoding variations that need to be handled within the XML interchanges used in this API specification. However, byte ordering and conversion issues can still arise. This section describes the behavior of the SOAP listeners that run at *Operator Sites* in regards to the way they convert data received into XML encoded in Unicode.

UTF-8 allows data to be transmitted with an optional three-position byte order mark (BOM) preceding the XML data. This BOM does not contain information that is useful for decoding the contents, but tells the receiving program the order that bytes within double-byte pairs occur within the data. Further analysis can then be performed to determine whether the XML received contains ASCII or Unicode characters. The BOM is not required to perform this analysis however, and it is safe for *Operator Sites* to remove the BOM prior to processing messages received.

Operator Sites must be prepared to accept messages that contain Byte Order Marks, but the BOM is not required to process SOAP messages successfully.

Data returned by all of the messages defined in this specification will not contain a BOM, and will be encoded as UTF-8 XML data.

Appendix C: XML Usage Details

This appendix explains the specifics of XML conventions employed across all UDDI *Operator Sites*. Implementations that desire to remain compliant with the behaviors of *Operator Sites* should follow these same conventions.

Use of multiple languages in the description elements.

Many of the messages defined in this programmers interface specification contain an element named *description*. Multiple descriptions are allowed to accommodate multiple language descriptions. These description elements are also permitted to be sent without an xml:lang attribute qualifier.

Only one description element is allowed to be passed to a save_xx API call without an xml:lang attribute qualifier. Elements passed in this way will be assigned the default language code of the registering party. This default language code is established at the time that publishing credentials are established with an individual *Operator Site*.

If more than one description element is sent in a document being stored, only the first description element in a particular structure may be sent without a xml:lang attribute qualifier. All subsequent description peers must contain an xml:lang qualifier.

Valid Language Codes

The valid values for language codes are to be specified as ISO language codes. Values for these codes and translation to other common language code sets can be found at:

<u>http://www.unicode.org/unicode/onlinedat/languages.html</u>

Only one description element is allowed for each language code used at any given container level.

Default Language Codes

A default ISO language code will be determined for a publisher at the time that a party establishes permissions to publish at a given *Operator Site* or implementation. This default language code will be applied to any description values that are provided with no language code.

On data returned via the SOAP interface, all descriptions will contain xml:lang qualifications.

ISSUE for Validation: XML namespace declaration

For use with the xml:lang language qualifiers, documents that contain this attribute will declare the xml namespace as:

xmlns:xml="<u>http://www.w3.org/1999/XMLSchema</u>"

This will occur at the top level of the instance document (in the Envelope element)

Support for XML Encoding

All messages to and from the Operator Site shall be encoded using the UTF-8 encoding, and all such messages shall have the 'encoding="UTF-8"' attribute on the initial line. Other encoding name variants, such as UTF8, UTF_8, etc. shall not be used. Therefore, to be explicit, the initial line shall be:

```
<?xml version="1.0" encoding="UTF-8" ?>
```

Appendix D: Security model in the publishers API

The Publishers API describes the messages that are used to control the content contained within an *Operator Site*, and can be used by compliant non-operator implementations that adhere to the behaviors described in this programmers reference specification.

Achieving wire level privacy: All methods are secured via SSL

All calls made to *Operator Sites* that use the messages defined in the publishers API will be transported using SSL encryption. *Operator Sites* will each provide a service description that exposes a bindingTemplate that makes use of HTTPS and SSL to secure the transmission of data.

Authentication

Each of the calls in the publishers API that change information at a given *Operator Site* requires the use of an opaque authentication token. These tokens are generated by or provided by each *Operator Site* independently, and are passed from the caller to the *Operator Site* in the element named *authInfo*.

These tokens are meaningful only to the *Operator Site* that provided them and are to be used according to the published policies of a given *Operator Site*.

Each party who has been granted publication access to a given *Operator Site* will be provided a token by the site. Obtaining this token is *Operator Site* specific.

Establishing credentials

Before any party can publish data within an *Operator Site*, credentials and permission to publish must be established with the individual operator. Generally, you will only need to interact with one *Operator Site* because all data published at any *Operator Site* is replicated automatically to all other *Operator Sites*. Establishing publishing credentials involves providing some verifiable identification information, contact information and establishing security credentials with the individual *Operator Site*. The specifics of these establishing credentials is *Operator Site* dependant, and all valid *Operator Sites* will provide a Web-based user interface via which to establish an identity and secure permissions to publish data.

Authentication tokens are not portable

Every registry implementation that adheres to these specifications will establish their own mechanism for token generation and authentication. The only requirement placed on token generation for use with the publishers API is that the tokens themselves must be valid string text that can be placed within the authInfo XML element. Given that binary to string translations are well understood and in common use, this requirement will not introduce hardships.

Authentication tokens are not required to be valid except at the *Operator Site* or implementation from which they originated. These tokens need only have meaning at a single *Operator Site* or implementation, and will not be expected to work across sites.

Generating Authentication Tokens

Many implementations are expected to require a login step. The get_authToken message is provided to accommodate those implementations that desire a login step. Security schemes that are based on the convention of exchanging User ID and password credentials fall into this category. For implementations that desire this kind of security, the get_authToken API is provided as an optional means for generating a temporary authentication token.

Certificate based authentication and similar security mechanisms do not require this additional step of "logging in" and can directly pass compatible authentication token information (such as a certificate value) within the authInfo element provided on each of the publishers API messages. If certificate based authentication or similar security is employed by the choice of a given *Operator Site*, the use of the get_authToken and discard_authToken messages is optional.

Per-account space limits

Operator Sites may impose limits on the amount of data that can be published by a given user. The initial limits for a new user are:

▼ businessEntity: 1 per user account

▼ businessService: 4 per businessEntity

▼ bindingTemplate: 2 per businessService

▼ tModel: 10 per user account

Individual user accounts can negotiate per-account limits with the *Operator Site*.

Appendix E: Search Qualifiers

The inquiry API functions *find_binding*, *find_business*, *find_service*, and *find_tModel* each will accept an optional element named findQualifiers. This element argument is provided as a means to allow the caller to override default search behaviors.

General form of search qualifiers

The general form of the findQualifiers structure is:

```
<findQualifiers>
    <findQualifier>fixedQualifierValue</findQualifier>
    [<findQualifier>fixedQualifierValue</findQualifier> ...]
</findQualifiers>
```

Search Qualifiers enumerated

The value passed in each findQualifier element represents the behavior change desired by the caller. These values must come from the following list of qualifiers:

▼ **exactNameMatch**: signifies that leftmost name match behavior should be overridden. When this behavior is specified, only entries that exactly match the entry passed in the name argument will be returned.

▼ **caseSentiveMatch**: signifies that the default case-insensitive behavior of a name match should be overridden. When this behavior is specified, case is relevant in the search results and only entries that match the case of the value passed in the name argument will be returned.

▼ **sortByNameAsc**: signifies that the result returned by a *find_x* or *get_x* inquiry call should be sorted on the name field in ascending alphabetic sort order. This sort is applied prior to any truncation of result sets. Only applicable on queries that return a *name* element in the topmost detail level of the result set. If no conflicting sort qualifier is specied, this is the default sort order for inquiries that return *name* values at this topmost detail level.

▼ **sortByNameDesc**: signifies that the result returned by a *find_x* or *get_x* inquiry call should be sorted on the name field in descending alphabetic sort order. This sort is applied prior to any truncation of result sets. Only applicable on queries that return a *name* element in the topmost detail level of the result set. This is the reverse of the default sort order for this kind of result.

▼ **sortByDateAsc**: signifies that that the result returned by a *find_x* or *get_x* inquiry call should be sorted based on the date last updated in ascending chronological sort order (earliest returns first). If no conflicting sort qualifier is specified, this is the default sort order for all result sets. Sort qualifiers involving date are secondary in precedence to the sortByName qualifiers. This causes sortByName elements to be sorted within name by date, oldest to newest.

▼ **sortByDateDesc**: (default) signifies that the result returned by a *find_x* or *get_x* inquiry call should be sorted based on the date last updated in descending chronological sort order (most recent change returns first). Sort qualifiers involving date are secondary in precedence to the sortByName qualifiers. This causes sortByName elements to be sorted within name by date, oldest to newest.

At this time, these are the only qualifiers defined. *Operator Sites* may define more search qualifier values than these – but all *Operator Sites* and fully compatible software must support these qualifiers and behaviors.

Search Qualifier Precedence

Precedence of search qualifiers, when combined is as follows:

1. **exactNameMatch**, **caseSensitiveMatch**: These can be combined but are equal in precedence.

2. **sortByNameAsc**, **sortByNameDesc**: These are mutually exclusive, but equal in precedence.

3. **sortByDateAsc**, **sortByDateDesc**: These are mutually exclusive, but equal in precedence.

The precedence order is used to determine the proper ordering of results when multiple search qualifiers are combined.

Locale Details

The US English (EN_US) locale shall be used whenever a string comparison or alphabetic sort is specified. This applies to sortByNameAsc, sortByNameDesc, exactNameMatch.

Appendix F: Response message reference

Here we explain each of the response messages. These are technically defined in the UDDI API schema:

▼ **authToken**: This structure is return by the optional get_authToken message to return authentication information. The value returned is used in subsequent calls that require an authInfo value.

▼ **bindingDetail**: This structure is the technical information required to make a method call to an advertised web service. It is returned in response to the get_bindingDetail message.

▼ **businessDetail**: This structure contains full details for zero or more businessEntity structures. It is returned in response to a get_businessDetail message, and optionally in response to the save_business message.

▼ **businessDetailExt**: This structure allows UDDI compatible registries to define and share extended information about a businessEntity. *Operator Sites* support this message but return no additional data. This structure contains zero or more businessEntityExt structures. It is returned in response to a get_businessDetailExt message.

▼ **businessList**: This structure contains abbreviated information about registered businessEntity information. This message contains zero or more businessInfo structures. It is returned in response to a find_business message.

▼ **dispositionReport**: This structure is used to report the outcome of message processing and to report errors discovered during processing. This message contains one or more result structures. A special case – success – contains only one result structure with the special errno attribute value of E_success (0).

▼ **registeredInfo**: This structure contains abbreviated information about all registered businessEntity and tModel information that are controlled by the party specified in the request. This message contains one or more businessInfo structures and zero or more tModelInfo structures. It is returned in response to a get_registeredInfo message.

▼ **serviceDetail**: This structure contains full details for zero or more business Service structures. It is returned in response to a get_serviceDetail message, and optionally in response to the save_binding and save_service messages.

▼ **serviceList**: This structure contains abbreviated information about registered businessService information. This message contains zero or more serviceInfo structures. It is returned in response to a find_service message.

▼ **tModelDetail**: This structure contains full details for zero or more tModel structures. It is returned in response to a get_tModelDetail message, and optionally in response to the save_tModel message.

▼ **tModelList**: This structure contains abbreviated information about registered tModel information. This message contains zero or more tModelInfo structures. It is returned in response to a find_tModel message.

Appendix G: redirection via hostingRedirector element

One of the main benefits of using a public *Operator* Site instance of an UDDI registry is to provide a single point of reference for determining the correct location to send a business service request to a remote web service. In general, the controller of a particular instance of bindingTemplate structure can be assured that by keeping the registered copy pointing to the proper server or invocation address, special conditions such as disaster recovery to a secondary site can be handled with a minimum of service disruption for customers or partners. The same holds true for those who choose to use a registry that is compatible with the UDDI API, but to a lesser degree.

In many cases, the API specified in the get_bindingDetail message is straightforward. Once a business or application knows of a service that needs to be invoked, the bindingTemplate information for this service can be cached until needed. In the event that the cached information fails at the time the partner web service is actually invoked (e.g. the accessPoint information in the cached bindingTemplate structure is used to invoke a remote partner service), the application can use the bindingKey in the cached information to get a fresh copy of the bindingTemplate information. This cached approach serves to prevent needless round trips to the registry.

Special situations requiring the hostingRedirector

Two special needs arise that cannot be directly supported by the *accessPoint* information in a bindingTemplate. These are:

▼ **Third Party Hosting of Technical Web Services**: A business chooses to expose a service that is actually hosted at a remote or third party site. Application Service Providers and Network Market Makers are common examples of this situation. In this situation, it is the actual third party that needs to control the actual value of the binding information.

▼ **Use specific access control to binding location**: In other situations, such as situation specific redirection based on the identity of the caller, or even time-of-day routing, it is necessary to provide the actual contact point information for the remote service in a more dynamic way than the cached accessPoint data would support.

For these cases, the bindingTemplate structures contain an alternative data element called *hostingRedirector*. The presence of a hostingRedirector element is mutually exclusive with the accessPoint information. This makes it possible to tell which method of gaining the actual bindingTemplate information that contains the accessPoint data to use.

Using the hostingRedirector data

When a bindingTemplate returned by UDDI registry contains a hosting-Redirector element, the programmer uses this information to locate the actual bindingTemplate for the hosted service. The content of the hostingRedirector element is a bindingKey reference that refers to another bindingTemplate that contains the address of a redirector service that will respond to a get_bindingDetail message. The argument that gets passed to this message is the original binding-Template *uuid_key* value for the redirected service. The bindingTemplate returned by this redirected call must have a accessPoint element in it – this being the actual binding information for the redirected web service request.

Stepwise overview

1. A business registers a bindingTemplate *A* for a remotely hosted or redirected business service *S*. This bindingTemplate contains a bindingKey value *Q* that references a second bindingTemplate *B*. The bindingTemplate *B* is typically controlled by the organization that hosts the redirection service. This bindingTemplate *B* contains an accessPoint element that points to the actual hostingRedirector service *R*.

2. A program that wants to call the service S that is registered in step one gets the binding information for the advertised service. This bindingTemplate information contains a hostingRedirector element with the bindingKey K for the bindingTemplate B.

3. The programmer takes the bindingKey K for and issues a get_bindingDetail message against the UDDI registry that the original bindingTemplate A came from. This returns the data for bindingTemplate B. The programmer now has the address of the service that implements the redirection. This information is in the accessPoint element found in bindingTemplate B. This service, to be compliant, knows how to respond to a get_bindingDetail message.

4. Using the original binding key Q and issues a get_bindingDetails to the redirector service R. This service is responsible for returning the actual binding information for the redirected business service S or returning an error. The programmer has the choice of caching this bindingTemplate if desired.

Using this algorithm, an organization that hosts services for other businesses to use can control the information that is used to actually access the hosted service. This not only provides this hosting organization with the ability to manage situations such as disaster recovery locations, but also lets them specify the actual URL that is used to make a call to the actual business service. This URL can be keyed specifically to the caller, or can be a general location for the hosted or redirected service.

In any case, the original caller is able to find the technical web service (binding Template) advertised within the actual business partner's data without having to know that any redirection occurred.

Appendix H: Details on the validate_categorization call

Whenever save_business, save_service or save_tModel are called, all contents of any included *categoryBag* information may be checked to see that it is properly coded to match existing categories. The reason given for this is to maximize consistency across category based searches.

Operator specific policy allows interpretation of various error returns to result in non-specified behavior. Consult the operations policy of the operator at which you register data to understand the specific behaviors of any validation performed.

validate_categorization

The validate_categorization service performs two functions. It is used to verify that a specific category (keyValue) exists within the given taxonomy. The service also optionally restricts the entities that may be classified within the category.

Syntax:

```
<validate_categorization generic="1.0" xmlns="name_qualifier" >
  <tModelKey/>
  <keyValue/>
  [ <businessEntity/> | <businessService/> | <tModel/> ]
</validate_categorization>
```

Arguments:

The optional businessEntity, businessService or tModel parameters are mutually exclusive.

▼ *tModelKey*: The identifier of a registered tModel that is used as a name-space qualifier that implies a specific taxonomy.

▼ **keyValue:** The *category identifier*[9] of the category within the identified taxonomy.

▼ **businessEntity:** (optional) The businessEntity structure being categorized

▼ **businessService:** (optional) The business service structure being categorized.

▼ **tModel:** (optional) The tModel structure being categorized.

Behavior:

To validate categorizations of registry entries, it is sufficient to verify the category identified by the keyValue parameter exists within the taxonomy identified by the tModelKey.

Optionally, a businessEntity, businessService, or tModel may be passed with the required values. This additional information may be used by the taxonomy

---

[9]A *category identifier* is the specific coded value that designates a category within taxonomy. An example would be NAICS code 247 with the appropriate category identifier being "247".

validation service to verify that the entity is properly classified within this taxonomy category.

Returns:

Upon successful completion, a dispositionReport is returned with a single success indicator.

Caveats:

If any error occurs in processing this message, a dispositionReport structure will be returned to the caller. The following error number information will be relevant:

▼ **E_invalidKeyPassed**: the tModelKey value passed didn't match any known tModel.

▼ **E_invalidCategory**: one of the keyValue values supplied did not correspond to a category within the taxonomy identified by the tModel Key.

▼ **E_categorizationNotAllowed**: The optional businessEntity, businessService, or tModel provided does not conform to restrictions placed on the given category by the taxonomy publisher.

Appendix I: Utility tModels and Conventions

In order to facilitate consistency in Service Description (tModel) registration, and provide a framework for their basic organization within the UDDI registry, a set of conventions has been established. This section describes the conventions for registration of Service Descriptions, as well as a set of Utility tModels that facilitate registration of common information and the services provided by the UDDI registry itself.

UDDI Type Taxonomy

The UDDI specifications provide a great deal of flexibility in terms of the types of information that may be registered. A type taxonomy has been established to assist in general categorization of the types of information registered. In this release, the type taxonomy has been developed for the categorization of Service Descriptions, or tModels. Business or Service types may be incorporated into this taxonomy at a later date.

The approach to categorization of tModels within the UDDI Type Taxonomy is consistent with that used for each of the other taxonomies. The categorization information for each tModel is added to the **<categoryBag>** elements in a **save_tModel** message. A **<keyedReference>** element is added to the category bag to indicate the type of tModel that is being registered.

The values used for keyed references are defined in the UDDI Type Taxonomy shown in the tModel description table below.

tModel Name:	`uddi-org:types`
tModel Description:	UDDI Type Taxonomy
tModel UUID:	`uuid:C1ACF26D-9672-4404-9D70-39B756E62AB4`

Taxonomy Values

The table below describes the UDDI types taxonomy. As the structure is hierarchical, the ParentID column indicates the parent-child relationships. The tModel key is the root of the structure. Categorization is allowed at all levels of the taxonomy, with the exception of the root key.

ID	ParentID	Allowed	Description
tModel	tModel	no	These types are used for tModels
identifier	tModel	yes	Unique identifier
namespace	tModel	yes	Namespace
categorization	tModel	yes	Categorization (taxonomy)
specification	tModel	yes	Specification for a Web Service
xmlSpec	specification	yes	Specification for a Web Service using XML messages
soapSpec	xmlSpec	yes	Specification for interaction with a Web Service using SOAP messages
wsdlSpec	specification	yes	Specification for a Web Service described in WSDL
protocol	tModel	yes	Protocol
transport	protocol	yes	Wire/transport protocol
signature-Component	tModel	yes	Signature component

tModel: The UDDI type taxonomy is structured to allow for categorization of registry entries other than tModels. This key is the root of the branch of the taxonomy that is intended for use in categorization of tModels within the UDDI registry. Categorization is not allowed with this key.

identifier: An identifier tModel represents a specific set of values used to uniquely identify information. For example, a Dun & Bradstreet D-U-N-S® Number uniquely identifies companies globally. The D-U-N-S® Number taxonomy is an identifier taxonomy.

namespace: A namespace tModel represents a scoping constraint or domain for a set of information. In contrast to an identifier, a namespace does not have a predefined set of values within the domain, but acts to avoid collisions. It is similar to the namespace functionality used for XML.

categorization: A categorization tModel is used for information taxonomies within the UDDI registry. NAICS and UNSPSC are examples of categorization tModels.

specification: A specification tModel is used for tModels that define interactions with a Web Service. These interactions typically include the definition of the set of requests and responses or other types of interaction that are prescribed by the service. tModels describing XML, COM, Corba, or any other services are specification tModels.

xmlSpec: An xmlSpec tModel is a refinement of the specification tModel type. It is used to indicate that the interaction with the service is via XML. The UDDI API tModels are xmlSpec tModels.

soapSpec: Further refining the xmlSpec tModel type, a soapSpec is used to indicate that the interaction with the service is via SOAP. The UDDI API tModels are soapSpe tModels, in addition to xmlSpec tModels.

wsdlSpec: A tModel for a Web Service described using WSDL is categorized as a wsdlSpec.

protocol: A tModel describing a protocol of any sort.

transport: A transport tModel is a specific type of protocol. HTTP, FTP, and SMTP are types of transport tModels.

signatureComponent: A signature component is used to for cases where a single tModel can not represent a complete specification for a Web Service. This is the case for specifications like RosettaNet, where implementation requires the composition of three tModels to be complete - a general tModel indicating RNIF, one for the specific PIP, and one for the error handling services.

Each of these tModels would be of type signature component, in addition to any others as appropriate.

UDDI Registry tModels

The UDDI registry defines a number of tModels to define its core services. Each of the core tModels are listed in this section.

tModel Name:	`uddi-org:inquiry`
tModel Description:	UDDI Inquiry API - Core Specification
tModel UUID:	`uuid:4CD7E4BC-648B-426D-9936-443EAAC8AE23`
Categorization:	`specification, xmlSpec, soapSpec`

This tModel defines the inquiry API calls for interacting with the UDDI registry.

tModel Name:	`uddi-org:publication`
tModel Description:	UDDI Publication API - Core Specification
tModel UUID:	`uuid:64C756D1-3374-4E00-AE83-EE12E38FAE63`
Categorization:	`specification, xmlSpec, soapSpec`

This tModel defines the publication API calls for interacting with the UDDI registry.

tModel Name:	`uddi-org:taxonomy`
tModel Description:	UDDI Taxonomy API
tModel UUID:	`uuid:3FB66FB7-5FC3-462F-A351-C140D9BD8304`
Categorization:	`specification, xmlSpec, soapSpec`

This tModel defines the taxonomy maintenance API calls for interacting with the UDDI registry.

UDDI Core tModels - Taxonomies

An additional set of tModels has been established to assist in categorization within industry taxonomies. There tModels are described below.

tModel Name:	`ntis-gov:naics:1997`
tModel Description:	Business Taxonomy: NAICS (1997 Release)

tModel UUID:	`uuid:C0B9FE13-179F-413D-8A5B-5004DB8E5BB2`
Categorization:	`categorization`

This tModel defines the NAICS industry taxonomy.

tModel Name:	`unspsc-org:unspsc:3-1`
tModel Description:	Product Taxonomy: UNSPSC (Version 3.1)
tModel UUID:	`uuid:DB77450D-9FA8-45D4-A7BC-04411D14E384`
Categorization:	`categorization`

This tModel defines the UNSPSC product taxonomy.

tModel Name:	`uddi-org:misc-taxonomy`
tModel Description:	Other Taxonomy
tModel UUID:	`uuid:A035A07C-F362-44dd-8F95-E2B134BF43B4`
Categorization:	`categorization`

This tModel defines an unidentified taxonomy.

UDDI Core tModels - Other

Additional tModels are defined to help register within leading industry encoding schemes and standard protocols. This list is expected to be expanded as appropriate as the UDDI business registry expands.

tModel Name:	`dnb-com:D-U-N-S`
tModel Description:	Dun & Bradstreet D-U-N-S® Number
tModel UUID:	`uuid:8609C81E-EE1F-4D5A-B202-3EB13AD01823`
Categorization:	`identifier`

This tModel is used for the Dun & Bradstreet D-U-N-S® Number identifier. Note that this tModel is initially registered as part of the UDDI core tModels. Once the registry is in production, management of this tModel is expected to be transferred to the Dun & Bradstreet publisher account. For more information, see http://www.dnb.com.

tModel Name:	`thomasregister-com:supplierID`
tModel Description:	Thomas Registry Suppliers
tModel UUID:	`uuid:B1B1BAF5-2329-43E6-AE13-BA8E97195039`
Categorization:	`identifier`

This tModel is used for the Thomas Register supplier identifier codes. Note that this tModel is initially registered as part of the UDDI core tModels. Once the registry is in production, custody of this tModel is expected to be transferred to the Thomas Register publisher account. For more information, see http://www.thomasregister.com.

tModel Name:	`uddi-org:smtp`
tModel Description:	E-mail based web service
tModel UUID:	`uuid:93335D49-3EFB-48A0-ACEA-EA102B60DDC6`
Categorization:	`transport`

This tModel is used to describe a web service that is invoked through SMTP email transmissions. These transmissions may be either between people or applications.

tModel Name:	`uddi-org:fax`
tModel Description:	Fax based web service
tModel UUID:	`uuid:1A2B00BE-6E2C-42F5-875B-56F32686E0E7`
Categorization:	`protocol`

This tModel is used to describe a web service that is invoked through fax transmissions. These transmissions may be either between people or applications.

tModel Name:	`uddi-org:ftp`
tModel Description:	File transfer protocol (ftp) based web service
tModel UUID:	`uuid:5FCF5CD0-629A-4C50-8B16-F94E9CF2A674`
Categorization:	`transport`

This tModel is used to describe a web service that is invoked through file transfers via the ftp protocol.

tModel Name:	`uddi-org:telephone`
tModel Description:	Telephone based web service

tModel UUID:	`uuid:38E12427-5536-4260-A6F9-` `B5B530E63A07`
Categorization:	`specification`

This tModel is used to describe a web service that is invoked through a telephone call and interaction by voice and/or touch-tone.

tModel Name:	`uddi-org:http`
tModel Description:	An http or web browser based web service
tModel UUID:	`uuid:68DE9E80-AD09-469D-8A37-` `088422BFBC36`
Categorization:	`transport`

This tModel is used to describe a web service that is invoked through a web browser and/or the http protocol.

Registering tModels within the Type Taxonomy

When a new tModel is registered within UDDI, its type can be classified within the framework of the UDDI Type Taxonomy. This classification provides additional hints to applications for what type of tModel is being registered. For each appropriate classification, and keyed reference is added to the category bag element for the tModel.

As an example, the Dun & Bradstreet D-U-N-S® Number is a type of identifier for an organization. Within the UDDI type taxonomy, the `dnb-com:D-U-N-S` tModel is classified as type identifier.

The categoryBag element of the tModel registered would be as follows :

```
<categoryBag>
 <keyedReference
   tModelKey = "uuid:C1ACF26D-9672-4404-9D70-39B756E62AB4"
   keyValue = "identifier"
   keyName = "tModel is a unique identifier">
</categoryBag>
```

tModelKey: This is the GUID for the UDDI Types taxonomy. It is required.

keyValue: This is the identifier for the categorization within the UDDI Types taxonomy. It is required.

keyName: This is the description of the identifier within the UDDI Types taxonomy. It is not required as a part of the registration, but simply provides additional information about the key selected.

References

This section contains URL pointers to various specifications and other documents that are pertinent in understanding this specification.

W3C specifications, notes and drafts

- ▼ XML 1.0
- ▼ XML Schema
- ▼ XML namespaces
- ▼ SOAP 1.1

UDDI specifications, white-papers and schemas

- ▼ UDDI API schema
- ▼ UDDI overview
- ▼ UDDI technical overview
- ▼ UDDI Operators specification
- ▼ UDDI.org
- ▼ UDDI XML structure reference

Change History

V1.00 30 September 2000 (Christopher Kurt). Added Appendix I, and updated table of contents as appropriate. Revised document date for final publication.

V1.01 27 March 2001 (Tom Glover). Corrected typographical errors.

CHAPTER
4

UDDI Data Structure Reference V1.0

UDDI Open Draft Specification 30 September 2000

This version:

http://www.uddi.org/pubs/DataStructure-V1.00-Open-20000930.html

Latest version:

http://www.uddi.org/pubs/DataStructure-V1.00-Open-20000930.html

Authors (alphabetically):

Toufic Boubez, IBM

Maryann Hondo, IBM

Chris Kurt, Microsoft

Jared Rodriguez, Ariba

Daniel Rogers, Microsoft

CONTENTS

Introduction

The programmatic interface provided for interacting with systems that follow the Universal Description, Discovery and Integration (UDDI) specifications make use of Extensible Markup Language (XML) and a related technology called Simple Object Access Protocol (SOAP), which is a specification for using XML in simple message-based exchanges.

The UDDI Programmer's API Specification defines approximately 30 SOAP messages that are used to perform inquiry and publishing functions against any UDDI-compliant Business Registry. This document outlines the details of each of the XML structures associated with these messages.

Note: This document is a co-requisite to the UDDI XML Schema document.

Service discovery

The purpose of UDDI-compliant registries is to provide a business discovery platform on the World Wide Web. Service discovery is related to being able to advertise and locate information about different technical interfaces exposed by different parties. Services are interesting when you can discover them, determine their purpose, and then have software that is equipped for using a particular type of Web service complete a connection and derive benefit from a service.

A UDDI-compliant registry provides an information framework for describing services exposed by an entity or business. Using this framework the description of a service that is managed by a UDDI registry is information about the service itself. In order to promote cross platform service description that is suitable to a "black-box[1]" Web environment, this description is rendered in cross-platform XML.

---

[1]The term "black box" in this context implies that the descriptive information found in a UDDI compliant registry is provided in a neutral format that allows any kind of service, without regard to a given services platform requirements or technology requirements. UDDI provides a framework for describing any kind of service, and allows storage of as much detail about a service and its implementation as desired.

Four data structure types

The information that makes up a registration consists of four data structure types. This division by information type provides simple partitions to assist in the rapid location and understanding of the different information that makes up a registration.

The four core types are shown below:

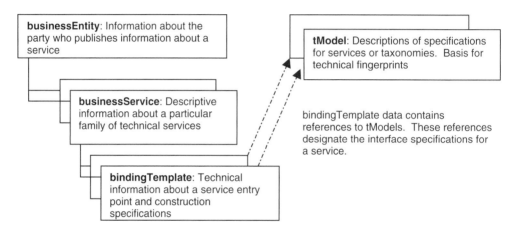

FIGURE 1

These four structure types make up the complete amount of information provided within the UDDI service description framework. Each of these XML structures contains a number of data fields[2] that serve a business or technical descriptive purpose. Explaining each of these structures and the meaning and placement of each field is the primary purpose of this document.

These structures are described in the UDDI API Programmer's API Specification and XML Schema. The schema defines approximately 20 requests and 10 responses, each of which contain these structures, references to these structures, or summary versions of these structures. In this document we first explain the core structures, and then provide descriptions of the individual structures used for the request/response XML SOAP interface.

---

[2]In XML vernacular, fields are called either elements or attributes.

Core structure reference

This section outlines each of the four core structures and provides in-depth technical descriptions of each of the fields contained within each structure.

Overall principles

Each of the four structure types is used to express specific types of data, arranged in the relationship shown in Figure 1. A particular instance of an individual fact or set of related facts is expressed using XML according to the definition of these core types. For instance, two separate businesses may publish information about the Web services they offer, whether these services are entry points for interfacing with accounting systems, or services that allow customers to query the status of a factory order. Each business, and the corresponding service descriptions (both logical and technical descriptions) exist as separate instances of data within a UDDI registry.

Unique identifiers

The individual facts about a business, its services, technical information, or information about specifications for services are kept separate, and are accessed individually by way of unique identifiers, or keys. A UDDI registry assigns these unique identifiers when information is first saved, and these identifiers can be used later as keys to access the specific data instances on demand.

Each unique identifier generated by a UDDI registry takes the form of a Universally Unique ID (UUID). Technically, a UUID is an octet of hexadecimal characters that has been generated according to a very exacting algorithm that is sufficiently precise as to prevent any two UUIDS from ever being generated in duplicate.

Containment

The individual instance data managed by a UDDI registry are sensitive to the parent/child relationships in the XML schema. This same containment relationship is seen in Figure 1 for the core structures. The businessEntity structure contains one or more unique businessService structures. Similarly, individual businessService structures contain specific instances of bindingTemplate data, which in turn contains information that includes pointers to specific instances of tModel structures.

It is important to note that no single instance of a core structure type is ever "contained" by more than one parent structure. This means that only one specific businessEntity structure (identified by its unique key value) will ever contain or be used to express information about a specific instance of a businessService structure (also identified by its own unique key value).

References, on the other hand, operate differently. We can see an example of this in Figure 1 where the bindingTemplate structures contain references to unique instances of tModel structures. References can be repeated within any number of the core typed data instances such that many references to a single unique instance are allowed.

Determining what is a reference to an instance of a core data type and what is a key for a core data type within a specific instance is straightforward. Besides being able to reference this document, which will make the distinction clear in the field-by-field descriptions, you can also use your knowledge that there are four core data types, and that each of these types are key. Thus you know that the businessKey found within the businessEntity structure is a key, and not a reference. Similarly, the serviceKey and bindingKey values found respectively within the businessService and bindingTemplate structures are keys. The same holds true for the tModelKey value found within the tModel structure.

References on the other hand, occur in only two places today. When tModels are referenced, as seen within a bindingTemplate structure, these occur within a list structure designed for the purpose of holding references to tModels. This list, not being one of the four core data structure types, is not keyed as an individual instance. Rather, its own identity is derived from the parent structure that contains it – and it cannot be separated. Thus any key values directly contained in structures that are not themselves one of the four core structure types, are references. Examples include tModelKey values found in lists within bindingTemplate and categorization and identification schemes – in which context the tModel itself represents a uniquely identifiable namespace reference and qualifier.

The businessEntity structure

The businessEntity structure represents all known information about a business or entity that publishes descriptive information about the entity as well as the services that it offers. From an XML standpoint, the businessEntity is the top-level data structure that accommodates holding descriptive information about a business or entity. Service descriptions and technical information are expressed within a businessEntity by a containment relationship.

Structure specification

```
<element name = "businessEntity">
        <type content = "elementOnly">
                <group order = "seq">
                        <element ref = "discoveryURLs" min
                          Occurs = "0" maxOccurs = "1"/>
                        <element ref = "name"/>
                        <element ref = "description" minOccurs
                          = "0" maxOccurs = "*"/>
                        <element ref = "contacts" minOccurs =
                          "0" maxOccurs = "1"/>
                        <element ref = "businessServices"
                          minOccurs = "0" maxOccurs = "1"/>
                        <element ref = "identifierBag" min
                          Occurs = "0" maxOccurs = "1"/>
                        <element ref = "categoryBag" minOccurs
                          = "0" maxOccurs = "1"/>
                </group>
                <attribute name = "businessKey" minOccurs = "1"
                  type = "string"/>
                <attribute name = "operator" type = "string"/>
                <attribute name = "authorizedName" type =
                  "string"/>
        </type>
</element>
```

Descriptive matrix

At the top level, a businessEntity contains the following data. Required data is designated by bold field names:

Field Name	Description	Data Type	Length
businessKey	Attribute. This is the unique identifier for a given instance of a businessEntity data set.	UUID	128 bits (hex)
authorizedName	Attribute. This is the recorded name of the individual that published the businessEntity data. This data is	string	64

	calculated by the controlling operator and should not be supplied within save_business operations.		
operator	Attribute. This is the certified name of the UDDI registry site operator that manages the master copy of the businessEntity data. The controlling operator records this data at the time data is saved. This data is calculated and should not be supplied within save_business operations.	string	48
discoveryURLs	Optional element. This is a list of Uniform Resource Locators (URL) that point to alternate, file based service discovery mechanisms. Each recorded businessEntity structure is automatically assigned a URL that returns the individual businessEntity structure. URL search is provided via find_business call.	structure	
name	Required element. This is the name recorded for the businessEntity. Name search is provided via find_business call. Names may not be blank.	string	128
description	Optional repeating element. One or more short business descriptions. One description is allowed per national language code supplied.	string	255
contacts	Optional element. This is an optional list ofcontact information.	structure	
businessServices	Optional repeating element. This is a list of one or more logical or business service descriptions. If no services are registered with a businessEntity structure for a period of X days, businessEntity data will be subject to clean-up operations.	structure	
identifierBag	Optional element. This is an optional list of name-value pairs that can be used to record identificaton numbers for a businessEntity. These can be used during search via find_business.	structure	
categoryBag	Optional element. This is an optional list of name-value pairs that are used to tag a businessEntity with specific taxonomy information (e.g. industry, product or geographic codes). These can be used during search via find_business.	structure	

Substructure breakdown

DiscoveryURLs

The discoveryURLs structure is used to hold pointers to URL-addressable discovery documents. The expected retrieval mechanism for URLs referenced in the data within this structure is HTTP-GET. The expected return document is not defined. Rather, a framework for establishing convention is provided, and two such conventions are defined within UDDI behaviors. It is the hope that other conventions come about and use this structure to accommodate alternate means of discovery.[3]

Field Name	Description	Data Type	Length
discoveryURL	These are attribute qualified repeating elements holding strings that represent web addressable (via HTTP-GET) discovery documents.	String w/ attributes	255

DiscoveryURL

Each individual discovery URL consists of an attribute whose value designates the URL use-type convention, and a string, found within the body of the element. Each time a businessEntity structure is saved via a call to save_business, the UDDI registry node will generate one URL. The generated URL will point to an instance of either a businessEntity or businessEntityExt structure. The use Type attribute of the discoveryURL will be set to either "businessEntity" or "businessEntityExt" according to the data type found while processing the save_business message. The discoveryURL collection will be augmented so that it includes this generated URL. This URL can then be used to retrieve a specific instance of a businessEntity. The XML returned will be formatted as a normal businessDetail message.

---

[3]An example of an alternate form of service discovery is seen in the ECO Framework as defined by the commerce.net initiative. A convention to provide pointers to ECO discovery entry points could take advantage of the structures provided in discoveryURLs by adopting the useType value "ECO".

Field Name	Description	Data Type	Length
useType	Required attribute that designates the name of the convention that the referenced document follows. Two reserved convention values are "businessEntity" and "businessEntityExt". URL's qualified with these values should point to XML documents of the same type as the useType value.	String	20

Example: An example of the generated data for a given businessEntity might look similar to the following:

```
<discoveryURLs>
    <discoveryURL useType="businessEntity">
    http://www.someOperator?businessKey=BE3D2F08-CEB3-11D3-849F-
      0050DA1803C0
    </discoveryURL>
<discoveryURLs>
```

Contacts

The contacts structure provides a way for information to be registered with a businessEntity record so that someone finding the information can make human contact. Because the information held within the UDDI *Registry Sites* is freely available, some care should be taken when considering the amount of contact information to register. Electronic mail addresses in particular may be the greatest concern if you are sensitive to receiving unsolicited mail.

The contacts structure itself is a simple collection of *contact* structures. You'll find that there are many collections in the UDDI XML schema. Like the *discoveryURLs* structure – which is a container for one or more discoveryURL structures, the *contacts* structure is a simple container where one or more contact structures reside.

Contact

The contact structure lets you record contact information for a person. This information can consist of one or more optional elements, along with a person's name. Contact information exists by containment relationship alone, and no mechanisms for tracking individual contact instances is provided by UDDI specifications.

Field Name	Description	Data Type	Length
useType	Optional attribute that is used to describe the type of contact in freeform text. Suggested examples include "technical questions", "technical contact", "establish account", "sales contact", etc.	String	20
description	Optional element. Zero or more language-qualified [4]descriptions of the reason the contact should be used.	string	255
personName	Required element. Contacts should list the name of the person or name of the job role that will be available behind the contact. Examples of roles include "administrator" or "webmaster".	string	32
phone	Optional repeating element. Used to hold telephone numbers for the contact. This string value can be adorned with an optional useType attribute for descriptive purposes. If more than one phone element is saved, useType attributes are required on each.	string	50
email	Optional repeating element. This string value can be adorned with an optional useType attribute for descriptive purposes. If more than one email element is saved, useType attributes are required on each.	string	128
address	Optional repeating element. This structure represents the printable lines suitable for addressing an envelope.	structure	

Address

The address structure is a simple list of AddressLine elements within the address container. Each addressLine element is a simple string. UDDI compliant registries are responsible for preserving the order of any addressLine data provided.

---

[4]All fields named *description* behave the same way and are subject to the same language identifier rules as described in the XML usage appendix found in the UDDI programmers API specification. Embedded HTML is prohibited in description fields.

Address structures also have two optional attributes for recording the useType (freeform text) and sortCode data. The sortCode values are not significant within a UDDI registry, but may be used by user interfaces that present contact information in some ordered fashion using the values provided in the sortCode attribute.

AddressLine

AddressLine elements contain string data with a suggested line length limit of 40 character positions. Each addressLine element can be adorned with two optional descriptive attributes. Address line order is significant and will always be returned by the UDDI compliant registry in the order originally provided during a call to save_business.

Field Name	Description	Data Type	Length
useType	Optional attribute that is used to describe the type of address in freeform text. Suggested examples include "headquarters", "sales office", "billing department", etc.	String	20
sortCode	Optional attribute that can be used to drive the behavior of external display mechanisms that sort addresses. The suggested values for sortCode include numeric ordering values (e.g. 1, 2, 3), alphabetic character ordering values (e.g. a, b, c) or the first n positions of relevant data within the address.	String	10

businessServices

The businessServices structure provides a way for describing information about families of services. This simple collection accessor contains zero or more businessService structures and has no other associated structures.

identifierBag

The identifierBag element allows business, entity, or tModel data to include information about common forms of identification such as Dun & Bradstreet D-U-N-S® numbers, tax identifiers, etc. This data can be used to signify the identity of the busienssEntity, or can be used to signify the identity of the publishing party. Including data of this sort is optional, but when used greatly enhances the search behaviors exposed via the *find_xx* messages defined in the UDDI Programmers API specification. For a full description of the structures involved in establishing an identity, see the appendix in this document called "Using Identifiers".

categoryBag

The categoryBag element allows businessEntity, businessService and tModel data to be categorized according to any of several available taxonomy based classification schemes. *Operator Registry Sites* automatically provide validated categorization support for three taxonomies that cover industry codes (via NAICS), product and service classifications (via UNSPSC) and geography. Including data of this sort is optional, but when used greatly enhances the search behaviors exposed by the *find_xx* messages defined in the UDDI Programmers API specification. For a full description of structures involved in establishing categorization information, see the appendex in this document called "Using Categorization".

Information included in categoryBag may be used as hints for locating and referencing your published UDDI information. Expect that third party classification services will crawl and index the information found in the UDDI *Registry* Site registry stores, and use the categorization information as a first pass in establishing business level searching facilities. For this reason, it is not necessary to include all possible variants of category information for a given purpose. The sheer volume of data within the UDDI replicated *Registry Sites* makes it impractical as a first source of business level searching using category information.

The businessService structure

The businessService structures each represent a logical service classification. The name of the element includes the term "business" in an attempt to describe the purpose of this level in the service description hierarchy. Each businessService structure is the logical child of a single businessEntity structure. The identity of the containing (parent) businessEntity is determined by examining the embedded businessKey value. If no businessKey value is present, the businessKey must be obtainable by searching for a businessKey value in any parent structure containing the businessService. Each businessService element contains descriptive information in business terms outlining the type of technical services found within each businessService element.

Structure specification

```
<element name = "businessService">
        <type content = "elementOnly">
                <group order = "seq">
                        <element ref = "name"/>
                        <element ref = "description" minOccurs
                          = "0" maxOccurs = "*"/>
                        <element ref = "bindingTemplates"/>
                        <element ref = "categoryBag" minOccurs
                          = "0" maxOccurs = "1"/>
                </group>
                <attribute name = "serviceKey" minOccurs = "1"
                  type = "string"/>
                <attribute name = "businessKey" type =
                  "string"/>
        </type>
</element>
```

Substructure breakdown

Field Name	Description	Data Type	Length
businessKey	This attribute is optional when the businessService data is contained within a fully expressed parent that already contains a businessKey value. If the businessService data is rendered into XML and has no containing parent that has within its data a businessKey, the value of the businessKey that is the parent of the businessService is required to be provided. This behavior supports the ability to browse through the parent-child relationships given any of the core elements as a starting point.	UUID	128 bits (hex)
serviceKey	This is the unique key for a given businessService. When saving a new businessService structure, pass an empty serviceKey value. This signifies that a UUID value is to be generated. To update an existing businessService	UUID	128 bits (hex)

	structure, pass the UUID value that corresponds to the existing service. If this data is received via an inquiry operation, the serviceKey values may not be blank.		
name	This is a human readable name for this service family. Name values may not be blank.	string	40
description	Optional element. Zero or more language-qualified text descriptions of the logical service family.	string	255
binding-Templates	This structure holds the technical service description information related to a given business service family.	structure	
categoryBag	Optional element. This is an optional list of name-value pairs that are used to tag a businessService with specific taxonomy information (e.g. industry, product or geographic codes). These can be used during search via find_service. See categoryBag under businessEntity for a full description.	structure	

bindingTemplates

The bindingTemplates structure is a container for one or more bindingTemplate structures. This simple collection accessor has no other associated structure.

The bindingTemplate structure

Technical descriptions of Web services are accommodated via individual contained instances of bindingTemplate structures. These structures provide support for determining a technical entry point or optionally support remotely hosted services, as well as a lightweight facility for describing unique technical characteristics of a given implementation. Support for technology and application specific parameters and settings files are also supported.

Since UDDI's main purpose is to enable description and discovery of Web Service information, it is the bindingTemplate that provides the most interesting technical data.

Each bindingTemplate structure has a single logical businessService parent, which in turn has a single logical businessEntity parent.

Structure specification

```
<element name = "bindingTemplate">
        <type content = "elementOnly">
            <group order = "seq">
                <element ref = "description" minOccurs = "0"
                  maxOccurs = "*"/>
                <group order = "choice">
                        <element ref = "accessPoint" minOccurs
                            = "0" maxOccurs = "1"/>
                        <element ref = "hostingRedirector"
                            minOccurs = "0"maxOccurs = "1"/>
                </group>
                <element ref = "tModelInstanceDetails"/>
            </group>
            <attribute name = "bindingKey" minOccurs = "1" type
              = "string"/>
            <attribute name = "serviceKey" type = "string"/>
        </type>
</element>
```

Substructure breakdown

Field Name	Description	Data Type	Length
bindingKey	This is the unique key for a given bindingTemplate. When saving a new bindingTemplate structure, pass an empty bindingKey value. This signifies that a UUID value is to be generated. To update an existing bindingTemplate structure, pass the UUID value that corresponds to the existing binding Template instance. If this data is received via an inquiry operation, the bindingKey values may not be blank.	UUID	128 bits (hex)

serviceKey	This is the unique key for a given businessService. When saving a new businessService structure, pass an empty serviceKey value. This signifies that a UUID value is to be generated. To update an existing businessService structure, pass the UUID value that corresponds to the existing service. If this data is received via an inquiry operation, the serviceKey values may not be blank.	UUID	128 bits (hex)
description	Optional element. Zero or more language-qualified text descriptions of the technical service entry point.	string	255
accessPoint	Required attribute qualified data element[5]. This element is a text field that is used to convey the entry point address suitable for calling a particular Web service. This may be a URL, an electronic mail address, or even a telephone number. No assumptions about the type of data in this field can be made without first understanding the technical requirements associated with the Web service[6].	string	255
hostingRedirector	Required element if *accessPoint* not provided. This field is redirected reference to a different bindingTemplate. If you query a bindingTemplate and find a hostingRedirector value, you should retrieve that bindingTemplate and use it in place of the one containing the hostingRedirector data.	structure	
tModelInstance-Details	This structure is a list of tModelInfos. This data, taken in total, should form a distinct fingerprint that can be used to identify compatible services.	structure	

[5]One of accessPoint or hostingRedirector is required.

[6]The content of the structure named tModelInstanceDetails that is found within a bindingTemplate structure serves as a technical fingerprint. This fingerprint is a series of references to uniquely keyed specifications and/or concepts. To build a new service that is compatible with a tModel, the specifications must be understood. To register a service compatible with a specification, reference a tModelKey within the tModelInstanceDetails data for a bindingTemplate instance.

AccessPoint

The accessPoint element is an attribute-qualified pointer to a service entry point. The notion of service at the metadata level seen here is fairly abstract and many types of entry points are accommodated.

A single attribute is provided (named URLType). The purpose of the URLType attribute is to facilitate searching for entry points associated with a particular type of entry point. An example might be a purchase order service that provides three entry points, one for HTTP, one for SMTP, and one for FAX ordering. In this example, we'd find a businessService element that contains three binding-Template entries, each with identical data with the exception of the accessPoint value and URLType value.

The valid values for URLType are:

▼ **mailto**: designates that the accessPoint string is formatted as an electronic mail address reference. (Ex. mailto:purch@fabrikam.com)

▼ **http**: designates that the accessPoint string is formatted as an HTTP compatible Uniform Resource Locator (URL). (Ex. http://www.fabrikam.com/purchasing)

▼ **https**: designates that the accessPoint string is formatted as a secure HTTP compatible URL. (Ex. https://www.fabrikam.com/purchasing)

▼ **ftp**: designates that the accessPoint string is formatted as a writable FTP directory address. (Ex. ftp://ftp.fabrikam.com/public)

▼ **fax**: designates that the accessPoint string is formatted as a telephone number that will connect to a facsimile machine. (Ex. 1 425 555 5555)

▼ **phone**: designates that the accessPoint string is formatted as a telephone number that will connect to human or suitable voice or tone response based system. (Ex. 1 425 555 5555)

▼ **other**: designates that the accessPoint string is formatted as some other address format. When this value is used, one or more of the tModel signatures found in the tModelInstanceInfo collection must imply that a particular format or transport type is required.

hostingRedirector

The hostingRedirector element is used to designate that a bindingTemplate entry is a pointer to a different bindingTemplate entry. The value in providing this facility is seen when a business or entity wants to expose a service description (e.g. advertise that they have a service available that suits a specific purpose) that is actually a service that is described in a separate bindingTemplate record. This might occur when a service is remotely hosted (hence the name of this element), or when many service descriptions could benefit from a single service description.

The hostingRedirector element has a single attribute and no element content. The attribute is a bindingKey value (UUID Hex Octet) that is suitable within the same UDDI registry instance for querying and obtaining the bindingDetail data that is to be used.

There is more information on the hostingRedirector is in the appendices for the UDDI Programmer's API Specification.

tModelInstanceDetails

This structure is a simple accessor container for one or more tModelInstance-Info structures. When taken as a group, the data that is presented in a tModel-InstanceDetails structures forms a technically descriptive fingerprint by virtue of the unordered list of tModelKey references contained within this structure. What this means in English is that when someone registers a bindingTemplate (within a businessEntity data set), it will contain one or more references to specific and identifiable specifications that are implied by the tModelKey values provided with the registration. During an inquiry for a service, an interested party could use this information to look for a specific bindingTemplate that contains a specific tModel reference, or even a set of tModel references. By registering a specific fingerprint in this manner, a software developer can readily signify that they are compatible with the specifications implied in the tModelKeys exposed in this manner.

tModelInstanceInfo

A tModelInstanceInfo structure represents the bindingTemplate instance specific details for a single tModel by reference.

Field Name	Description	Data Type	Length
tModelKey	Required Attribute. This is the unique key reference that implies that the service being described has implementation details that are specified by the	string	255 128 bits (Hex GUID)[7]

---

[7]The data type for tModelKey allows for using URN values in a later revision. In the beta release, the key is a generated GUID. Design work around managing duplicate urn claims will allow user supplied URN keys on tModels in the future.

	specifications associated with the tModel that is referenced		
description	Optional repeating element. This is one or more language qualified text descriptions that designate what role a tModel reference plays in the overall service description.	string	255
instanceDetails	Optional element. This element can be used when tModel reference specific settings or other descriptive information are required to either describe a tModel specific component of a service description or support services that require additional technical data support (e.g. via settings or other handshake operations)	structure	

InstanceDetails

This structure holds service instance specific information that is required to either understand the service implementation details relative to a specific tModelKey reference, or to provide further parameter and settings support. If present, this element should not be empty. Because no single contained element is required in the schema description, this rule is called out here for clarity.

Field Name	Description	Data Type	Length
description	Optional repeating element. This language-qualfied text element is intended for holding a description of the purpose and/or use of the particular instance-Details entry.	string	255
overviewDoc	Optional element. Used to house references to remote descriptive or instructions related to proper use of a bindingTemplate technical sub-element.	Structure	
instanceParms	Optional data element. Used to contain settings parameters or a URL reference to a file that contains settings or parameters required to use a specific facet of a bindingTemplate description. If used to house the parameters themselves, the suggested content is a namespace qualified XML string – using a	string	

namespace outside of the UDDI schema. If
used to house a URL pointer to a file,
the suggested format is URL that is
suitable for retrieving the settings or
parameters via HTTP-GET.

overviewDoc

This optional structure is provided as a placeholder for metadata that describes
overview information about a particular tModel use within a bindingTemplate.

Field Name	Description	Data Type	Length
description	Optional repeating element. This language-qualified string is intended to hold a short descriptive overview of how a particular tModel is to be used.	string	255
overviewURL	Optional element. This string data element is to be used to hold a URL reference to a long form of an overview document that covers the way a particular tModel specific reference is used as a component of an overall web service description. The suggested format is a URL that is suitable for retrieving an HTML based description via a web browser or HTTP-GET operation.	string	255

The tModel structure

Being able to describe a Web service and then make the description meaningful
enough to be useful during searches is an important UDDI goal. Another goal is
to provide a facility to make these descriptions useful enough to learn about how
to interact with a service that you don't know much about. In order to do this,
there needs to be a way to mark a description with information that designates
how it behaves, what conventions it follows, or what specifications or standards
the service is compliant with. Providing the ability to describe compliance with a
specification, concept, or even a shared design is one of the roles that the tModel
structure fills.

The tModel structure takes the form of keyed metadata (data about data). In a general sense, the purpose of a tModel within the UDDI registry is to provide a reference system based on abstraction. Thus, the kind of data that a tModel represents is pretty nebulous. In other words, a tModel registration can define just about anything, but in the current revision, two conventions have been applied for using tModels as sources for determining compatibility and as keyed namespace references.

The information that makes up a tModel is quite simple. There's a key, a name, an optional description, and then a URL that points somewhere – presumably somewhere where the curious can go to find out more about the actual concept represented by the metadata in the tModel itself.

Two main uses

There are two places within a businessEntity registration that you'll find references to tModels. In this regard, tModels are special. Whereas the other data within the businessEntity (e.g. businessService and bindingTemplate data) exists uniquely with one uniquely keyed instance as a member of one unique parent businessEntity, tModels are used as references. This means that you'll find references to specific tModel instances in many businessEntity data sets.

Defining the technical fingerprint

The primary role that a tModel plays is to represent a technical specification. An example might be a specification that outlines wire protocols, interchange formats and interchange sequencing rules. One such specification can be seen in the RosettaNet RNIF 1.0 specification. Other examples can be found in standards efforts such as ebXML[8], ECO[9] and various Electronic Document Interchange (EDI) efforts.

Software that communicates with other software across some communication medium invariably adheres to some pre-agreed specifications. In situations where this is true, the designers of the specifications can establish a unique technical identity within a UDDI registry by registering information about the specification in a tModel.

Once registered in this way, other parties can express the availability of Web services that are compliant with a specification by simply including a reference to

---

[8]OASIS – see xml.org

[9]Eco Framework – see commerce.net

the tModel identitifier (called a tModelKey) in their technical service descriptions bindingTemplate data.

This approach facilitates searching for registered Web services that are compatible with a particular specification. Once you know the proper tModelKey value, you can find out whether a particular business or entity has registered a Web service that references that tModel key. In this way, the tModelKey becomes a technical fingerprint that is unique to a given specification.

Defining an abstract namespace reference

The other place where tModel references is used is within the identifierBag and categoryBag structures that are used to define organizational identity and various classifications. Used in this context, the tModel reference represents a relationship between the keyed name-value pairs to the super-name, or namespace within which the name-value pairs are meaningful.

An example of this can be seen in the way a business or entity can express the fact that their U.S. tax code identifier (which they are sure they are known by to their partners and customers) is a particular value. To do this, let's assume that we find a tModel that is named "US Tax Codes", with a description "United States business tax code numbers as defined by the United States Internal Revenue Service". In this regard, the tModel still represents a specific concept – but instead of being a technical specification, it represents a unique area within which tax code ID's have a particular meaning.

When the meaning is established, a business can use the tModelKey for the tax code tModel as a unique reference that qualifies the remainder of the data that makes up an entry in the identifierBag data. *Operator Registry Sites* have registered a number of useful tModels, including U.S. Tax Codes, NAICS (an industry code taxonomy), UNSPSC (a product and service code taxonomy), and a geographic taxonomy to be determined.

Structure specification

```
<element name = "tModel">
        <type content = "elementOnly">
                <group order = "seq">
                        <element ref = "name"/>
                        <element ref = "description" minOccurs
                          = "0" maxOccurs = "*"/>
                        <element ref = "overviewDoc" minOccurs
                          = "0" maxOccurs = "1"/>
```

```
                                    <element ref = "identifierBag" min
                                      Occurs = "0" maxOccurs = "1"/>
                                    <element ref = "categoryBag" minOccurs
                                      = "0" maxOccurs = "1"/>
                        </group>
                        <attribute name = "tModelKey" minOccurs = "1"
                          type = "string"/>
                        <attribute name = "operator" type = "string"/>
                        <attribute name = "authorizedName" type =
                          "string"/>
            </type>
</element>
```

Substructure breakdown

Field Name	Description	Data Type	Length
tModelKey	Required Attribute. This is the unique key for a given tModel structure. When saving a new tModel structure, pass an empty tModelKey value. This signifies that a UUID value is to be generated[10]. To update an existing tModel structure, pass the tModelKey value that corresponds to an existing tModel instance.	string	255
authorizedName	Attribute. This is the recorded name of the individual that published the tModel data. This data is calculated by the controlling operator and should not be supplied within save_tModel operations.	string	64
operator	Attribute. This is the certified name of the UDDI registry site operator that manages the master copy of the tModel data. The controlling operator records this data at the time data is saved. This data is calculated and should not be supplied within save_tModel operations.	string	48

---

[10] In the beta release (September 2000), tModelKey values will be generated as UUID strings. Subsequent work will focus on defining the tModel keys to be more useful by using URN/URI values that are supplied by the data owners. Process specifics around URN values prevented this feature from being part of the beta. Facilities to convert references to URN/URI values will be provided at the appropriate time.

name	Required element. This is the name recorded for the tModel. Name search is provided via find_tModel call. Names may not be blank, and should be meaningful to someone that looks at the tModel	string	128
description	Optional repeating element. One or more short language-qualified descriptions. One description is allowed per national language code supplied.	string	255
overviewDoc	Optional element. Used to house references to remote descriptive or instructions related to the tModel. See the substructure breakdown for Overview doc in the bindingTemplate section of this document.	Structure	
identifierBag	Optional element. This is an optional list of name-value pairs that can be used to record identificatonnumbers for a tModel. These can be used during search via find_tModel. See the full description of this element in the businessEntity section of this document and in the appendix "Using Identifiers"	structure	
categoryBag	Optional element. This is an optional list of name-value pairs that are used to tag a tModel with specific taxonomy information (e.g. industry, product or geographic codes). These can be used during search via find_tModel. See the full description of of this element in the businessEntity section of this document and in the appendix "Using Categorization"	structure	

Appendix A: Using Identifiers

The identifier dilemma

One of the design goals associated with the UDDI registration data is the ability to mark information with identifiers. The purpose of identifiers in the UDDI registration data is to allow others to find the published information using more formal identifiers such as Dun & Bradstreet D-U-N-S® Numbers, tax identifiers, or any other kind of organizational identifiers, regardless of whether these are private or shared.

When you look at an identifier, such as a D-U-N-S® Number, it is not always immediately apparent what the identifier represents. For instance, consider the following identifier:

```
123-45-6789
```

Standing alone, we could try and guess what this combination of digits and formatting characters implies. However, if we knew that this was a United States Social Security number, we would then have a better context and understand that the meaning, while still not clear, at least identifies one or more persons, perhaps even a living one. Expressed as a name / value pair, the identifier might then look like the following:

```
United States Social Security Number, 123-45-6789
```

Even with this new information, a search mechanism based on loosely qualified pairs (name of identifier type, identifier value), two different parties might spell or format either part of the information differently, and with the end result being a diminished value for searching.

The goal, of course, is to define a simple mechanism that disambiguates the conceptual meanings behind identifiers and exposes them in ways that are reliable and predictable enough to use, and yet are simple enough structurally to be easy to understand and extend.

Identifier characteristics

When we look at various types of simple identifiers, some common desirable characteristics become evident. In general terms, a system of identifiers that are used to facilitate searching need to be:

▼ **Resolvable**: Identifiers can be used in a way that allows the meaning of the identifier to be determined. For instance, a popular business identifier mechanism is provided by Dun & Bradstreet in the form of D-U-N-S® numbers. When you know an organization's D-U-N-S® Number, you can use this to reliably distinguish one organization from another.

▼ **Distinguishable**: Identifiers can be used in a way that you can tell what kind of identifier is being used, or you can specify what kind of identifier you are using to search for something. This means you can tell that two identifiers are the same kind of identifier or are different types (e.g. two D-U-N-S® Numbers, versus a tax identifier or an organizational membership number.)

▼ **Extensible**: The way that searchable identifiers are defines should be easy to extend so that anyone can register another type of identifier without having to create costly or difficult infrastructure. The search mechanisms that use Identifiers should be able to accommodate newly registered types without any changes to software, and anyone should be able to start using the new types immediately.

With this in mind, let's look at the way that identifiers are used in the UDDI data structures.

Using identifiers

Instead of defining a simple property where you could attach a keyword or a simple identifier field, UDDI defines the notion of annotating or attaching identifiers to data. Two of the core data types specified by UDDI provide a structure to support attaching identifiers to data. These are the businessEntity and the tModel structures. By providing a placeholder for attaching identifiers to these two root data types, any number of identifiers can be used for a variety of purposes.

In Figure 2 we see that businessEntity and tModel structures both have a placeholder element named identifierBag[11]. This structure is a general-purpose

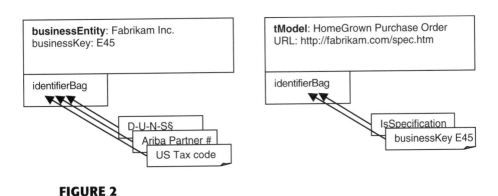

FIGURE 2

---

[11]The term "bag" is from the object design naming convention that places collections of like things within an outer container. From outside, it behaves like a bag – that is has a collection of things in it. To see what's in it, you have to look inside.

placeholder for any number of distinct identifiers. In this example, we see five types of identifiers in use in a way that accommodates the kinds of searching that might be required to locate businesses or tModels.

For instance, it is likely that someone who wants to find the types of technical Web services that are exposed by a given business would search by a business identifier. Used in this way, identifiers can represent business identifier types. In the example shown in figure 2, we see that the individual who registered the businessEntity data specified a D-U-N-S® Number, an Ariba partner number, and a US Tax Code identifier[12].

On the other hand, since a tModel is a fairly abstract concept, I might care more that a tModel represents an identifier, and that it was registered by a particular businessEntity. In the example shown in figure 2, we have shown some more abstract identifier types and can tell that the tModel that describes the way that Fabrikam's purchasing Web service has been marked with information that identifies the data as being related to the businessEntity record with the theoretical businessKey value E45. A second identifier marks the tModel as a specification.

Structure specification

```
<element name = "identifierBag">
        <type content = "elementOnly">
                <group order = "seq">
                        <element ref = "keyedReference" min
                        Occurs = "0" maxOccurs = "*"/>
                </group>
        </type>
</element>
```

From this structure definition we see that an identifier bag is an element that holds zero or more instances of something called a keyedReference. When we look at that structure, we see:

```
<element name = "keyedReference">
        <type content = "empty">
                <attribute name = "tModelKey" type = "string"/>
                <attribute name = "keyName" minOccurs = "1" type
                = "string"/>
```

---

[12]In the diagram, the actual name/value properties were abbreviated for the sake of simplicity.

```
                  <attribute name = "keyValue" minOccurs = "1"
                  type = "string"/>
        </type>
</element>
```

Upon examining this, we see a general-purpose structure for a name-value pair, with one curious additional reference to a tModel structure. It is this extra (optional) attribute that makes the identifier scheme extensible by allowing tModels to be used as conceptual namespace qualifiers.

Understanding this, it then should be easy to see how the example in figure two functioned. Assuming that the identifiers were fully defined, each of the five types shown would each reference one of 5 other tModels. Using the information we've learned already from the discussion of the tModel structure in this document and related texts, we should then be able to see how the tModel structure is useful as a general purpose concept registry with specific UDDI emphasis on the concepts of software specifications, identification schemes, and as we see in the next appendix, as a way to define a general taxonomy namespace key.

The net result is that you can register a tModel to represent an idea, and then use a reference to that tModel as part of a general discovery mechanism that allows unknown facts to be discovered and explained.

Appendix B: Using categorization

Categorization and the ability to voluntarily assign category information to data in the UDDI distributed registry was a key design goal. Without categorization and the ability to specify that information be tangentially related to some well-known industry, product or geographic categorization code set, locating data within the UDDI registry would prove to be too difficult.

At the same time, it is impractical to assume that the UDDI registry will be useful for general-purpose business search. With a projected near-term population of several hundred thousand to million distinct entities, the notion of searching for businesses that satisfy a particular set of criteria will yield a manageably sized result set is unlikely. For example, suppose we searched for all of the business information for businesses that have classified themselves with a particular industry code – retail. Even if we searched within this specific industry classification, the breadth of the category makes it likely that we'll find tens of thousands of companies that are retailers or in some way think of themselves as belonging to a retail category.

Secondary considerations include the accuracy with which categories are applied and the exact value match nature of the UDDI categorization facility. When you register a specific category along with your UDDI registration data, only people searching for that exact category will find your results. For example, in the case where one business marks itself as "retail – pet-food", and another simply uses "retail", the specialization and generalization across categories of any particular categorization scheme or taxonomy is not known to the UDDI search facility.

More intelligent search facilities are required that have some apriori knowledge of the meanings of specific categories and that provide the ability to cross-reference across related categories. Such is the role of more traditional search engines. The design of UDDI allows simplified forms of searching and allows the parties that publish data about themselves, and their advertised Web services to voluntarily provide categorization data that can be used by richer search facilities that will be created above the UDDI technical layer.

In Figure 1B we see the tiered search concept illustrated. The role of search portals and marketplaces will support the business level search facilities for such activities as finding partners with products in a certain price range or availability, or finding high quality partners with good reputations. The data in UDDI is not sufficient to accommodate this because of the cross category issues associated with high volumes and voluntary classification.

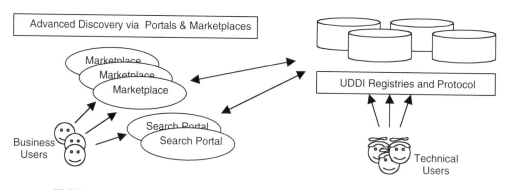

FIGURE 1B

Structure Specification

```
<element name = "categoryBag">
        <type content = "elementOnly">
                <group order = "seq">
                        <element ref ="keyedReference"</group>
        </type>
</element>
```

From this structure definition we see that categoryBag is an element that holds zero or more instances of keyedReference elements. This was described in the section on identifiers (Appendix A) and the basic structure is used in the same way.

The key difference is that while the contents of the identifierBag entries are checked only for a valid tModelKey reference (if supplied), extra validation is applied to the references found within the category Bag element. The thinking that drives this is that there may be a wish on the part of the organizations that publish taxonomies to limit or prevent certain parties from using the taxonomy or from using certain categories. For this reason, the *Operator Registry Sites* that implement the UDDI specifications are required to check with a Web service that validates the categorization data associated with a registration.

Initially, three categorization taxonomies have been identified and made a core part of the UDDI *Operator* registries. These are the North American Industry Classification System (NAICS), Universal Standard Products and Services Classification (UNSPSC), and a geographic taxonomy to be determined. A fourth category is also defined – named "Other" – for general-purpose keyword type classification[13].

Appendix C: Response message reference

All of the messages defined in the Programmer's API Specification return response messages upon successful completion. These structures are defined here for reference purposes. All of the structures shown will appear within SOAP 1.1

---

[13]*Operator Sites* are allowed to promote invalid category entries, or entries that are otherwise rejected by the category classification services, to this Other classification.

compliant envelope structures according the specifications described in the UDDI Programmers API specification. Only the SOAP <body> element contents are shown in the examples in this section.

authtoken

This message returns the authentication information that should be used in subsequent calls to the publishers API messages.

Sample

```
<authToken generic="1.0" operator="uddi.someoperator" xmlns="urn:
  uddi-org:api" >
        <authInfo>some opaque token value</authInfo>
</authToken>
```

The authToken message contains a single authInfo element that contains an access token that is to be passed back in all of the publisher API messages that change data. This message is always returned using SSL encryption as a synchronous response to the get_authToken message.

bindingDetail

This message returns specific bindingTemplate information in response to a get_bindingDetail or find_binding inquiry message.

Sample

```
<bindingDetail generic="1.0" operator="uddi.someoperator"
  truncated="true"
                  xmlns="urn:uddi-org:api">
        <bindingTemplate bindingKey="F5E65…" serviceKey="E4D6…" >
                ...
        </bindingTemplate>
        [<bindingTemplate/>…]
</bindingDetail>
```

In this message, one or more bindingTemplate structures are returned according to the data requested in the request message. The serviceKey attributes are always returned when bindingTemplate data is packaged in this way. The truncated flag shown in the example indicates that not all of the requested data was returned due to an unspecified processing limit. Ordinarily, the truncated flag is not included unless the result set has been truncated.

businessDetail

This message returns one or more complete businessEntity data sets in response to a get_businessDetail inquiry message.

Sample

```
<businessDetail generic="1.0" operator="uddi.sourceOperator"
  truncated="true"
                  xmlns="urn:uddi-org:api">
       <businessEntity businessKey="F5E65…" authorizedName="J.
         Doe"
                ...
       </businessEntity>
       [<businessEntity/>…]
</businessDetail>
```

In this message, we see that the businessEntity contains the proper output information (e.g. authorizedName, and operator). The two *operator* attributes shown
in the businessDetail element and the businessEntity element reflect the distinguished name of the *Operator Registry Site* providing the response message and
the distinguished name of the operator where the data is controlled, respectively.
Additionally, notice the name of the person who registered the data shown in the
authorizedName attribute.

businessDetailExt

This message returns one or more complete businessEntity data sets in response
to a get_businessDetailExt inquiry message. This is the same data returned by
the businessDetail messages, but is provided for consistency with third party extensions to businessEntity information.

Sample

```
<businessDetailExt generic="1.0" operator="uddi.sourceOperator"
  truncated="true"
                  xmlns="urn:uddi-org:api">
       <businessEntityExt>
               <businessEntity businessKey="F5E65…"
                 authorizedName="J. Doe"
                        operator="uddi.publishingOperator" >
                   ...
               </businessEntity>
       <businessEntityExt>
       [<businessEntityExt/>…]
</businessDetail>
```

The message API design allows third party registries (e.g. non-operator sites) to
implement the UDDI API Specifications while at the same time extending the
details collected in a way that will not break tools that are written to UDDI
specifications. *Operator Registry Sites* are required to support the *Ext* form of the

businessDetail message for compatibility with tools, but are not allowed to manage extended data.

businessList

This message returns one or more businessInfo data sets in response to a find_business inquiry message. BusinessInfo structures are abbreviated versions of businessEntity data suitable for populating lists of search results in anticipation of further "drill-down" detail inquiries.

Sample

```
<businessList generic="1.0" operator="uddi.sourceOperator"
  truncated="true"
              xmlns="urn:uddi-org:api">
        <businessInfos>
                <businessInfo businessKey="F5E65…" >
                        <name>My Company</name>
                        <serviceInfos>
                                    <serviceInfo serviceKey=
                                        "3D45…">
                                            <name>Purchase
                                                Orders</name>
                                    </serviceInfo>
                        </serviceInfos>
                </businessInfo>
                [<businessInfo/>…]
        <businessInfos>
</businessList>
```

This message returns overview data in the form of one or more businessInfo structures. Each businessInfo structure contains company name and optional description data, along with a collection element named serviceInfos that in turn can contain one or more serviceInfo structures[14]. Notice that the businessKey attribute is not expressed in the serviceInfo structure due to the fact that this information is available from the containing businessInfo structure.

registeredInfo

This message returns overview information that is suitable for identifying all of the data published by the requester. Provided as part of the publishers API message set, this information is only provided when requested via a get_registered-Info message over an SSL connection.

---

[14]Refer to the UDDI schema for structure details.

Sample

```
<registeredInfo generic="1.0" operator="uddi.sourceOperator"
  [truncated="false"]
                    xmlns="urn:uddi-org:api">
        <businessInfos>
                <businessInfo businessKey="F5E65…" >
                        <name>My Company</name>
                        <serviceInfos>
                                <serviceInfo
                                  serviceKey="3D45…">
                                        <name>Purchase
                                          Orders</name>
                                </serviceInfo>
                        </serviceInfos>
                </businessInfo>
                [<businessInfo/>…]
        <businessInfos>
        <tModelInfos>
                <tModelInfo tModelKey="34D5…">
                        <name>Proprietary XML purchase
                          order</name>
                </tModelInfo>
                [<tModelInfo/>…]
        </tModelInfos>
</registeredInfo>
```

This message contains overview data about all of the types of information published by a given publisher. This information is sufficient for driving tools that
display lists of registered information and then provide drill-down features. This
is the recommended structure for use after a network problem results in an unknown status of saved information.

serviceDetail

This message returns one or more complete businessService structures in response to a get_serviceDetail inquiry message.

Sample

```
<serviceDetail generic="1.0" operator="uddi.sourceOperator"
  [truncated="false"]
                    xmlns="urn:uddi-org:api">
        <businessService businessKey="F5E65…" serviceKey="3D21…">
                …
        </businessService>
        [<businessService/>…]
</serviceDetail>
```

One can use serviceDetail messages to get complete descriptive and technical details about registered services by providing one or more serviceKey values in the get_serviceDetail message. Notice that the businessKey value is expressed in this message because the container does not provide a link to the parent businessEntity structure.

serviceList

This message returns one or more serviceInfo data sets in response to a find_service inquiry message.

Sample

```
<serviceList generic="1.0" operator="uddi.sourceOperator"
  [truncated="false"]
                    xmlns="urn:uddi-org:api">
        <serviceInfos>
                <serviceInfo serviceKey="3D45…"
                  businessKey="2E4C…">
                                <name>Purchase Orders</name>
                </serviceInfo>
        </serviceInfos>
</serviceList>
```

This data is suitable for populating a list of services associated with a business and that match a pattern as specified in the inputs to the find_service message. Notice that the businessKey attribute is expressed in the serviceInfo elements found in this message. This is because this information is not available from a containing element.

tModelDetail

This message returns one or more complete tModel data sets in response to a get_tModelDetail inquiry message.

Sample

```
<tModelDetail generic="1.0" operator="uddi.sourceOperator"
  [truncated="false"]
                    xmlns="urn:uddi-org:api">
        <tModel tModelKey="F5E65…" authorizedName="J. Doe"
          operator="uddi.publishingOperator" >
          …
        </tModel>
        [<tModel/>…]
</tModelDetail>
```

Because tModel structures are top-level data (e.g. able to stand alone with no parent containers) the authorizedName value is expressed. This is the name of the person whose account was used to register the data. The two expressions of the *operator* attribute each express the distinguished name of the *Operator Registry Site* that is providing the data and the operator where the data is managed.

tModelList

This message returns one or more abbreviated tModelInfo data sets in response to a find_tModel inquiry message.

Sample

```
<tModelList generic="1.0" operator="uddi.sourceOperator"
  [truncated="false"
                  xmlns="urn:uddi-org:api">
      <tModelInfos>
              <tModelInfo tModelKey="34D5…">
                      <name>Proprietary XML purchase
                      order</name>
              </tModelInfo>
              [<tModelInfo/>…]
      </tModelInfos>
</tModelList>
```

This data is suitable for finding candidate tModels, populating lists of results and then providing drill-down features that rely on the get_xxDetail messages.

Appendix D: Data Field Lengths

The following table summarizes all known stored element and attribute names based on the names of the fields defined in the XML schema. These are the storage length limits for information that is saved in the UDDI Registry. The *Operator Registry Sites* will truncate data that exceeds these lengths. Fields that are generated by the Operator Registry site (ignored on input) are not listed. Keys are listed even though they are generated. Since keys are referenced by other structures, they are shown here.

Field Name	
accessPoint	255
addressLine	40
	409
authInfo	6
authorizedName	64
bindingKey	41
businessKey	41
description	255
discoveryURL	255
email	128
hostingRedirector	41
instanceParms	255
keyName	128
keyType	16
keyValue	128
name	128
overviewUrl	255
personName	32
phone	50
serviceKey	41
sortCode	10
tModelKey	255
uploadRegister	255
URLType	16
useType	32

CHAPTER
5

UDDI XML Schema 1.0 (1999)

```
<?xml version ="1.0"?>
<schema targetNamespace = "urn:uddi-org:api"
  xmlns = "http://www.w3.org/1999/XMLSchema">
<annotation>
 <appInfo>UDDI API schema.Version 1.0, revision 0.Last change 2000-09-06
 Version 1.0, revision 1.  Last change 2001-10-26
Removed incorrect comment line claiming this schema conforms to the TR
 < /appInfo>
</annotation>
<element name = "addressLine" type = "string"/>
<element name = "bindingKey" type = "string"/>
<element name = "businessKey" type = "string"/>
<element name = "description" type = "string"/>
<element name = "keyValue" type="string" />
<element name = "name" type = "string"/>
<element name = "overviewURL" type = "string"/>
<element name = "personName" type = "string"/>
<element name = "serviceKey" type = "string"/>
<element name = "tModelKey" type = "string"/>
<element name = "uploadRegister" type = "string"/>
<element name = "address">
 <type content = "elementOnly">
  <annotation>
   <appInfo>Data: a printable, free form address. Typed by
     convention. Sort not used.</appInfo>
  </annotation>
  <group order = "seq">
   <element ref = "addressLine" minOccurs = "0" maxOccurs = "*"/>
  </group>
  <attribute name = "useType" type = "string"/>
  <attribute name = "sortCode" type = "string"/>
 </type>
</element>
<element name = "contacts">
 <type content = "elementOnly">
  <annotation>
   <appInfo>Service element: accessor for one or more contacts.</appInfo>
  </annotation>
  <group order = "seq">
   <element ref = "contact" minOccurs = "0" maxOccurs = "*"/>
  </group>
 </type>
</element>
<element name = "contact">
 <type content = "elementOnly">
  <annotation>
   <appInfo>Data: a contact</appInfo>
```

```
   </annotation>
   <group order = "seq">
    <element ref = "description" minOccurs = "0" maxOccurs = "*"/>
    <element ref = "personName"/>
    <element ref = "phone" minOccurs = "0" maxOccurs = "*"/>
    <element ref = "email" minOccurs = "0" maxOccurs = "*"/>
    <element ref = "address" minOccurs = "0" maxOccurs = "*"/>
   </group>
   <attribute name = "useType" type = "string"/>
  </type>
 </element>
 <element name = "discoveryURL">
  <type source = "string" content = "textOnly">
   <annotation>
    <appInfo>Data: A url pointing to an external (typed by convention)
      discovery doc.</appInfo>
   </annotation>
   <attribute name = "useType" minOccurs = "1" type = "string"/>
  </type>
 </element>
 <element name = "discoveryURLs">
  <type content = "elementOnly">
   <annotation>
    <appInfo>Service Element: accessor for one or more discoveryURL
      elements</appInfo>
   </annotation>
   <group order = "seq">
    <element ref = "discoveryURL" minOccurs = "1" maxOccurs = "*"/>
   </group>
  </type>
 </element>
 <element name = "phone">
  <type content = "textOnly">
   <annotation>
    <appInfo>Data: an telephone number.</appInfo>
   </annotation>
   <attribute name = "useType" type = "string"/>
  </type>
 </element>
 <element name = "email">
  <type content = "textOnly">
   <annotation>
    <appInfo>Data: an email address.</appInfo>
   </annotation>
   <attribute name = "useType" type = "string"/>
  </type>
 </element>
```

```
<element name = "businessEntity">
 <type content = "elementOnly">
  <annotation>
   <appInfo>Primary Data type: Describes an instance of a business or
     business unit.</appInfo>
  </annotation>
  <group order = "seq">
   <element ref = "discoveryURLs" minOccurs = "0" maxOccurs = "1"/>
   <element ref = "name"/>
   <element ref = "description" minOccurs = "0" maxOccurs = "*"/>
   <element ref = "contacts" minOccurs = "0" maxOccurs = "1"/>
   <element ref = "businessServices" minOccurs = "0" maxOccurs =  "1"/>
   <element ref = "identifierBag" minOccurs = "0" maxOccurs = "1"/>
   <element ref = "categoryBag" minOccurs = "0" maxOccurs = "1"/>
  </group>
  <attribute name = "businessKey" minOccurs = "1" type =  "string"/>
  <attribute name = "operator" type = "string"/>
  <attribute name = "authorizedName" type = "string"/>
 </type>
</element>
<element name = "businessServices">
 <type content = "elementOnly">
  <annotation>
   <appInfo>Service element. Accessor collection point for businessService
     data.</appInfo>
  </annotation>
  <group order = "seq">
   <element ref = "businessService" minOccurs = "0" maxOccurs = "*"/>
  </group>
 </type>
</element>
<element name = "businessService">
 <type content = "elementOnly">
  <annotation>
   <appInfo>Primary Data type: Describes a logical service type in
     business terms.</appInfo>
  </annotation>
  <group order = "seq">
   <element ref = "name"/>
   <element ref = "description" minOccurs = "0" maxOccurs = "*"/>
   <element ref = "bindingTemplates"/>
   <element ref = "categoryBag" minOccurs = "0" maxOccurs = "1"/>
  </group>
  <attribute name = "serviceKey" minOccurs = "1" type = "string"/>
  <attribute name = "businessKey" type = "string"/>
 </type>
</element>
```

```
<element name = "bindingTemplates">
 <type content = "elementOnly">
  <annotation>
   <appInfo>Service element. Collection accessor for bindingTemplate
    information.</appInfo>
  </annotation>
  <group order = "seq">
   <element ref = "bindingTemplate" minOccurs = "0" maxOccurs = "*"/>
  </group>
 </type>
</element>
<element name = "identifierBag">
 <type content = "elementOnly">
  <annotation>
   <appInfo>Service element. Used in searching and categorization.
     </appInfo>
  </annotation>
  <group order = "seq">
   <element ref = "keyedReference" minOccurs = "0" maxOccurs = "*"/>
  </group>
 </type>
</element>
<element name = "keyedReference">
 <type content = "empty">
  <annotation>
   <appInfo>Service element. Represents a namespace qualified
    name-value pair. Depending on use context, this structure can
    be used within different convention frameworks.</appInfo>
  </annotation>
  <attribute name = "tModelKey" type = "string"/>
  <attribute name = "keyName" minOccurs = "1" type = "string"/>
  <attribute name = "keyValue" minOccurs = "1" type = "string"/>
 </type>
</element>
<element name = "categoryBag">
 <type content = "elementOnly">
  <annotation>
   <appInfo>Service element. Used in searching and categorization.
     </appInfo>
  </annotation>
  <group order = "seq">
   <element ref = "keyedReference" minOccurs = "0" maxOccurs = "*"/>
  </group>
 </type>
</element>
<element name = "bindingTemplate">
 <type content = "elementOnly">
```

```
    <annotation>
     <appInfo>Primary Data type: Describes an instance of a web service
       in technical terms.</appInfo>
    </annotation>
    <group order = "seq">
     <element ref = "description" minOccurs = "0" maxOccurs = "*"/>
    <group order = "choice">
      <element ref = "accessPoint" minOccurs = "0" maxOccurs = "1"/>
      <element ref = "hostingRedirector" minOccurs = "0" maxOccurs = "1"/>
     </group>
     <element ref = "tModelInstanceDetails"/>
    </group>
    <attribute name = "bindingKey" minOccurs = "1" type = "string"/>
    <attribute name = "serviceKey" type = "string"/>
   </type>
 </element>
 <element name = "accessPoint">
  <type source = "string" content = "textOnly">
   <annotation>
    <appInfo>Data: present when a service is directly accessible at a
      particular address (e.g. URL, etc).Mutually exclusive with
      hostingRedirector.</appInfo>
   </annotation>
   <attribute name = "URLType" minOccurs = "1">
    <datatype source = "NMTOKEN">
     <enumeration value = "mailto"/>
     <enumeration value = "http"/>
     <enumeration value = "https"/>
     <enumeration value = "ftp"/>
     <enumeration value = "fax"/>
     <enumeration value = "phone"/>
     <enumeration value = "other"/>
    </datatype>
   </attribute>
  </type>
 </element>
 <element name = "hostingRedirector">
  <type content = "empty">
   <annotation>
    <appInfo>Data: present only when the service is provisioned
      via remote hosting,load balancing, etc.  Mutually exclusive
      with accessPoint.</appInfo>
   </annotation>
   <attribute name = "bindingKey" minOccurs = "1" type = "string"/>
  </type>
 </element>
 <element name = "tModelInstanceDetails">
```

```
 <type content = "elementOnly">
  <annotation>
   <appInfo>Support element used as a container for tModel references
   within a web service bindingTemplate metadata set.</appInfo>
  </annotation>
  <group order = "seq">
   <element ref = "tModelInstanceInfo" minOccurs = "0" maxOccurs = "*"/>
  </group>
 </type>
</element>
<element name = "tModelInstanceInfo">
 <type content = "elementOnly">
  <annotation>
   <appInfo>Support element used to contain implementation instance
    specific information about compatible specications (via tModel
    reference) and optional settings details.</appInfo>
  </annotation>
  <group order = "seq">
   <element ref = "description" minOccurs = "0" maxOccurs = "*"/>
   <element ref = "instanceDetails" minOccurs = "0" maxOccurs = "1"/>
  </group>
  <attribute name = "tModelKey" minOccurs = "1" type = "string"/>
 </type>
</element>
<element name = "instanceDetails">
 <type content = "elementOnly">
  <annotation>
   <appInfo>Support element used to contain optional information
    about the way an instance of a web service is implemented or
    varies from the general specifications outlined in a specific
    tModel.</appInfo>
  </annotation>
  <group order = "seq">
   <element ref = "description" minOccurs = "0" maxOccurs = "*"/>
   <element ref = "overviewDoc" minOccurs = "0" maxOccurs = "1"/>
   <element ref = "instanceParms" minOccurs = "0" maxOccurs = "1"/>
  </group>
 </type>
</element>
<element name = "instanceParms" type = "string">
 <annotation>
  <appInfo>This is a URL pointing to the settings file, or the settings
   themselves that are needed to invoke a registered service (for getting
   fixed parm values prior to call)
   </appInfo>
 </annotation>
</element>
```

```
<element name = "tModel">
 <type content = "elementOnly">
  <annotation>
   <appInfo>This structure defines a metadata about a technology,
     specification or namespace qualified list (e.g. taxonomy,
     organizaton, etc.) </appInfo>
  </annotation>
  <group order = "seq">
   <element ref = "name"/>
   <element ref = "description" minOccurs = "0" maxOccurs = "*"/>
   <element ref = "overviewDoc" minOccurs = "0" maxOccurs = "1"/>
   <element ref = "identifierBag" minOccurs = "0" maxOccurs = "1"/>
   <element ref = "categoryBag" minOccurs = "0" maxOccurs = "1"/>
  </group>
  <attribute name = "tModelKey" minOccurs = "1" type = "string"/>
  <attribute name = "operator" type = "string"/>
  <attribute name = "authorizedName" type = "string"/>
 </type>
</element>
<element name = "tModelBag">
 <type content = "elementOnly">
  <annotation>
   <appInfo>Support element used in searches by tModel key
     values</appInfo>
  </annotation>
  <group order = "seq">
   <element ref = "tModelKey" minOccurs = "1" maxOccurs = "*"/>
  </group>
 </type>
</element>
<element name = "overviewDoc">
 <type content = "elementOnly">
  <annotation>
   <appInfo>Support element - used to contain an on-line description and a
     URL pointer to more in-depth or external documentation.
</appInfo>
  </annotation>
  <group order = "seq">
   <element ref = "description" minOccurs = "0" maxOccurs = "*"/>
   <element ref = "overviewURL" minOccurs = "0" maxOccurs = "1"/>
  </group>
 </type>
</element>
<element name = "authInfo" type = "string">
 <annotation>
  <appInfo>This structure is used in all messages that update data on
    behalf of a user initiated request.</appInfo>
```

```
  </annotation>
</element>
<element name = "get_authToken">
 <type content = "empty">
  <annotation>
   <appInfo>This optional message is used to request an authentication
   token. The response is an authToken message.</appInfo>
  </annotation>
  <attribute name = "generic" minOccurs = "1" type = "string"/>
  <attribute name = "userID" minOccurs = "1" type = "string"/>
  <attribute name = "cred" minOccurs = "1" type = "string"/>
 </type>
</element>
<element name = "authToken">
 <type content = "elementOnly">
  <annotation>
   <appInfo>This message is used to return an authentication token in
     response to a "get_authToken" message.</appInfo>
  </annotation>
  <group order = "seq">
   <element ref = "authInfo"/>
  </group>
  <attribute name = "generic" minOccurs = "1" type = "string"/>
  <attribute name = "operator" minOccurs = "1" type = "string"/>
 </type>
</element>
<element name = "discard_authToken">
 <type content = "elementOnly">
  <annotation>
   <appInfo>This optional message is used to deactivate an authentication
   token that was obtained by a call to get_authToken.</appInfo>
  </annotation>
  <group order = "seq">
   <element ref = "authInfo"/>
  </group>
  <attribute name = "generic" minOccurs = "1" type = "string"/>
 </type>
</element>
<element name = "save_tModel">
 <type content = "elementOnly">
  <annotation>
   <appInfo>This message is used to register or update a tModel. One of
     tModel or uploadRegister is required.  Invalid if contains both or
     neither type.</appInfo>
  </annotation>
  <group order = "seq">
   <element ref = "authInfo"/>
```

```
   <element ref = "tModel" minOccurs = "0" maxOccurs = "*"/>
   <element ref = "uploadRegister" minOccurs = "0" maxOccurs = "*"/>
  </group>
  <attribute name = "generic" minOccurs = "1" type = "string"/>
 </type>
</element>
<element name = "delete_tModel">
 <type content = "elementOnly">
  <annotation>
   <appInfo>This message is used to delete information about a previously
     registered tModel.</appInfo>
  </annotation>
  <group order = "seq">
   <element ref = "authInfo"/>
   <element ref = "tModelKey" minOccurs = "1" maxOccurs = "*"/>
  </group>
  <attribute name = "generic" minOccurs = "1" type = "string"/>
 </type>
</element>
<element name = "save_business">
 <type content = "elementOnly">
  <annotation>
   <appInfo>This message is used to save (add/update) information
     describing one or more businessEntity structures. One of
     businessEntity or uploadRegister is required.  Invalid if contains
     both or neither type.</appInfo>
  </annotation>
  <group order = "seq">
   <element ref = "authInfo"/>
   <element ref = "businessEntity" minOccurs = "0" maxOccurs = "*"/>
   <element ref = "uploadRegister" minOccurs = "0" maxOccurs = "*"/>
  </group>
  <attribute name = "generic" minOccurs = "1" type = "string"/>
 </type>
</element>
<element name = "delete_business">
 <type content = "elementOnly">
  <annotation>
   <appInfo>This message is used to delete information about a previously
     registered businessEntity.</appInfo>
  </annotation>
  <group order = "seq">
   <element ref = "authInfo"/>
   <element ref = "businessKey" minOccurs = "1" maxOccurs = "*"/>
  </group>
  <attribute name = "generic" minOccurs = "1" type = "string"/>
 </type>
```

```
</element>
<element name = "save_service">
 <type content = "elementOnly">
  <annotation>
   <appInfo>This message is used to save (add/update) information
     about one or more businessService structures.</appInfo>
  </annotation>
  <group order = "seq">
   <element ref = "authInfo"/>
   <element ref = "businessService" minOccurs = "1" maxOccurs = "*"/>
  </group>
  <attribute name = "generic" minOccurs = "1" type = "string"/>
 </type>
</element>
<element name = "delete_service">
 <type content = "elementOnly">
  <annotation>
   <appInfo>This message is used to delete information about a previously
     registered businessService structure.</appInfo>
  </annotation>
  <group order = "seq">
   <element ref = "authInfo"/>
   <element ref = "serviceKey" minOccurs = "1" maxOccurs = "*"/>
  </group>
  <attribute name = "generic" minOccurs = "1" type = "string"/>
 </type>
</element>
<element name = "save_binding">
 <type content = "elementOnly">
  <annotation>
   <appInfo>This message is used to save (add/update) information
     about one or more bindingTemplate structures.</appInfo>
  </annotation>
  <group order = "seq">
   <element ref = "authInfo"/>
   <element ref = "bindingTemplate" minOccurs = "1" maxOccurs = "*"/>
  </group>
  <attribute name = "generic" minOccurs = "1" type = "string"/>
 </type>
</element>
<element name = "delete_binding">
 <type content = "elementOnly">
  <annotation>
   <appInfo>This message is used to delete information about a
     previously registered bindingTemplate structure. </appInfo>
  </annotation>
  <group order = "seq">
```

```
      <element ref = "authInfo"/>
      <element ref = "bindingKey" minOccurs = "1" maxOccurs = "*"/>
    </group>
    <attribute name = "generic" minOccurs = "1" type = "string"/>
  </type>
</element>
<element name = "dispositionReport">
  <type content = "elementOnly">
    <annotation>
      <appInfo>This message is used report the outcome of calls.  It is used
        within error (fault) messages, and can stand alone when indicating
        success.</appInfo>
    </annotation>
    <group order = "seq">
      <element ref = "result" minOccurs = "1" maxOccurs = "*"/>
    </group>
    <attribute name = "generic" minOccurs = "1" type = "string"/>
    <attribute name = "operator" minOccurs = "1" type = "string"/>
    <attribute name = "truncated">
      <datatype source = "NMTOKEN">
        <enumeration value = "true"/>
        <enumeration value = "false"/>
      </datatype>
    </attribute>
  </type>
</element>
<element name = "result">
  <type content = "elementOnly">
    <annotation>
      <appInfo> This structure supports the dispositionReport structure.
        </appInfo>
    </annotation>
    <group order = "seq">
      <element ref = "errInfo" minOccurs = "0" maxOccurs = "1"/>
    </group>
    <attribute name = "keyType" minOccurs = "0">
      <datatype source = "NMTOKEN">
        <enumeration value = "businessKey"/>
        <enumeration value = "tModelKey"/>
        <enumeration value = "serviceKey"/>
        <enumeration value = "bindingKey"/>
      </datatype>
    </attribute>
    <attribute name = "errno" minOccurs = "1" type = "integer"/>
  </type>
</element>
<element name = "errInfo">
```

```
<type content = "textOnly">
 <annotation>
  <appInfo>Supports the DispositionReport structure. This structure is
    provided for conveying text and structured error code (alphanumeric)
    information. Error message text is contained by this element.
    </appInfo>
 </annotation>
 <attribute name = "errCode" minOccurs = "1" type = "string"/>
</type>
</element>
<element name = "findQualifiers">
 <type content = "elementOnly">
  <annotation>
   <appInfo>container/accessor for findQualifiers</appInfo>
  </annotation>
  <group order = "seq">
   <element ref = "findQualifier" minOccurs = "0" maxOccurs = "*"/>
  </group>
 </type>
</element>
<element name = "findQualifier" type = "string">
 <annotation>
  <appInfo>This structure is provided to signal the behavior of the find
    operations. See appropriate appendix in API specification.</appInfo>
 </annotation>
</element>
<element name = "find_tModel">
 <type content = "elementOnly">
  <annotation>
   <appInfo>This message is used to search for summary results listing
     registered tModel data matching specific criteria. </appInfo>
  </annotation>
  <group order = "seq">
   <element ref = "findQualifiers" minOccurs = "0" maxOccurs = "1"/>
   <element ref = "name" minOccurs = "0" maxOccurs = "1"/>
   <element ref = "identifierBag" minOccurs = "0" maxOccurs = "1"/>
   <element ref = "categoryBag" minOccurs = "0" maxOccurs = "1"/>
  </group>
  <attribute name = "generic" minOccurs = "1" type = "string"/>
  <attribute name = "maxRows" type = "integer"/>
 </type>
</element>
<element name = "find_business">
 <type content = "elementOnly">
  <annotation>
   <appInfo>This message is used to search for summary results listing
     registered businessEntity data matching specific criteria.</appInfo>
```

```
   </annotation>
   <group order = "seq">
    <element ref = "findQualifiers" minOccurs = "0" maxOccurs = "1"/>
    <element ref = "name" minOccurs = "0" maxOccurs = "1"/>
    <element ref = "identifierBag" minOccurs = "0" maxOccurs = "1"/>
    <element ref = "categoryBag" minOccurs = "0" maxOccurs = "1"/>
    <element ref = "tModelBag" minOccurs = "0" maxOccurs = "1"/>
    <element ref = "discoveryURLs" minOccurs = "0" maxOccurs = "1"/>
   </group>
   <attribute name = "generic" minOccurs = "1" type = "string"/>
   <attribute name = "maxRows" type = "integer"/>
  </type>
 </element>
 <element name = "find_binding">
  <type content = "elementOnly">
   <annotation>
    <appInfo>This message is used to search for summary results listing
      registered bindingTemplate data within a businessService matching
      specific criteria.</appInfo>
   </annotation>
   <group order = "seq">
    <element ref = "findQualifiers" minOccurs = "0" maxOccurs = "1"/>
    <element ref = "tModelBag"/>
   </group>
   <attribute name = "generic" minOccurs = "1" type = "string"/>
   <attribute name = "maxRows" type = "integer"/>
   <attribute name = "serviceKey" minOccurs = "1" type = "string"/>
  </type>
 </element>
 <element name = "find_service">
  <type content = "elementOnly">
   <annotation>
    <appInfo>This message is used to search for summary results listing
      registered businessService data matching specific criteria.</appInfo>
   </annotation>
   <group order = "seq">
    <element ref = "findQualifiers" minOccurs = "0" maxOccurs = "1"/>
    <element ref = "name" minOccurs = "0" maxOccurs = "1"/>
    <element ref = "categoryBag" minOccurs = "0" maxOccurs = "1"/>
    <element ref = "tModelBag" minOccurs = "0" maxOccurs = "1"/>
   </group>
   <attribute name = "generic" minOccurs = "1" type = "string"/>
   <attribute name = "maxRows" type = "integer"/>
   <attribute name = "businessKey" minOccurs = "1" type = "string"/>
  </type>
 </element>
 <element name = "serviceList">
```

```
  <type content = "elementOnly">
   <annotation>
    <appInfo>This message is used to return results of a find_service
      request.</appInfo>
   </annotation>
   <group order = "seq">
    <element ref = "serviceInfos"/>
   </group>
   <attribute name = "generic" minOccurs = "1" type = "string"/>
   <attribute name = "operator" minOccurs = "1" type = "string"/>
   <attribute name = "truncated">
    <datatype source = "NMTOKEN">
     <enumeration value = "true"/>
     <enumeration value = "false"/>
    </datatype>
   </attribute>
  </type>
</element>
<element name = "businessList">
 <type content = "elementOnly">
  <annotation>
   <appInfo>This is a report - a list of businesses in short form. This
     message is the response to a find_businessEntity query. </appInfo>
  </annotation>
  <group order = "seq">
   <element ref = "businessInfos"/>
  </group>
  <attribute name = "generic" minOccurs = "1" type = "string"/>
  <attribute name = "operator" minOccurs = "1" type = "string"/>
  <attribute name = "truncated">
   <datatype source = "NMTOKEN">
    <enumeration value = "true"/>
    <enumeration value = "false"/>
   </datatype>
  </attribute>
 </type>
</element>
<element name = "tModelList">
 <type content = "elementOnly">
  <annotation>
   <appInfo>This is a report - a list of tModels in short form. This
     message is the response to a find_tModel query.</appInfo>
  </annotation>
  <group order = "seq">
   <element ref = "tModelInfos"/>
  </group>
  <attribute name = "generic" minOccurs = "1" type = "string"/>
```

```
    <attribute name = "operator" minOccurs = "1" type = "string"/>
    <attribute name = "truncated">
     <datatype source = "NMTOKEN">
      <enumeration value = "true"/>
      <enumeration value = "false"/>
     </datatype>
    </attribute>
   </type>
  </element>
  <element name = "businessInfo">
   <type content = "elementOnly">
    <annotation>
     <appInfo>This element is used as a short form of the BusinessEntity
      element as a first pass result set for "find businesses" queries.
       </appInfo>
    </annotation>
    <group order = "seq">
     <element ref = "name"/>
     <element ref = "description" minOccurs = "0" maxOccurs = "*"/>
     <element ref = "serviceInfos"/>
    </group>
    <attribute name = "businessKey" minOccurs = "1" type = "string"/>
   </type>
  </element>
  <element name = "businessInfos">
   <type content = "elementOnly">
    <annotation>
     <appInfo> Accessor container for one or more businessInfo   structures
      </appInfo>
    </annotation>
    <group order = "seq">
     <element ref = "businessInfo" minOccurs = "0" maxOccurs = "*"/>
    </group>
   </type>
  </element>
  <element name = "serviceInfo">
   <type content = "elementOnly">
    <annotation>
     <appInfo>This structure is used as the short form of a service for list
      purposes.</appInfo>
    </annotation>
    <group order = "seq">
     <element ref = "name"/>
    </group>
    <attribute name = "serviceKey" minOccurs = "1" type =  "string"/>
    <attribute name = "businessKey" type = "string"/>
   </type>
```

```
 </element>
<element name = "serviceInfos">
 <type content = "elementOnly">
  <annotation>
   <appInfo>Accessor container for one or more serviceInfo structures
      </appInfo>
  </annotation>
  <group order = "seq">
   <element ref = "serviceInfo" minOccurs = "0" maxOccurs = "*"/>
  </group>
 </type>
</element>
<element name = "get_businessDetail">
 <type content = "elementOnly">
  <annotation>
   <appInfo>This message is used to get the detailed information
     registered about businessEntity data matching specific key
     value(s).</appInfo>
  </annotation>
  <group order = "seq">
   <element ref = "businessKey" minOccurs = "1" maxOccurs = "*"/>
  </group>
  <attribute name = "generic" minOccurs = "1" type = "string"/>
 </type>
</element>
<element name = "businessDetail">
 <type content = "elementOnly">
  <annotation>
   <appInfo>This structure is used to return businessEntity
     structures.</appInfo>
  </annotation>
  <group order = "seq">
   <element ref = "businessEntity" minOccurs = "0" maxOccurs =
     "*"/>
  </group>
  <attribute name = "generic" minOccurs = "1" type = "string"/>
  <attribute name = "operator" minOccurs = "1" type = "string"/>
  <attribute name = "truncated">
   <datatype source = "NMTOKEN">
    <enumeration value = "true"/>
    <enumeration value = "false"/>
   </datatype>
  </attribute>
 </type>
</element>
<element name = "get_serviceDetail">
 <type content = "elementOnly">
```

```
    <annotation>
     <appInfo>This message is used to get the detailed information
       registered about businessService data matching specific key
       value(s).</appInfo>
    </annotation>
    <group order = "seq">
     <element ref = "serviceKey" minOccurs = "1" maxOccurs = "*"/>
    </group>
    <attribute name = "generic" minOccurs = "1" type = "string"/>
  </type>
</element>
<element name = "serviceDetail">
  <type content = "elementOnly">
    <annotation>
     <appInfo>This structure is used to return full businessService
       details.</appInfo>
    </annotation>
    <group order = "seq">
     <element ref = "businessService" minOccurs = "0" maxOccurs = "*" />
    </group>
    <attribute name = "generic" minOccurs = "1" type = "string"/>
    <attribute name = "operator" minOccurs = "1" type = "string"/>
    <attribute name = "truncated">
     <datatype source = "NMTOKEN">
      <enumeration value = "true"/>
      <enumeration value = "false"/>
     </datatype>
    </attribute>
  </type>
</element>
<element name = "get_registeredInfo">
  <type content = "elementOnly">
    <annotation>
     <appInfo>This message is used to support tool resynch by allowing a
       query to get summarized information about registered businessEntity
       and tModels for a given userID. This API is intended to let
       publishers determine what they've published.  As such, authentication
       is required.  The response is a registeredInfo message.</appInfo>
    </annotation>
    <group order = "seq">
     <element ref = "authInfo"/>
    </group>
    <attribute name = "generic" minOccurs = "1" type = "string"/>
  </type>
</element>
<element name = "registeredInfo">
  <type content = "elementOnly">
```

```
    <annotation>
     <appInfo>This structure is used in the resynch process and is
       a response to a get_registeredInfo message.</appInfo>
    </annotation>
    <group order = "seq">
     <element ref = "businessInfos"/>
     <element ref = "tModelInfos"/>
    </group>
    <attribute name = "generic" minOccurs = "1" type = "string"/>
    <attribute name = "operator" minOccurs = "1" type = "string"/>
    <attribute name = "truncated">
     <datatype source = "NMTOKEN">
      <enumeration value = "true"/>
      <enumeration value = "false"/>
     </datatype>
    </attribute>
   </type>
  </element>
  <element name = "tModelInfo">
   <type content = "elementOnly">
    <annotation>
     <appInfo>This structure is used to enumerate short form tModel
       information.</appInfo>
    </annotation>
    <group order = "seq">
     <element ref = "name"/>
    </group>
    <attribute name = "tModelKey" minOccurs = "1" type = "string"/>
   </type>
  </element>
  <element name = "tModelInfos">
   <type content = "elementOnly">
    <annotation>
     <appInfo>Support element - accessor container for tModelInfo.</appInfo>
    </annotation>
    <group order = "seq">
     <element ref = "tModelInfo" minOccurs = "0" maxOccurs = "*"/>
    </group>
   </type>
  </element>
  <element name = "get_tModelDetail">
   <type content = "elementOnly">
    <annotation>
     <appInfo>This message is used to request the details about a specific
       tModel. Results are returned in a tModelDetail message. </appInfo>
    </annotation>
    <group order = "seq">
```

```
      <element ref = "tModelKey" minOccurs = "1" maxOccurs = "*"/>
     </group>
     <attribute name = "generic" minOccurs = "1" type = "string"/>
    </type>
   </element>
  <element name = "tModelDetail">
    <type content = "elementOnly">
     <annotation>
      <appInfo>This is a response message that returns all exposed details
        about a tModel.</appInfo>
     </annotation>
     <group order = "seq">
      <element ref = "tModel" minOccurs = "1" maxOccurs = "*"/>
     </group>
     <attribute name = "generic" minOccurs = "1" type = "string"/>
     <attribute name = "operator" minOccurs = "1" type = "string"/>
     <attribute name = "truncated">
      <datatype source = "NMTOKEN">
       <enumeration value = "true"/>
       <enumeration value = "false"/>
      </datatype>
     </attribute>
    </type>
  </element>
  <element name = "businessEntityExt">
   <type content = "elementOnly">
    <annotation>
     <appInfo>This structure is the container for safely extending the
       businessEntity information in private implementations of UDDI
       compatible registries. Official operator nodes may not provide
       extended data but must return a properly populated businessEntity
       structure within this structure in response to a get_business
       DetailExt message.</appInfo>
    </annotation>
    <group order = "seq">
     <element ref = "businessEntity"/>
    </group>
   </type>
  </element>
  <element name = "get_businessDetailExt">
   <type content = "elementOnly">
    <annotation>
     <appInfo>The extended businessDetail messages define an API that allows
       non-operator nodes to provide extended information via a consistent
       API. This message is the request that will cause a businessDetailExt
       message to be returned.</appInfo>
    </annotation>
```

```
  <group order = "seq">
   <element ref = "businessKey" minOccurs = "1" maxOccurs = "*"/>
  </group>
  <attribute name = "generic" minOccurs = "1" type = "string"/>
 </type>
</element>
<element name = "businessDetailExt">
 <type content = "elementOnly">
  <annotation>
   <appInfo>The extended businessDetail messages define an API that allows
    non-operator nodes to provide extended information via a consistent
    API.  This message is the response to get_businessDetailExt.
    </appInfo>
  </annotation>
  <group order = "seq">
   <element ref = "businessEntityExt" minOccurs = "1" maxOccurs = "*"/>
  </group>
  <attribute name = "generic" minOccurs = "1" type = "string"/>
  <attribute name = "operator" minOccurs = "1" type = "string"/>
  <attribute name = "truncated">
   <datatype source = "NMTOKEN">
    <enumeration value = "true"/>
    <enumeration value = "false"/>
   </datatype>
  </attribute>
 </type>
</element>
<element name = "get_bindingDetail">
 <type content = "elementOnly">
  <group order = "seq">
   <element ref = "bindingKey" minOccurs = "1" maxOccurs = "*"/>
  </group>
  <attribute name = "generic" minOccurs = "1" type = "string"/>
 </type>
</element>
<element name = "bindingDetail">
 <type content = "elementOnly">
  <group order = "seq">
   <element ref = "bindingTemplate" minOccurs = "0" maxOccurs = "*" />
  </group>
  <attribute name = "generic" minOccurs = "1" type = "string"/>
  <attribute name = "operator" minOccurs = "1" type = "string"/>
  <attribute name = "truncated">
   <datatype source = "NMTOKEN">
    <enumeration value = "true"/>
    <enumeration value = "false"/>
   </datatype>
```

```
      </attribute>
    </type>
  </element>
  <element name = "validate_categorization">
   <type content = "elementOnly">
    <group order = "seq">
     <element ref = "tModelKey"/>
     <element ref = "keyValue"/>
     <element ref = "businessEntity" minOccurs = "0" maxOccurs =
       "1" />
     <element ref = "businessService" minOccurs = "0" maxOccurs =
       "1" />
     <element ref = "tModel" minOccurs = "0" maxOccurs = "1" />
    </group>
    <attribute name = "generic" minOccurs = "1" type = "string"/>
   </type>
  </element>
</schema>
```

UDDI XML Schema
1.0 (2001)

```
<?xml version="1.0" encoding="UTF-8" ?>
<xsd:schema id="uddi" attributeFormDefault="qualified" element
  FormDefault="qualified" targetNamespace="urn:uddi-org:api"
  xmlns:xsd="http://www.w3.org/2001/XMLSchema" xmlns:uddi="urn:
  uddi-org:api">
 <xsd:import namespace="http://www.w3.org/XML/1998/namespace" />
 <xsd:complexType name="AccessPoint" mixed="true">
  <xsd:attribute name="URLType" type="uddi:URLType"use="required" />
 </xsd:complexType>
 <xsd:complexType name="Address">
  <xsd:sequence>
   <xsd:element minOccurs="0" maxOccurs="unbounded" name="addressLine"
    type="xsd:string" />
  </xsd:sequence>
  <xsd:attribute name="sortCode" type="xsd:string" use= "optional" />
  <xsd:attribute name="useType" type="xsd:string" use="optional" />
 </xsd:complexType>
 <xsd:element name="authToken" type="uddi:AuthToken" />
 <xsd:complexType name="AuthToken">
  <xsd:sequence>
   <xsd:element minOccurs="1" maxOccurs="1" name="authInfo"
    type="xsd:string" />
  </xsd:sequence>
  <xsd:attribute name="generic" type="xsd:string" use= "required"/>
  <xsd:attribute name="operator" type="xsd:string" use="required" />
 </xsd:complexType>
<xsd:element name="bindingDetail" type="uddi:BindingDetail" />
 <xsd:complexType name="BindingDetail">
  <xsd:sequence>
   <xsd:element minOccurs="0" maxOccurs="unbounded" name=
    "bindingTemplate" type="uddi:BindingTemplate" />
  </xsd:sequence>
  <xsd:attribute name="generic" type="xsd:string" use= "required"/>
  <xsd:attribute name="operator" type="xsd:string" use="required" />
  <xsd:attribute name="truncated" type="uddi:Truncated" use="optional" />
 </xsd:complexType>
 <xsd:complexType name="BindingTemplate">
  <xsd:sequence>
   <xsd:element minOccurs="0" maxOccurs="unbounded" name="description"
    type="uddi:Description" />
   <xsd:choice minOccurs="1" maxOccurs="1">
    <xsd:element name="accessPoint" type="uddi:AccessPoint" />
    <xsd:element name="hostingRedirector"
    type="uddi:HostingRedirector" />
   </xsd:choice>
   <xsd:element minOccurs="1" maxOccurs="1" name="tModelInstanceDetails"
    type="uddi:TModelInstanceDetails" />
```

```
    </xsd:sequence>
    <xsd:attribute name="serviceKey" type="xsd:string" use="optional" />
    <xsd:attribute name="bindingKey" type="xsd:string" use="required" />
  </xsd:complexType>
<xsd:complexType name="BindingTemplates">
    <xsd:sequence>
      <xsd:element minOccurs="0" maxOccurs="unbounded"
      name="bindingTemplate" type="uddi:BindingTemplate" />
    </xsd:sequence>
    </xsd:complexType>
  <xsd:element name="businessDetail" type="uddi:BusinessDetail" />
  <xsd:complexType name="BusinessDetail">
    <xsd:sequence>
      <xsd:element minOccurs="0" maxOccurs="unbounded" name=
        "businessEntity" type="uddi:BusinessEntity" />
    </xsd:sequence>
    <xsd:attribute name="generic" type="xsd:string" use="required"/>
    <xsd:attribute name="operator" type="xsd:string" use="required" />
    <xsd:attribute name="truncated" type="uddi:Truncated" use="optional" />
  </xsd:complexType>
  <xsd:element name="businessDetailExt" type="uddi:Business DetailExt" />
  <xsd:complexType name="BusinessDetailExt">
    <xsd:sequence>
      <xsd:element minOccurs="1" maxOccurs="unbounded"
      name="businessEntityExt" type="uddi:BusinessEntityExt" />
    </xsd:sequence>
    <xsd:attribute name="generic" type="xsd:string" use="required"/>
    <xsd:attribute name="operator" type="xsd:string" use="required" />
    <xsd:attribute name="truncated" type="uddi:Truncated" use="optional" />
  </xsd:complexType>
  <xsd:complexType name="BusinessEntity">
    <xsd:sequence>
      <xsd:element minOccurs="0" maxOccurs="1" name="discovery URLs"
        type="uddi:DiscoveryURLs" />
      <xsd:element minOccurs="1" maxOccurs="1" name="name" type=
        "xsd:string" />
      <xsd:element minOccurs="0" maxOccurs="unbounded" name=
        "description" type="uddi:Description" />
      <xsd:element minOccurs="0" maxOccurs="1" name="contacts"
        type="uddi:Contacts" />
      <xsd:element minOccurs="0" maxOccurs="1" name="business
        Services" type="uddi:BusinessServices" />
      <xsd:element minOccurs="0" maxOccurs="1" name= "identifierBag"
        type="uddi:IdentifierBag" />
      <xsd:element minOccurs="0" maxOccurs="1" name="categoryBag"
        type="uddi:CategoryBag" />
    </xsd:sequence>
```

```
        <xsd:attribute name="businessKey" type="xsd:string" use="required" />
        <xsd:attribute name="operator" type="xsd:string" use="optional" />
        <xsd:attribute name="authorizedName" type="xsd:string" use="optional" />
      </xsd:complexType>
  <xsd:complexType name="BusinessEntityExt">
      <xsd:sequence>
        <xsd:element minOccurs="1" maxOccurs="1" name="businessEntity"
          type="uddi:BusinessEntity" />
      </xsd:sequence>
    </xsd:complexType>
  <xsd:complexType name="BusinessInfo">
      <xsd:sequence>
        <xsd:element minOccurs="1" maxOccurs="1" name="name" type=
          "xsd:string" />
        <xsd:element minOccurs="0" maxOccurs="unbounded" name=
          "description" type="uddi:Description" />
        <xsd:element minOccurs="1" maxOccurs="1" name="serviceInfos"
          type="uddi:ServiceInfos" />
      </xsd:sequence>
      <xsd:attribute name="businessKey" type="xsd:string" use="required" />
    </xsd:complexType>
  <xsd:complexType name="BusinessInfos">
      <xsd:sequence>
        <xsd:element minOccurs="0" maxOccurs="unbounded" name="businessInfo"
          type="uddi:BusinessInfo" />
      </xsd:sequence>
    </xsd:complexType>
  <xsd:element name="businessList" type="uddi:BusinessList" />
    <xsd:complexType name="BusinessList">
      <xsd:sequence>
        <xsd:element minOccurs="1" maxOccurs="1" name="business-
          Infos" type="uddi:BusinessInfos" />
      </xsd:sequence>
      <xsd:attribute name="generic" type="xsd:string" use="required"/>
      <xsd:attribute name="operator" type="xsd:string" use="required" />
      <xsd:attribute name="truncated" type="uddi:Truncated" use="optional" />
    </xsd:complexType>
  <xsd:complexType name="BusinessService">
      <xsd:sequence>
        <xsd:element minOccurs="1" maxOccurs="1" name="name"
          type="xsd:string" />
        <xsd:element minOccurs="0" maxOccurs="unbounded" name=
          "description" type="uddi:Description" />
        <xsd:element minOccurs="1" maxOccurs="1" name="binding
          Templates" type="uddi:BindingTemplates" />
```

```xml
        <xsd:element minOccurs="0" maxOccurs="1" name="categoryBag"
          type="uddi:CategoryBag" />
      </xsd:sequence>
      <xsd:attribute name="serviceKey" type="xsd:string" use="required" />
      <xsd:attribute name="businessKey" type="xsd:string" use="optional" />
    </xsd:complexType>
<xsd:complexType name="BusinessServices">
    <xsd:sequence>
        <xsd:element minOccurs="0" maxOccurs="unbounded" name=
          "businessService" type="uddi:BusinessService" />
    </xsd:sequence>
  </xsd:complexType>
<xsd:complexType name="CategoryBag">
    <xsd:sequence>
        <xsd:element minOccurs="0" maxOccurs="unbounded" name=
          "keyedReference" type="uddi:KeyedReference" />
    </xsd:sequence>
  </xsd:complexType>
<xsd:complexType name="Contact">
    <xsd:sequence>
        <xsd:element minOccurs="0" maxOccurs="unbounded" name=
          "description" type="uddi:Description" />
        <xsd:element minOccurs="1" maxOccurs="1" name="personName"
          type="xsd:string" />
        <xsd:element minOccurs="0" maxOccurs="unbounded" name="phone"
          type="uddi:Phone" />
        <xsd:element minOccurs="0" maxOccurs="unbounded" name="email"
          type="uddi:Email" />
        <xsd:element minOccurs="0" maxOccurs="unbounded" name="address"
          type="uddi:Address" />
    </xsd:sequence>
    <xsd:attribute name="useType" type="xsd:string" use="optional"/>
  </xsd:complexType>
<xsd:complexType name="Contacts">
    <xsd:sequence>
        <xsd:element minOccurs="0" maxOccurs="unbounded" name="contact"
          type="uddi:Contact" />
    </xsd:sequence>
  </xsd:complexType>
<xsd:element name="delete_binding" type="uddi:DeleteBinding" />
  <xsd:complexType name="DeleteBinding">
    <xsd:sequence>
        <xsd:element minOccurs="1" maxOccurs="1" name="authInfo"
          type="xsd:string" />
        <xsd:element minOccurs="1" maxOccurs="unbounded" name="bindingKey"
          type="xsd:string" />
```

```xml
      </xsd:sequence>
      <xsd:attribute name="generic" type="xsd:string" use="required"/>
    </xsd:complexType>
  <xsd:element name="delete_business" type="uddi:DeleteBusiness" />
    <xsd:complexType name="DeleteBusiness">
      <xsd:sequence>
        <xsd:element minOccurs="1" maxOccurs="1" name="authInfo"
          type="xsd:string" />
        <xsd:element minOccurs="1" maxOccurs="unbounded" name="businessKey"
          type="xsd:string" />
      </xsd:sequence>
      <xsd:attribute name="generic" type="xsd:string" use="required"/>
    </xsd:complexType>
  <xsd:element name="delete_service" type="uddi:DeleteService" />
    <xsd:complexType name="DeleteService">
      <xsd:sequence>
        <xsd:element minOccurs="1" maxOccurs="1" name="authInfo"
          type="xsd:string" />
        <xsd:element minOccurs="1" maxOccurs="unbounded" name="serviceKey"
          type="xsd:string" />
      </xsd:sequence>
      <xsd:attribute name="generic" type="xsd:string" use="required"/>
    </xsd:complexType>
  <xsd:element name="delete_tModel" type="uddi:DeleteTModel" />
    <xsd:complexType name="DeleteTModel">
      <xsd:sequence>
        <xsd:element minOccurs="1" maxOccurs="1" name="authInfo"
          type="xsd:string" />
        <xsd:element minOccurs="1" maxOccurs="unbounded" name="tModelKey"
          type="xsd:string" />
      </xsd:sequence>
      <xsd:attribute name="generic" type="xsd:string" use="required"/>
    </xsd:complexType>
  <xsd:complexType name="Description" mixed="true">
      <xsd:attribute ref="xml:lang" use="optional" />
    </xsd:complexType>
  <xsd:element name="discard_authToken" type="uddi:DiscardAuthToken"/>
    <xsd:complexType name="DiscardAuthToken">
      <xsd:sequence>
        <xsd:element minOccurs="1" maxOccurs="1" name="authInfo"
          type="xsd:string" />
      </xsd:sequence>
      <xsd:attribute name="generic" type="xsd:string" use="required"/>
    </xsd:complexType>
  <xsd:complexType name="DiscoveryUrl" mixed="true">
      <xsd:attribute name="useType" type="xsd:string" use="required"/>
    </xsd:complexType>
```

```xml
<xsd:complexType name="DiscoveryURLs">
    <xsd:sequence>
       <xsd:element minOccurs="1" maxOccurs="unbounded" name="discoveryUrl"
         type="uddi:DiscoveryUrl" />
    </xsd:sequence>
  </xsd:complexType>
<xsd:element name="dispositionReport" type="uddi: DispositionReport" />
  <xsd:complexType name="DispositionReport">
    <xsd:sequence>
       <xsd:element minOccurs="1" maxOccurs="unbounded" name="result"
         type="uddi:Result" />
    </xsd:sequence>
    <xsd:attribute name="generic" type="xsd:string" use="required"/>
    <xsd:attribute name="operator" type="xsd:string" use="required" />
    <xsd:attribute name="truncated" type="uddi:Truncated" use="optional" />
  </xsd:complexType>
<xsd:complexType name="Email" mixed="true">
    <xsd:attribute name="useType" type="xsd:string" use="optional"/>
  </xsd:complexType>
<xsd:complexType name="ErrInfo" mixed="true">
    <xsd:attribute name="errCode" type="xsd:string" use="required"/>
  </xsd:complexType>
<xsd:element name="find_binding" type="uddi:FindBinding" />
  <xsd:complexType name="FindBinding">
    <xsd:sequence>
       <xsd:element minOccurs="0" maxOccurs="1" name="findQualifiers"
         type="uddi:FindQualifiers" />
       <xsd:element minOccurs="1" maxOccurs="1" name="tModelBag"
         type="uddi:TModelBag" />
    </xsd:sequence>
    <xsd:attribute name="generic" type="xsd:string" use="required"/>
    <xsd:attribute name="maxRows" type="xsd:int" use="optional" />
    <xsd:attribute name="serviceKey" type="xsd:string" use="required" />
  </xsd:complexType>
<xsd:element name="find_business" type="uddi:FindBusiness" />
  <xsd:complexType name="FindBusiness">
    <xsd:sequence>
       <xsd:element minOccurs="0" maxOccurs="1" name="findQualifiers"
         type="uddi:FindQualifiers" />
       <xsd:element minOccurs="0" maxOccurs="1" name="name"
         type="xsd:string" />
       <xsd:element minOccurs="0" maxOccurs="1" name= "identifierBag"
         type="uddi:IdentifierBag" />
       <xsd:element minOccurs="0" maxOccurs="1" name="categoryBag"
         type="uddi:CategoryBag" />
       <xsd:element minOccurs="0" maxOccurs="1" name="tModelBag"
         type="uddi:TModelBag" />
```

```
        <xsd:element minOccurs="0" maxOccurs="1" name= "discoveryURLs"
          type="uddi:DiscoveryURLs" />
      </xsd:sequence>
      <xsd:attribute name="generic" type="xsd:string" use="required"/>
      <xsd:attribute name="maxRows" type="xsd:int" use="optional" />
    </xsd:complexType>
  <xsd:element name="find_service" type="uddi:FindService" />
    <xsd:complexType name="FindService">
      <xsd:sequence>
        <xsd:element minOccurs="0" maxOccurs="1" name="findQualifiers"
          type="uddi:FindQualifiers" />
        <xsd:element minOccurs="0" maxOccurs="1" name="name"
          type="xsd:string" />
        <xsd:element minOccurs="0" maxOccurs="1" name="categoryBag"
          type="uddi:CategoryBag" />
        <xsd:element minOccurs="0" maxOccurs="1" name="tModelBag"
          type="uddi:TModelBag" />
      </xsd:sequence>
      <xsd:attribute name="generic" type="xsd:string" use="required"/>
      <xsd:attribute name="maxRows" type="xsd:int" use="optional" />
      <xsd:attribute name="businessKey" type="xsd:string" use="required" />
    </xsd:complexType>
  <xsd:element name="find_tModel" type="uddi:FindTModel" />
    <xsd:complexType name="FindTModel">
      <xsd:sequence>
        <xsd:element minOccurs="0" maxOccurs="1" name="findQualifiers"
          type="uddi:FindQualifiers" />
        <xsd:element minOccurs="0" maxOccurs="1" name="name" type=
          "xsd:string" />
        <xsd:element minOccurs="0" maxOccurs="1" name= "identifierBag"
          type="uddi:IdentifierBag" />
        <xsd:element minOccurs="0" maxOccurs="1" name="categoryBag"
          type="uddi:CategoryBag" />
      </xsd:sequence>
      <xsd:attribute name="generic" type="xsd:string" use="required"/>
      <xsd:attribute name="maxRows" type="xsd:int" use="optional" />
    </xsd:complexType>
  <xsd:complexType name="FindQualifiers">
      <xsd:sequence>
        <xsd:element minOccurs="0" maxOccurs="unbounded" name="findQualifier"
          type="xsd:string" />
      </xsd:sequence>
    </xsd:complexType>
  <xsd:element name="get_authToken" type="uddi:GetAuthToken" />
    <xsd:complexType name="GetAuthToken">
      <xsd:attribute name="generic" type="xsd:string" use="required"/>
```

```xml
        <xsd:attribute name="userID" type="xsd:string" use="required"/>
        <xsd:attribute name="cred" type="xsd:string" use="required" />
      </xsd:complexType>
<xsd:element name="get_bindingDetail" type="uddi:GetBindingDetail"/>
  <xsd:complexType name="GetBindingDetail">
    <xsd:sequence>
      <xsd:element minOccurs="1" maxOccurs="unbounded" name="bindingKey"
        type="xsd:string" />
    </xsd:sequence>
    <xsd:attribute name="generic" type="xsd:string" use="required"/>
  </xsd:complexType>
<xsd:element name="get_businessDetail" type="uddi:GetBusinessDetail" />
  <xsd:complexType name="GetBusinessDetail">
    <xsd:sequence>
      <xsd:element minOccurs="1" maxOccurs="unbounded" name="businessKey"
        type="xsd:string" />
    </xsd:sequence>
    <xsd:attribute name="generic" type="xsd:string" use="required"/>
  </xsd:complexType>
<xsd:element name="get_businessDetailExt" type="uddi:GetBusiness
  DetailExt" />
  <xsd:complexType name="GetBusinessDetailExt">
    <xsd:sequence>
      <xsd:element minOccurs="1" maxOccurs="unbounded" name="businessKey"
        type="xsd:string" />
    </xsd:sequence>
    <xsd:attribute name="generic" type="xsd:string" use="required"/>
  </xsd:complexType>
<xsd:element name="get_registeredInfo" type="uddi:GetRegisteredInfo" />
  <xsd:complexType name="GetRegisteredInfo">
    <xsd:sequence>
      <xsd:element minOccurs="1" maxOccurs="1" name="authInfo"
        type="xsd:string" />
    </xsd:sequence>
    <xsd:attribute name="generic" type="xsd:string" use="required"/>
  </xsd:complexType>
<xsd:element name="get_serviceDetail" type="uddi:GetServiceDetail"/>
  <xsd:complexType name="GetServiceDetail">
    <xsd:sequence>
      <xsd:element minOccurs="1" maxOccurs="unbounded" name="serviceKey"
        type="xsd:string" />
    </xsd:sequence>
    <xsd:attribute name="generic" type="xsd:string" use="required"/>
  </xsd:complexType>
<xsd:element name="get_tModelDetail" type="uddi:GetTModelDetail"/>
  <xsd:complexType name="GetTModelDetail">
```

```xml
          <xsd:sequence>
            <xsd:element minOccurs="1" maxOccurs="unbounded" name="tModelKey"
              type="xsd:string" />
          </xsd:sequence>
          <xsd:attribute name="generic" type="xsd:string" use="required"/>
        </xsd:complexType>
  <xsd:complexType name="HostingRedirector">
          <xsd:attribute name="bindingKey" type="xsd:string" use="required" />
        </xsd:complexType>
  <xsd:complexType name="IdentifierBag">
          <xsd:sequence>
            <xsd:element minOccurs="0" maxOccurs="unbounded" name=
              "keyedReference" type="uddi:KeyedReference" />
          </xsd:sequence>
        </xsd:complexType>
  <xsd:complexType name="InstanceDetails">
          <xsd:sequence>
            <xsd:element minOccurs="0" maxOccurs="unbounded" name="description"
              type="uddi:Description" />
            <xsd:element minOccurs="0" maxOccurs="1" name="overviewDoc"
              type="uddi:OverviewDoc" />
            <xsd:element minOccurs="0" maxOccurs="1" name="instanceParms"
              type="xsd:string" />
          </xsd:sequence>
        </xsd:complexType>
  <xsd:complexType name="KeyedReference">
          <xsd:attribute name="tModelKey" type="xsd:string" use="optional" />
          <xsd:attribute name="keyName" type="xsd:string" use="required"/>
          <xsd:attribute name="keyValue" type="xsd:string" use="required" />
        </xsd:complexType>
  <xsd:simpleType name="KeyType">
          <xsd:restriction base="xsd:string">
            <xsd:enumeration value="businessKey" />
            <xsd:enumeration value="tModelKey" />
            <xsd:enumeration value="serviceKey" />
            <xsd:enumeration value="bindingKey" />
          </xsd:restriction>
        </xsd:simpleType>
  <xsd:complexType name="OverviewDoc">
          <xsd:sequence>
            <xsd:element minOccurs="0" maxOccurs="unbounded" name="description"
              type="uddi:Description" />
            <xsd:element minOccurs="0" maxOccurs="1" name="overviewURL"
              type="xsd:string" />
          </xsd:sequence>
        </xsd:complexType>
  <xsd:complexType name="Phone" mixed="true">
```

```xml
        <xsd:attribute name="useType" type="xsd:string" use="optional"/>
    </xsd:complexType>
<xsd:element name="registeredInfo" type="uddi:RegisteredInfo" />
    <xsd:complexType name="RegisteredInfo">
        <xsd:sequence>
            <xsd:element minOccurs="1" maxOccurs="1" name="businessInfos"
                type="uddi:BusinessInfos" />
            <xsd:element minOccurs="1" maxOccurs="1" name="tModelInfos"
                type="uddi:TModelInfos" />
        </xsd:sequence>
        <xsd:attribute name="generic" type="xsd:string" use="required"/>
        <xsd:attribute name="operator" type="xsd:string" use="required" />
        <xsd:attribute name="truncated" type="uddi:Truncated" use="optional" />
    </xsd:complexType>
<xsd:complexType name="Result">
        <xsd:sequence>
            <xsd:element minOccurs="0" maxOccurs="1" name="errInfo"
                type="uddi:ErrInfo" />
        </xsd:sequence>
        <xsd:attribute name="keyType" type="uddi:KeyType" use="optional" />
        <xsd:attribute name="errno" type="xsd:int" use="required" />
    </xsd:complexType>
<xsd:element name="save_binding" type="uddi:SaveBinding" />
    <xsd:complexType name="SaveBinding">
        <xsd:sequence>
            <xsd:element minOccurs="1" maxOccurs="1" name="authInfo"
                type="xsd:string" />
            <xsd:element minOccurs="1" maxOccurs="unbounded" name=
                "bindingTemplate" type="uddi:BindingTemplate" />
        </xsd:sequence>
        <xsd:attribute name="generic" type="xsd:string" use="required"/>
    </xsd:complexType>
<xsd:element name="save_business" type="uddi:SaveBusiness" />
    <xsd:complexType name="SaveBusiness">
        <xsd:sequence>
            <xsd:element minOccurs="1" maxOccurs="1" name="authInfo"
                type="xsd:string" />
            <xsd:element minOccurs="0" maxOccurs="unbounded" name=
                "businessEntity" type="uddi:BusinessEntity" />
            <xsd:element minOccurs="0" maxOccurs="unbounded" name=
                "uploadRegister" type="xsd:string" />
        </xsd:sequence>
        <xsd:attribute name="generic" type="xsd:string" use="required"/>
    </xsd:complexType>
<xsd:element name="save_service" type="uddi:SaveService" />
    <xsd:complexType name="SaveService">
        <xsd:sequence>
```

```xml
        <xsd:element minOccurs="1" maxOccurs="1" name="authInfo" type=
          "xsd:string" />
        <xsd:element minOccurs="1" maxOccurs="unbounded" name=
          "businessService" type="uddi:BusinessService" />
      </xsd:sequence>
      <xsd:attribute name="generic" type="xsd:string" use="required"/>
    </xsd:complexType>
<xsd:element name="save_tModel" type="uddi:SaveTModel" />
  <xsd:complexType name="SaveTModel">
    <xsd:sequence>
      <xsd:element minOccurs="1" maxOccurs="1" name="authInfo"
        type="xsd:string" />
      <xsd:element minOccurs="0" maxOccurs="unbounded" name="tModel"
        type="uddi:TModel" />
      <xsd:element minOccurs="0" maxOccurs="unbounded" name=
        "uploadRegister" type="xsd:string" />
    </xsd:sequence>
    <xsd:attribute name="generic" type="xsd:string" use="required"/>
  </xsd:complexType>
<xsd:element name="serviceDetail" type="uddi:ServiceDetail" />
  <xsd:complexType name="ServiceDetail">
    <xsd:sequence>
      <xsd:element minOccurs="0" maxOccurs="unbounded" name=
        "businessService" type="uddi:BusinessService" />
    </xsd:sequence>
    <xsd:attribute name="generic" type="xsd:string" use="required"/>
    <xsd:attribute name="operator" type="xsd:string" use="required" />
    <xsd:attribute name="truncated" type="uddi:Truncated" use="optional" />
  </xsd:complexType>
<xsd:complexType name="ServiceInfo">
    <xsd:sequence>
      <xsd:element minOccurs="1" maxOccurs="1" name="name" type=
        "xsd:string" />
    </xsd:sequence>
    <xsd:attribute name="serviceKey" type="xsd:string" use="required" />
    <xsd:attribute name="businessKey" type="xsd:string" use="optional" />
  </xsd:complexType>
<xsd:complexType name="ServiceInfos">
    <xsd:sequence>
      <xsd:element minOccurs="0" maxOccurs="unbounded" name="serviceInfo"
        type="uddi:ServiceInfo" />
    </xsd:sequence>
  </xsd:complexType>
<xsd:element name="serviceList" type="uddi:ServiceList" />
  <xsd:complexType name="ServiceList">
    <xsd:sequence>
      <xsd:element minOccurs="1" maxOccurs="1" name="serviceInfos"
        type="uddi:ServiceInfos" />
```

```xml
    </xsd:sequence>
    <xsd:attribute name="generic" type="xsd:string" use="required"/>
    <xsd:attribute name="operator" type="xsd:string" use="required" />
    <xsd:attribute name="truncated" type="uddi:Truncated" use="optional" />
  </xsd:complexType>
<xsd:complexType name="TModel">
    <xsd:sequence>
      <xsd:element minOccurs="1" maxOccurs="1" name="name"
        type="xsd:string" />
      <xsd:element minOccurs="0" maxOccurs="unbounded" name="description"
        type="uddi:Description" />
      <xsd:element minOccurs="0" maxOccurs="1" name="overviewDoc"
        type="uddi:OverviewDoc" />
      <xsd:element minOccurs="0" maxOccurs="1" name= "identifierBag"
        type="uddi:IdentifierBag" />
      <xsd:element minOccurs="0" maxOccurs="1" name="categoryBag"
        type="uddi:CategoryBag" />
    </xsd:sequence>
    <xsd:attribute name="tModelKey" type="xsd:string" use="required" />
    <xsd:attribute name="operator" type="xsd:string" use="optional" />
    <xsd:attribute name="authorizedName" type="xsd:string" use="optional" />
  </xsd:complexType>
<xsd:complexType name="TModelBag">
    <xsd:sequence>
      <xsd:element minOccurs="1" maxOccurs="unbounded" name="tModelKey"
        type="xsd:string" />
    </xsd:sequence>
  </xsd:complexType>
<xsd:element name="tModelDetail" type="uddi:TModelDetail" />
  <xsd:complexType name="TModelDetail">
    <xsd:sequence>
      <xsd:element minOccurs="1" maxOccurs="unbounded" name="tModel"
        type="uddi:TModel" />
    </xsd:sequence>
    <xsd:attribute name="generic" type="xsd:string" use="required"/>
    <xsd:attribute name="operator" type="xsd:string" use="required" />
    <xsd:attribute name="truncated" type="uddi:Truncated" use="optional" />
  </xsd:complexType>
<xsd:complexType name="TModelInfo">
    <xsd:sequence>
      <xsd:element minOccurs="1" maxOccurs="1" name="name" type=
        "xsd:string" />
    </xsd:sequence>
    <xsd:attribute name="tModelKey" type="xsd:string" use="required" />
  </xsd:complexType>
<xsd:complexType name="TModelInfos">
    <xsd:sequence>
```

```xsd
        <xsd:element minOccurs="0" maxOccurs="unbounded" name="tModelInfo"
          type="uddi:TModelInfo" />
      </xsd:sequence>
    </xsd:complexType>
  <xsd:complexType name="TModelInstanceDetails">
      <xsd:sequence>
        <xsd:element minOccurs="0" maxOccurs="unbounded" name=
          "tModelInstanceInfo" type="uddi:TModelInstanceInfo" />
      </xsd:sequence>
    </xsd:complexType>
  <xsd:complexType name="TModelInstanceInfo">
      <xsd:sequence>
        <xsd:element minOccurs="0" maxOccurs="unbounded" name="description"
          type="uddi:Description" />
        <xsd:element minOccurs="0" maxOccurs="1" name="instance Details"
          type="uddi:InstanceDetails" />
      </xsd:sequence>
      <xsd:attribute name="tModelKey" type="xsd:string" use="required" />
    </xsd:complexType>
  <xsd:element name="tModelList" type="uddi:TModelList" />
    <xsd:complexType name="TModelList">
      <xsd:sequence>
        <xsd:element minOccurs="1" maxOccurs="1" name="tModelInfos"
          type="uddi:TModelInfos" />
      </xsd:sequence>
      <xsd:attribute name="generic" type="xsd:string" use="required"/>
      <xsd:attribute name="operator" type="xsd:string" use="required" />
      <xsd:attribute name="truncated" type="uddi:Truncated" use="optional" />
    </xsd:complexType>
  <xsd:simpleType name="Truncated">
      <xsd:restriction base="xsd:string">
        <xsd:enumeration value="true" />
        <xsd:enumeration value="false" />
      </xsd:restriction>
    </xsd:simpleType>
  <xsd:simpleType name="URLType">
      <xsd:restriction base="xsd:string">
        <xsd:enumeration value="mailto" />
        <xsd:enumeration value="http" />
        <xsd:enumeration value="https" />
        <xsd:enumeration value="ftp" />
        <xsd:enumeration value="fax" />
        <xsd:enumeration value="phone" />
        <xsd:enumeration value="other" />
      </xsd:restriction>
    </xsd:simpleType>
```

```xml
<xsd:element name="validate_categorization"
  type="uddi:ValidateCategorization" />
  <xsd:complexType name="ValidateCategorization">
    <xsd:sequence>
      <xsd:element minOccurs="1" maxOccurs="1" name="tModelKey"
        type="xsd:string" />
      <xsd:element minOccurs="1" maxOccurs="1" name="keyValue"
        type="xsd:string" />
      <xsd:element minOccurs="0" maxOccurs="1" name="businessEntity"
        type="uddi:BusinessEntity" />
      <xsd:element minOccurs="0" maxOccurs="1" name="businessService"
        type="uddi:BusinessService" />
      <xsd:element minOccurs="0" maxOccurs="1" name="tModel"
        type="uddi:TModel" />
    </xsd:sequence>
    <xsd:attribute name="generic" type="xsd:string" use="required"/>
  </xsd:complexType>
</xsd:schema>
```

PART
2

Simple Object Access Protocol (SOAP) 1.1

CHAPTER
7

W3C Simple Object Access Protocol (SOAP) 1.1

W3C Note 08 May 2000

This version:

http://www.w3.org/TR/2000/NOTE-SOAP-20000508

Latest version:

http://www.w3.org/TR/SOAP

Authors (alphabetically):

> Don Box, DevelopMentor
> David Ehnebuske, IBM
> Gopal Kakivaya, Microsoft
> Andrew Layman, Microsoft
> Noah Mendelsohn, Lotus Development Corp.
> Henrik Frystyk Nielsen, Microsoft
> Satish Thatte, Microsoft
> Dave Winer, UserLand Software, Inc.

Abstract

SOAP is a lightweight protocol for exchange of information in a decentralized, distributed environment. It is an XML based protocol that consists of three parts: an envelope that defines a framework for describing what is in a message and how to process it, a set of encoding rules for expressing instances of application-defined datatypes, and a convention for representing remote procedure calls and responses. SOAP can potentially be used in combination with a variety of other protocols; however, the only bindings defined in this document describe how to use SOAP in combination with HTTP and HTTP Extension Framework.

Status

This document is a submission to the World Wide Web Consortium (see Submission Request, W3C Staff Comment) to propose the formation of a working group in the area of XML-based protocols. Comments are welcome to the authors but you are encouraged to share your views on the W3C's public mailing list <xml-dist-app@w3.org> (see archives).

This document is a NOTE made available by the W3C for discussion only. Publication of this Note by W3C indicates no endorsement by W3C or the W3C Team, or any W3C Members. W3C has had no editorial control over the preparation of this Note. This document is a work in progress and may be updated, replaced, or rendered obsolete by other documents at any time.

A list of current W3C technical documents can be found at the Technical Reports page.

TABLE OF CONTENTS

1. Introduction

SOAP provides a simple and lightweight mechanism for exchanging structured and typed information between peers in a decentralized, distributed environment using XML. SOAP does not itself define any application semantics such as a programming model or implementation specific semantics; rather it defines a simple mechanism for expressing application semantics by providing a modular packaging model and encoding mechanisms for encoding data within modules. This allows SOAP to be used in a large variety of systems ranging from messaging systems to RPC.

SOAP consists of three parts:

▼ The SOAP envelope (see section 4) construct defines an overall framework for expressing **what** is in a message; **who** should deal with it, and **whether** it is optional or mandatory.

▼ The SOAP encoding rules (see section 5) defines a serialization mechanism that can be used to exchange instances of application-defined datatypes.

▼ The SOAP RPC representation (see section 7) defines a convention that can be used to represent remote procedure calls and responses.

Although these parts are described together as part of SOAP, they are functionally orthogonal. In particular, the envelope and the encoding rules are defined in different namespaces in order to promote simplicity through modularity.

In addition to the SOAP envelope, the SOAP encoding rules and the SOAP RPC conventions, this specification defines two protocol bindings that describe how a SOAP message can be carried in HTTP [5] messages either with or without the HTTP Extension Framework [6].

1.1 Design Goals

A major design goal for SOAP is simplicity and extensibility. This means that there are several features from traditional messaging systems and distributed object systems that are not part of the core SOAP specification. Such features include

▼ Distributed garbage collection

▼ Boxcarring or batching of messages

▼ Objects-by-reference (which requires distributed garbage collection)

▼ Activation (which requires objects-by-reference)

1.2 Notational Conventions

The keywords "MUST", "MUST NOT", "REQUIRED", "SHALL", "SHALL NOT", "SHOULD", "SHOULD NOT", "RECOMMENDED", "MAY", and "OPTIONAL" in this document are to be interpreted as described in RFC-2119 [2].

The namespace prefixes "SOAP-ENV" and "SOAP-ENC" used in this document are associated with the SOAP namespaces "http://schemas.xmlsoap.org/soap/envelope/" and "http://schemas.xmlsoap.org/soap/encoding/" respectively.

Throughout this document, the namespace prefix "xsi" is assumed to be associated with the URI "http://www.w3.org/1999/XMLSchema-instance" which is defined in the XML Schemas specification [11]. Similarly, the namespace prefix "xsd" is assumed to be associated with the URI "http://www.w3.org/1999/XMLSchema" which is defined in [10]. The namespace prefix "tns" is used to indicate whatever is the target namespace of the current document. All other namespace prefixes are samples only.

Namespace URIs of the general form "some-URI" represent some application-dependent or context-dependent URI [4].

This specification uses the augmented Backus-Naur Form (BNF) as described in RFC-2616 [5] for certain constructs.

1.3 Examples of SOAP Messages

In this example, a GetLastTradePrice SOAP request is sent to a StockQuote service. The request takes a string parameter, ticker symbol, and returns a float in the SOAP response. The SOAP Envelope element is the top element of the XML document representing the SOAP message. XML namespaces are used to disambiguate SOAP identifiers from application specific identifiers. The example illustrates the HTTP bindings defined in section 6. It is worth noting that the rules governing XML payload format in SOAP are entirely independent of the fact that the payload is carried in HTTP.

More examples are available in Appendix A.

Example 1   SOAP Message Embedded in HTTP Request

```
POST /StockQuote HTTP/1.1
Host: www.stockquoteserver.com
Content-Type: text/xml; charset="utf-8"
Content-Length: nnnn
```

```
SOAPAction: "Some-URI"

<SOAP-ENV:Envelope
 xmlns:SOAP-ENV="http://schemas.xmlsoap.org/soap/envelope/"
 SOAP-ENV:encodingStyle="http://schemas.xmlsoap.org/soap/
  encoding/">
 <SOAP-ENV:Body>
     <m:GetLastTradePrice xmlns:m="Some-URI">
        <symbol>DIS</symbol>
     </m:GetLastTradePrice>
 </SOAP-ENV:Body>
</SOAP-ENV:Envelope>
```

Following is the response message containing the HTTP message with the SOAP message as the payload:

Example 2   SOAP Message Embedded in HTTP Response

```
HTTP/1.1 200 OK
Content-Type: text/xml; charset="utf-8"
Content-Length: nnnn

<SOAP-ENV:Envelope
 xmlns:SOAP-ENV="http://schemas.xmlsoap.org/soap/envelope/"
 SOAP-ENV:encodingStyle="http://schemas.xmlsoap.org/soap/
  encoding/"/>
 <SOAP-ENV:Body>
     <m:GetLastTradePriceResponse xmlns:m="Some-URI">
        <Price>34.5</Price>
     </m:GetLastTradePriceResponse>
 </SOAP-ENV:Body>
</SOAP-ENV:Envelope>
```

2. The SOAP Message Exchange Model

SOAP messages are fundamentally one-way transmissions from a sender to a receiver, but as illustrated above, SOAP messages are often combined to implement patterns such as request/response.

SOAP implementations can be optimized to exploit the unique characteristics of particular network systems. For example, the HTTP binding described in <u>section 6</u> provides for SOAP response messages to be delivered as HTTP responses, using the same connection as the inbound request.

Regardless of the protocol to which SOAP is bound, messages are routed along a so-called "message path", which allows for processing at one or more intermediate nodes in addition to the ultimate destination.

A SOAP application receiving a SOAP message MUST process that message by performing the following actions in the order listed below:

1. Identify all parts of the SOAP message intended for that application (see <u>section 4.2.2</u>)

2. Verify that all mandatory parts identified in <u>step 1</u> are supported by the application for this message (see <u>section 4.2.3</u>) and process them accordingly. If this is not the case then discard the message (see <u>section 4.4</u>). The processor MAY ignore optional parts identified in step 1 without affecting the outcome of the processing.

3. If the SOAP application is not the ultimate destination of the message then remove all parts identified in <u>step 1</u> before forwarding the message.

Processing a message or a part of a message requires that the SOAP processor understands, among other things, the exchange pattern being used (one way, request/response, multicast, etc.), the role of the recipient in that pattern, the employment (if any) of RPC mechanisms such as the one documented in <u>section 7</u>, the representation or encoding of data, as well as other semantics necessary for correct processing.

While attributes such as the SOAP encodingStyle attribute (see <u>section 4.1.1</u>) can be used to describe certain aspects of a message, this specification does not mandate a particular means by which the recipient makes such determinations in general. For example, certain applications will understand that a particular <getStockPrice> element signals an RPC request using the conventions of <u>section 7</u>, while another application may infer that all traffic directed to it is encoded as one way messages.

3. Relation to XML

All SOAP messages are encoded using XML (see <u>[7]</u> for more information on XML).

A SOAP application SHOULD include the proper SOAP namespace on all elements and attributes defined by SOAP in messages that it generates. A SOAP application MUST be able to process SOAP namespaces in messages that it receives. It MUST discard messages that have incorrect namespaces (see section 4.4) and it MAY process SOAP messages without SOAP namespaces as though they had the correct SOAP namespaces.

SOAP defines two namespaces (see [8] for more information on XML namespaces):

▼ The SOAP envelope has the namespace identifier "http://schemas .xmlsoap.org/soap/envelope/"

▼ The SOAP serialization has the namespace identifier "http://schemas .xmlsoap.org/soap/encoding/"

A SOAP message MUST NOT contain a Document Type Declaration. A SOAP message MUST NOT contain Processing Instructions. [7]

SOAP uses the local, unqualified "id" attribute of type "ID" to specify the unique identifier of an encoded element. SOAP uses the local, unqualified attribute "href" of type "uri-reference" to specify a reference to that value, in a manner conforming to the XML Specification [7], XML Schema Specification [11], and XML Linking Language Specification [9].

With the exception of the SOAP mustUnderstand attribute (see section 4.2.3) and the SOAP actor attribute (see section 4.2.2), it is generally permissible to have attributes and their values appear in XML instances or alternatively in schemas, with equal effect. That is, declaration in a DTD or schema with a default or fixed value is semantically equivalent to appearance in an instance.

4. SOAP Envelope

A SOAP message is an XML document that consists of a mandatory SOAP envelope, an optional SOAP header, and a mandatory SOAP body. This XML document is referred to as a SOAP message for the rest of this specification. The namespace identifier for the elements and attributes defined in this section is "http://schemas.xmlsoap.org/soap/envelope/". A SOAP message contains the following:

▼ The Envelope is the top element of the XML document representing the message.

▼ The Header is a generic mechanism for adding features to a SOAP message in a decentralized manner without prior agreement between the communicating parties. SOAP defines a few attributes that can be used to indicate who should deal with a feature and whether it is optional or mandatory (see section 4.2)

▼ The Body is a container for mandatory information intended for the ultimate recipient of the message (see section 4.3). SOAP defines one element for the body, which is the Fault element used for reporting errors.

The grammar rules are as follows:

▼ 1 Envelope
  ▼ The element name is "Envelope".
  ▼ The element MUST be present in a SOAP message
  ▼ The element MAY contain namespace declarations as well as additional attributes. If present, such additional attributes MUST be namespace-qualified. Similarly, the element MAY contain additional sub elements. If present these elements MUST be namespace-qualified and MUST follow the SOAP Body element.

▼ Header (see section 4.2)
  ▼ The element name is "Header".
  ▼ The element MAY be present in a SOAP message. If present, the element MUST be the first immediate child element of a SOAP Envelope element.
  ▼ The element MAY contain a set of header entries each being an immediate child element of the SOAP Header element. All immediate child elements of the SOAP Header element MUST be namespace-qualified.

▼ Body (see section 4.3)
  ▼ The element name is "Body".
  ▼ The element MUST be present in a SOAP message and MUST be an immediate child element of a SOAP Envelope element. It MUST directly follow the SOAP Header element if present. Otherwise it MUST be the first immediate child element of the SOAP Envelope element.
  ▼ The element MAY contain a set of body entries each being an immediate child element of the SOAP Body element. Immediate child elements of the SOAP Body element MAY be namespace-qualified. SOAP defines the SOAP Fault element, which is used to indicate error messages (see section 4.4).

4.1.1 SOAP encodingStyle Attribute

The SOAP encodingStyle global attribute can be used to indicate the serialization rules used in a SOAP message. This attribute MAY appear on any element, and is scoped to that element's contents and all child elements not themselves containing such an attribute, much as an XML namespace declaration is scoped. There is no default encoding defined for a SOAP message.

The attribute value is an ordered list of one or more URIs identifying the serialization rule or rules that can be used to deserialize the SOAP message indicated in the order of most specific to least specific. Examples of values are

"http://schemas.xmlsoap.org/soap/encoding/"

"http://my.host/encoding/restricted http://my.host/encoding/"

""

The serialization rules defined by SOAP in section 5 are identified by the URI "http://schemas.xmlsoap.org/soap/encoding/". Messages using this particular serialization SHOULD indicate this using the SOAP encodingStyle attribute. In addition, all URIs syntactically beginning with "http://schemas.xmlsoap.org/soap/encoding/" indicate conformance with the SOAP encoding rules defined in section 5 (though with potentially tighter rules added).

A value of the zero-length URI ("") explicitly indicates that no claims are made for the encoding style of contained elements. This can be used to turn off any claims from containing elements.

4.1.2 Envelope Versioning Model

SOAP does not define a traditional versioning model based on major and minor version numbers. A SOAP message MUST have an Envelope element associated with the "http://schemas.xmlsoap.org/soap/envelope/" namespace. If a message is received by a SOAP application in which the SOAP Envelope element is associated with a different namespace, the application MUST treat this as a version error and discard the message. If the message is received through a request/response protocol such as HTTP, the application MUST respond with a SOAP VersionMismatch faultcode message (see section 4.4) using the SOAP "http://schemas.xmlsoap.org/soap/envelope/" namespace.

4.2 SOAP Header

SOAP provides a flexible mechanism for extending a message in a decentralized and modular way without prior knowledge between the communicating parties. Typical examples of extensions that can be implemented as header entries are authentication, transaction management, payment etc.

The Header element is encoded as the first immediate child element of the SOAP Envelope XML element. All immediate child elements of the Header element are called header entries.

The encoding rules for header entries are as follows:

1. A header entry is identified by its fully qualified element name, which consists of the namespace URI and the local name. All immediate child elements of the SOAP Header element MUST be namespace-qualified.

2. The SOAP encodingStyle attribute MAY be used to indicate the encoding style used for the header entries (see section 4.1.1).

3. The SOAP mustUnderstand attribute (see section 4.2.3) and SOAP actor attribute (see section 4.2.2) MAY be used to indicate how to process the entry and by whom (see section 4.2.1).

4.2.1 Use of Header Attributes

The SOAP Header attributes defined in this section determine how a recipient of a SOAP message should process the message as described in section 2. A SOAP application generating a SOAP message SHOULD only use the SOAP Header attributes on immediate child elements of the SOAP Header element. The recipient of a SOAP message MUST ignore all SOAP Header attributes that are not applied to an immediate child element of the SOAP Header element.

An example is a header with an element identifier of "Transaction", a "mustUnderstand" value of "1", and a value of 5. This would be encoded as follows:

```
<SOAP-ENV:Header>
 <t:Transaction
  xmlns:t="some-URI" SOAP-ENV:mustUnderstand="1">
    5
 </t:Transaction>
</SOAP-ENV:Header>
```

4.2.2 SOAP actor Attribute

A SOAP message travels from the originator to the ultimate destination, potentially by passing through a set of SOAP intermediaries along the message path. A SOAP intermediary is an application that is capable of both receiving and forwarding SOAP messages. Both intermediaries as well as the ultimate destination are identified by a URI.

Not all parts of a SOAP message may be intended for the ultimate destination of the SOAP message but, instead, may be intended for one or more of the intermediaries on the message path. The role of a recipient of a header element is similar to that of accepting a contract in that it cannot be extended beyond the recipient. That is, a recipient receiving a header element MUST NOT forward that header element to the next application in the SOAP message path. The recipient MAY insert a similar header element but in that case, the contract is between that application and the recipient of that header element.

The SOAP actor global attribute can be used to indicate the recipient of a header element. The value of the SOAP actor attribute is a URI. The special URI "http://schemas.xmlsoap.org/soap/actor/next" indicates that the header element is intended for the very first SOAP application that processes the message. This is similar to the hop-by-hop scope model represented by the Connection header field in HTTP.

Omitting the SOAP actor attribute indicates that the recipient is the ultimate destination of the SOAP message.

This attribute MUST appear in the SOAP message instance in order to be effective (see section 3 and 4.2.1).

4.2.3 SOAP mustUnderstand Attribute

The SOAP mustUnderstand global attribute can be used to indicate whether a header entry is mandatory or optional for the recipient to process. The recipient of a header entry is defined by the SOAP actor attribute (see section 4.2.2). The value of the mustUnderstand attribute is either "1" or "0". The absence of the SOAP mustUnderstand attribute is semantically equivalent to its presence with the value "0".

If a header element is tagged with a SOAP mustUnderstand attribute with a value of "1", the recipient of that header entry either MUST obey the semantics (as conveyed by the fully qualified name of the element) and process correctly to those semantics, or MUST fail processing the message (see section 4.4).

The SOAP mustUnderstand attribute allows for robust evolution. Elements tagged with the SOAP mustUnderstand attribute with a value of "1" MUST be presumed to somehow modify the semantics of their parent or peer elements. Tagging elements in this manner assures that this change in semantics will not be silently (and, presumably, erroneously) ignored by those who may not fully understand it.

This attribute MUST appear in the instance in order to be effective (see section 3 and 4.2.1).

4.3 SOAP Body

The SOAP Body element provides a simple mechanism for exchanging mandatory information intended for the ultimate recipient of the message. Typical uses of the Body element include marshalling RPC calls and error reporting.

The Body element is encoded as an immediate child element of the SOAP Envelope XML element. If a Header element is present then the Body element MUST immediately follow the Header element, otherwise it MUST be the first immediate child element of the Envelope element.

All immediate child elements of the Body element are called body entries and each body entry is encoded as an independent element within the SOAP Body element.

The encoding rules for body entries are as follows:

1. A body entry is identified by its fully qualified element name, which consists of the namespace URI and the local name. Immediate child elements of the SOAP Body element MAY be namespace-qualified.

2. The SOAP encodingStyle attribute MAY be used to indicate the encoding style used for the body entries (see section 4.1.1).

SOAP defines one body entry, which is the Fault entry used for reporting errors (see section 4.4).

4.3.1 Relationship between SOAP Header and Body

While the Header and Body are defined as independent elements, they are in fact related. The relationship between a body entry and a header entry is as follows: A body entry is semantically equivalent to a header entry intended for the default actor and with a SOAP mustUnderstand attribute with a value of "1". The default actor is indicated by not using the actor attribute (see section 4.2.2).

4.4 SOAP Fault

The SOAP Fault element is used to carry error and/or status information within a SOAP message. If present, the SOAP Fault element MUST appear as a body entry and MUST NOT appear more than once within a Body element.

The SOAP Fault element defines the following four subelements:

faultcode
: The faultcode element is intended for use by software to provide an algorithmic mechanism for identifying the fault. The faultcode MUST be present in a SOAP Fault element and the faultcode value MUST be a qualified name as defined in [8], section 3. SOAP defines a small set of SOAP fault codes covering basic SOAP faults (see section 4.4.1)

faultstring
: The faultstring element is intended to provide a human readable explanation of the fault and is not intended for algorithmic processing. The faultstring element is similar to the 'Reason-Phrase' defined by HTTP (see [5], section 6.1). It MUST be present in a SOAP Fault element and SHOULD

provide at least some information explaining the nature of the fault.

faultactor   The faultactor element is intended to provide information about who caused the fault to happen within the message path (see section 2). It is similar to the SOAP actor attribute (see section 4.2.2) but instead of indicating the destination of the header entry, it indicates the source of the fault. The value of the faultactor attribute is a URI identifying the source. Applications that do not act as the ultimate destination of the SOAP message MUST include the faultactor element in a SOAP Fault element. The ultimate destination of a message MAY use the faultactor element to indicate explicitly that it generated the fault (see also the detail element below).

detail   The detail element is intended for carrying application specific error information related to the Body element. It MUST be present if the contents of the Body element could not be successfully processed. It MUST NOT be used to carry information about error information belonging to header entries. Detailed error information belonging to header entries MUST be carried within header entries.

The absence of the detail element in the Fault element indicates that the fault is not related to processing of the Body element. This can be used to distinguish whether the Body element was processed or not in case of a fault situation.

All immediate child elements of the detail element are called detail entries and each detail entry is encoded as an independent element within the detail element.

The encoding rules for detail entries are as follows (see also example 10):

1. A detail entry is identified by its fully qualified element name, which consists of the namespace URI and the local name. Immediate child elements of the detail element MAY be namespace-qualified.

2. The SOAP encodingStyle attribute MAY be used to indicate the encoding style used for the detail entries (see section 4.1.1).

Other Fault subelements MAY be present, provided they are namespace-qualified.

4.4.1 SOAP Fault Codes

The faultcode values defined in this section MUST be used in the faultcode element when describing faults defined by this specification. The namespace identifier for these faultcode values is "http://schemas.xmlsoap.org/soap/envelope/". Use of this space is recommended (but not required) in the specification of methods defined outside of the present specification.

The default SOAP faultcode values are defined in an extensible manner that allows for new SOAP faultcode values to be defined while maintaining backwards compatibility with existing faultcode values. The mechanism used is very similar to the 1xx, 2xx, 3xx etc basic status classes classes defined in HTTP (see [5] section 10). However, instead of integers, they are defined as XML qualified names (see [8] section 3). The character "." (dot) is used as a separator of faultcode values indicating that what is to the left of the dot is a more generic fault code value than the value to the right. Example

Client.Authentication

The set of faultcode values defined in this document is:

Name	Meaning
VersionMismatch	The processing party found an invalid namespace for the SOAP Envelope element (see section 4.1.2)
MustUnderstand	An immediate child element of the SOAP Header element that was either not understood or not obeyed by the processing party contained a SOAP mustUnderstand attribute with a value of "1" (see section 4.2.3)
Client	The Client class of errors indicate that the message was incorrectly formed or did not contain the appropriate information in order to succeed. For example, the message could lack the proper authentication or payment information. It is generally an indication that the message should not be resent without change. See also section 4.4 for a description of the SOAP Fault detail sub-element.
Server	The Server class of errors indicate that the message could not be processed for reasons not directly attributable to the contents of the message itself but rather to the processing of the message. For example, processing could include communicating with an upstream processor, which didn't respond. The message may succeed at a later point in time. See also section 4.4 for a description of the SOAP Fault detail sub-element.

5. SOAP Encoding

The SOAP encoding style is based on a simple type system that is a generalization of the common features found in type systems in programming languages, databases and semi-structured data. A type either is a simple (scalar) type or is a compound type constructed as a composite of several parts, each with a type. This is described in more detail below. This section defines rules for serialization of a graph of typed objects. It operates on two levels. First, given a schema in any notation consistent with the type system described, a schema for an XML grammar may be constructed. Second, given a type-system schema and a particular graph of values conforming to that schema, an XML instance may be constructed. In reverse, given an XML instance produced in accordance with these rules, and given also the original schema, a copy of the original value graph may be constructed.

The namespace identifier for the elements and attributes defined in this section is "http://schemas.xmlsoap.org/soap/encoding/". The encoding samples shown assume all namespace declarations are at a higher element level.

Use of the data model and encoding style described in this section is encouraged but not required; other data models and encodings can be used in conjunction with SOAP (see section 4.1.1).

5.1 Rules for Encoding Types in XML

XML allows very flexible encoding of data. SOAP defines a narrower set of rules for encoding. This section defines the encoding rules at a high level, and the next section describes the encoding rules for specific types when they require more detail. The encodings described in this section can be used in conjunction with the mapping of RPC calls and responses specified in Section 7.

To describe encoding, the following terminology is used:

1. A "value" is a string, the name of a measurement (number, date, enumeration, etc.) or a composite of several such primitive values. All values are of specific types.

2. A "simple value" is one without named parts. Examples of simple values are particular strings, integers, enumerated values etc.

3. A "compound value" is an aggregate of relations to other values. Examples of Compound Values are particular purchase orders, stock reports, street addresses, etc.

4. Within a compound value, each related value is potentially distinguished by a role name, ordinal or both. This is called its "accessor." Examples of compound values include particular Purchase Orders, Stock Reports etc. Arrays are also compound values. It is possible to have compound values with several accessors each named the same, as for example, RDF does.

5. An "array" is a compound value in which ordinal position serves as the only distinction among member values.

6. A "struct" is a compound value in which accessor name is the only distinction among member values, and no accessor has the same name as any other.

7. A "simple type" is a class of simple values. Examples of simple types are the classes called "string," "integer," enumeration classes, etc.

8. A "compound type" is a class of compound values. An example of a compound type is the class of purchase order values sharing the same accessors (shipTo, totalCost, etc.) though with potentially different values (and perhaps further constrained by limits on certain values).

9. Within a compound type, if an accessor has a name that is distinct within that type but is not distinct with respect to other types, that is, the name plus the type together are needed to make a unique identification, the name is called "locally scoped." If however the name is based in part on a Uniform Resource Identifier, directly or indirectly, such that the name alone is sufficient to uniquely identify the accessor irrespective of the type within which it appears, the name is called "universally scoped."

10. Given the information in the schema relative to which a graph of values is serialized, it is possible to determine that some values can only be related by a single instance of an accessor. For others, it is not possible to make this determination. If only one accessor can reference it, a value is considered "single-reference". If referenced by more than one, actually or potentially, it is "multi-reference." Note that it is possible for a certain value to be considered "single-reference" relative to one schema and "multi-reference" relative to another.

11. Syntactically, an element may be "independent" or "embedded." An independent element is any element appearing at the top level of a serialization. All others are embedded elements.

Although it is possible to use the xsi:type attribute such that a graph of values is self-describing both in its structure and the types of its values, the serialization rules permit that the types of values MAY be determinate only by reference to a schema. Such schemas MAY be in the notation described by "XML Schema Part 1: Structures" [10] and "XML Schema Part 2: Datatypes" [11] or MAY be in any other notation. Note also that, while the serialization rules apply to compound types other than arrays and structs, many schemas will contain only struct and array types.

The rules for serialization are as follows:

1. All values are represented as element content. A multi-reference value MUST be represented as the content of an independent element. A single-reference value SHOULD not be (but MAY be).

2. For each element containing a value, the type of the value MUST be represented by at least one of the following conditions: (a) the containing element instance contains an xsi:type attribute, (b) the containing element instance is itself contained within an element containing a (possibly defaulted) SOAP-ENC:arrayType attribute or (c) or the name of the element bears a definite relation to the type, that type then determinable from a schema.

3. A simple value is represented as character data, that is, without any subelements. Every simple value must have a type that is either listed in the XML Schemas Specification, part 2 [11] or whose source type is listed therein (see also section 5.2).

4. A Compound Value is encoded as a sequence of elements, each accessor represented by an embedded element whose name corresponds to the name of the accessor. Accessors whose names are local to their containing types have unqualified element names; all others have qualified names (see also section 5.4).

5. A multi-reference simple or compound value is encoded as an independent element containing a local, unqualified attribute named "id" and of type "ID" per the XML Specification [7]. Each accessor to this value is an empty element having a local, unqualified attribute named "href" and of type "uri-reference" per the XML Schema Specification [11], with a "href" attribute value of a URI fragment identifier referencing the corresponding independent element.

6. Strings and byte arrays are represented as multi-reference simple types, but special rules allow them to be represented efficiently for common cases (see also section 5.2.1 and 5.2.3). An accessor to a string or byte-array value MAY have an attribute named "id" and of type "ID" per the XML Specification [7]. If so, all other accessors to the same value are encoded as empty elements having a local, unqualified attribute named "href" and of type "uri-reference" per the XML Schema Specification [11], with a "href" attribute value of a URI fragment identifier referencing the single element containing the value.

7. It is permissible to encode several references to a value as though these were references to several distinct values, but only when from context it is known that the meaning of the XML instance is unaltered.

8. Arrays are compound values (see also section 5.4.2). SOAP arrays are defined as having a type of "SOAP-ENC:Array" or a type derived there from.

SOAP arrays have one or more dimensions (rank) whose members are distinguished by ordinal position. An array value is represented as a series of elements reflecting the array, with members appearing in ascending ordinal sequence. For multi-dimensional arrays the dimension on the right side varies most rapidly. Each member element is named as an independent element (see rule 2).

SOAP arrays can be single-reference or multi-reference values, and consequently may be represented as the content of either an embedded or independent element.

SOAP arrays MUST contain a "SOAP-ENC:arrayType" attribute whose value specifies the type of the contained elements as well as the dimension(s) of the array. The value of the "SOAP-ENC:arrayType" attribute is defined as follows:

```
arrayTypeValue = atype asize
atype          = QName *( rank )
rank           = "[" *( "," ) "]"
asize          = "[" #length "]"
length         = 1*DIGIT
```

The "atype" construct is the type name of the contained elements expressed as a QName as would appear in the "type" attribute of an XML Schema element declaration and acts as a type constraint (meaning that all values of contained elements are asserted to conform to the indicated type; that is, the type cited in SOAP-ENC:arrayType must be the type or a supertype of every array member). In the case of arrays of arrays or "jagged arrays", the type component is encoded as the "innermost" type name followed by a rank construct for each level of nested arrays starting from 1. Multi-dimensional arrays are encoded using a comma for each dimension starting from 1.

The "asize" construct contains a comma separated list of zero, one, or more integers indicating the lengths of each dimension of the array. A value of zero integers indicates that no particular quantity is asserted but that the size may be determined by inspection of the actual members.

For example, an array with 5 members of type array of integers would have an arrayTypeValue value of "int[][5]" of which the atype value is "int[]" and the asize value is "[5]". Likewise, an array with 3 members of type two-dimensional arrays of integers would have an arrayTypeValue value of "int[,][3]" of which the atype value is "int[,]" and the asize value is "[3]".

A SOAP array member MAY contain a "SOAP-ENC:offset" attribute indicating the offset position of that item in the enclosing array. This can be used to indicate the offset position of a partially represented array (see section 5.4.2.1). Likewise, an array member MAY contain a "SOAP-ENC:position" attribute indicating the position of that item in the enclosing array. This can be used to describe members of sparse arrays (see section 5.4.2.2). The value of the "SOAP-ENC:offset" and the "SOAP-ENC:position" attribute is defined as follows:

```
arrayPoint = "[" #length "]"
```

with offsets and positions based at 0.

9 A NULL value or a default value MAY be represented by omission of the accessor element. A NULL value MAY also be indicated by an accessor element containing the attribute xsi:null with value '1' or possibly other application-dependent attributes and values.

Note that rule 2 allows independent elements and also elements representing the members of arrays to have names which are not identical to the type of the contained value.

5.2 Simple Types

For simple types, SOAP adopts all the types found in the section "Built-in datatypes" of the "XML Schema Part 2: Datatypes" Specification [11], both the value and lexical spaces. Examples include:

Type	Example
int	58502
float	314159265358979E+1
negativeInteger	-32768
string	Louis "Satchmo" Armstrong

The datatypes declared in the XML Schema specification may be used directly in element schemas. Types derived from these may also be used. An example of a schema fragment and corresponding instance data with elements of these types is:

```
<element name="age" type="int"/>
<element name="height" type="float"/>
<element name="displacement" type="negativeInteger"/>
<element name="color">
 <simpleType base="xsd:string">
   <enumeration value="Green"/>
   <enumeration value="Blue"/>
 </simpleType>
</element>

<age>45</age>
<height>5.9</height>
<displacement>-450</displacement>
<color>Blue</color>
```

All simple values MUST be encoded as the content of elements whose type is either defined in "XML Schema Part 2: Datatypes" Specification [11], or is based on a type found there by using the mechanisms provided in the XML Schema specification.

If a simple value is encoded as an independent element or member of a heterogenous array it is convenient to have an element declaration corresponding to the datatype. Because the "XML Schema Part 2: Datatypes" Specification [11] includes type definitions but does not include corresponding element declarations, the SOAP-ENC schema and namespace declares an element for every simple datatype. These MAY be used.

```
<SOAP-ENC:int id="int1">45</SOAP-ENC:int>
```

5.2.1 Strings

The datatype "string" is defined in "XML Schema Part 2: Datatypes" Specification [11]. Note that this is not identical to the type called "string" in many database or programming languages, and in particular may forbid some characters those languages would permit. (Those values must be represented by using some datatype other than xsd:string.)

A string MAY be encoded as a single-reference or a multi-reference value.

The containing element of the string value MAY have an "id" attribute. Additional accessor elements MAY then have matching "href" attributes.

For example, two accessors to the same string could appear, as follows:

```
<greeting id="String-0">Hello</greeting>
<salutation href="#String-0"/>
```

However, if the fact that both accessors reference the same instance of the string (or subtype of string) is immaterial, they may be encoded as two single-reference values as follows:

```
<greeting>Hello</greeting>
<salutation>Hello</salutation>
```

Schema fragments for these examples could appear similar to the following:

```
<element name="greeting" type="SOAP-ENC:string"/>
<element name="salutation" type="SOAP-ENC:string"/>
```

(In this example, the type SOAP-ENC:string is used as the element's type as a convenient way to declare an element whose datatype is "xsd:string" and which also allows an "id" and "href" attribute. See the SOAP Encoding schema for the exact definition. Schemas MAY use these declarations from the SOAP Encoding schema but are not required to.)

5.2.2 Enumerations

The "XML Schema Part 2: Datatypes" Specification [11] defines a mechanism called "enumeration." The SOAP data model adopts this mechanism directly. However, because programming and other languages often define enumeration somewhat differently, we spell-out the concept in more detail here and describe how a value that is a member of an enumerated list of possible values is to be encoded. Specifically, it is encoded as the name of the value.

"Enumeration" as a concept indicates a set of distinct names. A specific enumeration is a specific list of distinct values appropriate to the base type. For example the set of color names ("Green", "Blue", "Brown") could be defined as an enumeration based on the string built-in type. The values ("1", "3", "5") are a possible enumeration based on integer, and so on. "XML Schema Part 2: Datatypes" [11] supports enumerations for all of the simple types except for boolean. The language of "XML Schema Part 1: Structures" Specification [10] can be used to define enumeration types. If a schema is generated from another notation in which no specific base type is applicable, use "string". In the following schema example "EyeColor" is defined as a string with the possible values of "Green", "Blue", or "Brown" enumerated, and instance data is shown accordingly.

```
<element name="EyeColor" type="tns:EyeColor"/>
<simpleType name="EyeColor" base="xsd:string">
```

```
  <enumeration value="Green"/>
  <enumeration value="Blue"/>
  <enumeration value="Brown"/>
</simpleType>

<Person>
  <Name>Henry Ford</Name>
  <Age>32</Age>
  <EyeColor>Brown</EyeColor>
</Person>
```

5.2.3 Array of Bytes

An array of bytes MAY be encoded as a single-reference or a multi-reference value. The rules for an array of bytes are similar to those for a string.

In particular, the containing element of the array of bytes value MAY have an "id" attribute. Additional accessor elements MAY then have matching "href" attributes.

The recommended representation of an opaque array of bytes is the 'base64' encoding defined in XML Schemas [10][11], which uses the base64 encoding algorithm defined in 2045 [13]. However, the line length restrictions that normally apply to base64 data in MIME do not apply in SOAP. A "SOAP-ENC:base64" subtype is supplied for use with SOAP.

```
<picture xsi:type="SOAP-ENC:base64">
  aG93IG5vDyBicm73biBjb3cNCg==
</picture>
```

5.3 Polymorphic Accessor

Many languages allow accessors that can polymorphically access values of several types, each type being available at run time. A polymorphic accessor instance MUST contain an "xsi:type" attribute that describes the type of the actual value.

For example, a polymorphic accessor named "cost" with a value of type "xsd:float" would be encoded as follows:

```
<cost xsi:type="xsd:float">29.95</cost>
```

as contrasted with a cost accessor whose value's type is invariant, as follows:

```
<cost>29.95</cost>
```

5.4 Compound types

SOAP defines types corresponding to the following structural patterns often found in programming languages:

Struct   A "struct" is a compound value in which accessor name is the only distinction among member values, and no accessor has the same name as any other.

Array   An "array" is a compound value in which ordinal position serves as the only distinction among member values.

SOAP also permits serialization of data that is neither a Struct nor an Array, for example data such as is found in a Directed-Labeled-Graph Data Model in which a single node has many distinct accessors, some of which occur more than once. SOAP serialization does not require that the underlying data model make an ordering distinction among accessors, but if such an order exists, the accessors MUST be encoded in that sequence.

5.4.1 Compound Values, Structs and References to Values

The members of a Compound Value are encoded as accessor elements. When accessors are distinguished by their name (as for example in a struct), the accessor name is used as the element name. Accessors whose names are local to their containing types have unqualified element names; all others have qualified names.

The following is an example of a struct of type "Book":

```
<e:Book>
  <author>Henry Ford</author>
  <preface>Prefatory text</preface>
  <intro>This is a book.</intro>
</e:Book>
```

And this is a schema fragment describing the above structure:

```
<element name="Book">
<complexType>
 <element name="author" type="xsd:string"/>
 <element name="preface" type="xsd:string"/>
 <element name="intro" type="xsd:string"/>
</complexType>
</e:Book>
```

Below is an example of a type with both simple and complex members. It shows two levels of referencing. Note that the "href" attribute of the "Author" accessor element is a reference to the value whose "id" attribute matches. A similar construction appears for the "Address".

```
<e:Book>
  <title>My Life and Work</title>
  <author href="#Person-1"/>
</e:Book>
<e:Person id="Person-1">
  <name>Henry Ford</name>
  <address href="#Address-2"/>
</e:Person>
<e:Address id="Address-2">
  <email>mailto:henryford@hotmail.com</email>
  <web>http://www.henryford.com</web>
</e:Address>
```

The form above is appropriate when the "Person" value and the "Address" value are multi-reference. If these were instead both single-reference, they SHOULD be embedded, as follows:

```
<e:Book>
  <title>My Life and Work</title>
  <author>
      <name>Henry Ford</name>
      <address>
         <email>mailto:henryford@hotmail.com</email>
         <web>http://www.henryford.com</web>
      </address>
  </author>
</e:Book>
```

If instead there existed a restriction that no two persons can have the same address in a given instance and that an address can be either a Street-address or an Electronic-address, a Book with two authors would be encoded as follows:

```
<e:Book>
  <title>My Life and Work</title>
  <firstauthor href="#Person-1"/>
  <secondauthor href="#Person-2"/>
</e:Book>
<e:Person id="Person-1">
  <name>Henry Ford</name>
  <address xsi:type="m:Electronic-address">
      <email>mailto:henryford@hotmail.com</email>
      <web>http://www.henryford.com</web>
  </address>
```

```
</e:Person>
<e:Person id="Person-2">
  <name>Samuel Crowther</name>
  <address xsi:type="n:Street-address">
      <street>Martin Luther King Rd</street>
      <city>Raleigh</city>
      <state>North Carolina</state>
  </address>
</e:Person>
```

Serializations can contain references to values not in the same resource:

```
<e:Book>
  <title>Paradise Lost</title>
  <firstauthor href="http://www.dartmouth.edu/~milton/"/>
</e:Book>
```

And this is a schema fragment describing the above structures:

```
<element name="Book" type="tns:Book"/>
<complexType name="Book">
  <!-- Either the following group must occur or else the
       href attribute must appear, but not both. -->
  <sequence minOccurs="0" maxOccurs="1">
      <element name="title" type="xsd:string"/>
      <element name="firstauthor" type="tns:Person"/>
      <element name="secondauthor" type="tns:Person"/>
  </sequence>
  <attribute name="href" type="uriReference"/>
  <attribute name="id" type="ID"/>
  <anyAttribute namespace="##other"/>
</complexType>

<element name="Person" base="tns:Person"/>
<complexType name="Person">
  <!-- Either the following group must occur or else the
       href attribute must appear, but not both. -->
  <sequence minOccurs="0" maxOccurs="1">
      <element name="name" type="xsd:string"/>
      <element name="address" type="tns:Address"/>
  </sequence>
  <attribute name="href" type="uriReference"/>
  <attribute name="id" type="ID"/>
  <anyAttribute namespace="##other"/>
</complexType>
```

```
<element name="Address" base="tns:Address"/>
<complexType name="Address">
  <!-- Either the following group must occur or else the
       href attribute must appear, but not both. -->
  <sequence minOccurs="0" maxOccurs="1">
      <element name="street" type="xsd:string"/>
      <element name="city" type="xsd:string"/>
      <element name="state" type="xsd:string"/>
  </sequence>
  <attribute name="href" type="uriReference"/>
  <attribute name="id" type="ID"/>
  <anyAttribute namespace="##other"/>
</complexType>
```

5.4.2 Arrays

SOAP arrays are defined as having a type of "SOAP-ENC:Array" or a type derived there from (see also <u>rule 8</u>). Arrays are represented as element values, with no specific constraint on the name of the containing element (just as values generally do not constrain the name of their containing element).

Arrays can contain elements which themselves can be of any type, including nested arrays. New types formed by restrictions of SOAP-ENC:Array can also be created to represent, for example, arrays limited to integers or arrays of some user-defined enumeration.

The representation of the value of an array is an ordered sequence of elements constituting the items of the array. Within an array value, element names are not significant for distinguishing accessors. Elements may have any name. In practice, elements will frequently be named so that their declaration in a schema suggests or determines their type. As with compound types generally, if the value of an item in the array is a single-reference value, the item contains its value. Otherwise, the item references its value via an "href" attribute.

The following example is a schema fragment and an array containing integer array members.

```
<element name="myFavoriteNumbers"
    type="SOAP-ENC:Array"/>

<myFavoriteNumbers
 SOAP-ENC:arrayType="xsd:int[2]">
  <number>3</number>
  <number>4</number>
</myFavoriteNumbers>
```

In that example, the array "myFavoriteNumbers" contains several members each of which is a value of type SOAP-ENC:int. This can be determined by inspection of the SOAP-ENC:arrayType attribute. Note that the SOAP-ENC:Array type allows unqualified element names without restriction. These convey no type information, so when used they must either have an xsi:type attribute or the containing element must have a SOAP-ENC:arrayType attribute. Naturally, types derived from SOAP-ENC:Array may declare local elements, with type information.

As previously noted, the SOAP-ENC schema contains declarations of elements with names corresponding to each simple type in the "XML Schema Part 2: Datatypes" Specification [11]. It also contains a declaration for "Array". Using these, we might write

```
<SOAP-ENC:Array SOAP-ENC:arrayType="xsd:int[2]">
  <SOAP-ENC:int>3</SOAP-ENC:int>
  <SOAP-ENC:int>4</SOAP-ENC:int>
</SOAP-ENC:Array>
```

Arrays can contain instances of any subtype of the specified arrayType. That is, the members may be of any type that is substitutable for the type specified in the arrayType attribute, according to whatever substitutability rules are expressed in the schema. So, for example, an array of integers can contain any type derived from integer (for example "int" or any user-defined derivation of integer). Similarly, an array of "address" might contain a restricted or extended type such as "internationalAddress". Because the supplied SOAP-ENC:Array type admits members of any type, arbitrary mixtures of types can be contained unless specifically limited by use of the arrayType attribute.

Types of member elements can be specified using the xsi:type attribute in the instance, or by declarations in the schema of the member elements, as the following two arrays demonstrate respectively.

```
<SOAP-ENC:Array SOAP-ENC:arrayType="xsd:ur-type[4]">
  <thing xsi:type="xsd:int">12345</thing>
  <thing xsi:type="xsd:decimal">6.789</thing>
  <thing xsi:type="xsd:string">
    Of Mans First Disobedience, and the Fruit
    Of that Forbidden Tree, whose mortal tast
    Brought Death into the World, and all our woe,
  </thing>
  <thing xsi:type="xsd:uriReference">
    http://www.dartmouth.edu/~milton/reading_room/
  </thing>
</SOAP-ENC:Array>

<SOAP-ENC:Array SOAP-ENC:arrayType="xsd:ur-type[4]">
  <SOAP-ENC:int>12345</SOAP-ENC:int>
  <SOAP-ENC:decimal>6.789</SOAP-ENC:decimal>
```

```
 <xsd:string>
  Of Mans First Disobedience, and the Fruit
  Of that Forbidden Tree, whose mortal tast
  Brought Death into the World, and all our woe,
 </xsd:string>
 <SOAP-ENC:uriReference>
  http://www.dartmouth.edu/~milton/reading_room/
 </SOAP-ENC:uriReference >
</SOAP-ENC:Array>
```

Array values may be structs or other compound values. For example an array of "xyz:Order" structs :

```
<SOAP-ENC:Array SOAP-ENC:arrayType="xyz:Order[2]">
 <Order>
    <Product>Apple</Product>
    <Price>1.56</Price>
 </Order>
 <Order>
    <Product>Peach</Product>
    <Price>1.48</Price>
 </Order>
</SOAP-ENC:Array>
```

Arrays may have other arrays as member values. The following is an example of an array of two arrays, each of which is an array of strings.

```
<SOAP-ENC:Array SOAP-ENC:arrayType="xsd:string[][2]">
  <item href="#array-1"/>
  <item href="#array-2"/>
</SOAP-ENC:Array>
<SOAP-ENC:Array id="array-1" SOAP-ENC:arrayType="xsd:string[2]">
  <item>r1c1</item>
  <item>r1c2</item>
  <item>r1c3</item>
</SOAP-ENC:Array>
<SOAP-ENC:Array id="array-2" SOAP-ENC:arrayType="xsd:string[2]">
  <item>r2c1</item>
  <item>r2c2</item>
</SOAP-ENC:Array>
```

The element containing an array value does not need to be named "SOAP-ENC:Array". It may have any name, provided that the type of the element is either SOAP-ENC:Array or is derived from SOAP-ENC:Array by restriction. For example, the following is a fragment of a schema and a conforming instance array.

```
<simpleType name="phoneNumber" base="string"/>

<element name="ArrayOfPhoneNumbers">
 <complexType base="SOAP-ENC:Array">
   <element name="phoneNumber" type="tns:phoneNumber"
maxOccurs="unbounded"/>
 </complexType>
 <anyAttribute/>
</element>

<xyz:ArrayOfPhoneNumbers SOAP-ENC:arrayType="xyz:phoneNumber[2]">
  <phoneNumber>206-555-1212</phoneNumber>
  <phoneNumber>1-888-123-4567</phoneNumber>
</xyz:ArrayOfPhoneNumbers>
```

Arrays may be multi-dimensional. In this case, more than one size will appear within the asize part of the arrayType attribute:

```
<SOAP-ENC:Array SOAP-ENC:arrayType="xsd:string[2,3]">
  <item>r1c1</item>
  <item>r1c2</item>
  <item>r1c3</item>
  <item>r2c1</item>
  <item>r2c2</item>
  <item>r2c3</item>
</SOAP-ENC:Array>
```

While the examples above have shown arrays encoded as independent elements, array values MAY also appear embedded and SHOULD do so when they are known to be single reference.

The following is an example of a schema fragment and an array of phone numbers embedded in a struct of type "Person" and accessed through the accessor "phone-numbers":

```
<simpleType name="phoneNumber" base="string"/>

<element name="ArrayOfPhoneNumbers">
 <complexType base="SOAP-ENC:Array">
   <element name="phoneNumber" type="tns:phoneNumber"
maxOccurs="unbounded"/>
 </complexType>
 <anyAttribute/>
</element>

<element name="Person">
 <complexType>
```

```
    <element name="name" type="string"/>
    <element name="phoneNumbers" type="tns:ArrayOfPhoneNumbers"/>
 </complexType>
</element>

<xyz:Person>
  <name>John Hancock</name>
  <phoneNumbers SOAP-ENC:arrayType="xyz:phoneNumber[2]">
      <phoneNumber>206-555-1212</phoneNumber>
      <phoneNumber>1-888-123-4567</phoneNumber>
  </phoneNumbers>
</xyz:Person>
```

Here is another example of a single-reference array value encoded as an embedded element whose containing element name is the accessor name:

```
<xyz:PurchaseOrder>
  <CustomerName>Henry Ford</CustomerName>
  <ShipTo>
      <Street>5th Ave</Street>
      <City>New York</City>
      <State>NY</State>
      <Zip>10010</Zip>
  </ShipTo>
  <PurchaseLineItems SOAP-ENC:arrayType="Order[2]">
      <Order>
          <Product>Apple</Product>
          <Price>1.56</Price>
      </Order>
      <Order>
          <Product>Peach</Product>
          <Price>1.48</Price>
      </Order>
  </PurchaseLineItems>
</xyz:PurchaseOrder>
```

5.4.2.1 Partially Transmitted Arrays

SOAP provides support for partially transmitted arrays, known as "varying" arrays in some contexts [12]. A partially transmitted array indicates in an "SOAP-ENC:offset" attribute the zero-origin offset of the first element transmitted. If omitted, the offset is taken as zero.

The following is an example of an array of size five that transmits only the third and fourth element counting from zero:

```
<SOAP-ENC:Array SOAP-ENC:arrayType="xsd:string[5]" SOAP-ENC:-
offset="[2]">
```

```
  <item>The third element</item>
  <item>The fourth element</item>
</SOAP-ENC:Array>
```

5.4.2.2 Sparse Arrays

SOAP provides support for sparse arrays. Each element representing a member value contains a "SOAP-ENC:position" attribute that indicates its position within the array. The following is an example of a sparse array of two-dimensional arrays of strings. The size is 4 but only position 2 is used:

```
<SOAP-ENC:Array SOAP-ENC:arrayType="xsd:string[,][4]">
  <SOAP-ENC:Array href="#array-1" SOAP-ENC:position="[2]"/>
</SOAP-ENC:Array>
<SOAP-ENC:Array id="array-1" SOAP-
ENC:arrayType="xsd:string[10,10]">
  <item SOAP-ENC:position="[2,2]">Third row, third col</item>
  <item SOAP-ENC:position="[7,2]">Eighth row, third col</item>
</SOAP-ENC:Array>
```

If the only reference to array-1 occurs in the enclosing array, this example could also have been encoded as follows:

```
<SOAP-ENC:Array SOAP-ENC:arrayType="xsd:string[,][4]">
 <SOAP-ENC:Array SOAP-ENC:position="[2]" SOAP-
ENC:arrayType="xsd:string[10,10]>
    <item SOAP-ENC:position="[2,2]">Third row, third col</item>
    <item SOAP-ENC:position="[7,2]">Eighth row, third col</item>
 </SOAP-ENC:Array>
</SOAP-ENC:Array>
```

5.4.3 Generic Compound Types

The encoding rules just cited are not limited to those cases where the accessor names are known in advance. If accessor names are known only by inspection of the immediate values to be encoded, the same rules apply, namely that the accessor is encoded as an element whose name matches the name of the accessor, and the accessor either contains or references its value. Accessors containing values whose types cannot be determined in advance MUST always contain an appropriate xsi:type attribute giving the type of the value.

Similarly, the rules cited are sufficient to allow serialization of compound types having a mixture of accessors distinguished by name and accessors distinguished by both name and ordinal position. (That is, having some accessors repeated.) This does not require that any schema actually contain such types, but rather says that if a type-model schema does have such types, a corresponding XML syntactic schema and instance may be generated.

```
<xyz:PurchaseOrder>
  <CustomerName>Henry Ford</CustomerName>
  <ShipTo>
    <Street>5th Ave</Street>
    <City>New York</City>
    <State>NY</State>
    <Zip>10010</Zip>
  </ShipTo>
  <PurchaseLineItems>
    <Order>
      <Product>Apple</Product>
      <Price>1.56</Price>
    </Order>
    <Order>
      <Product>Peach</Product>
      <Price>1.48</Price>
    </Order>
  </PurchaseLineItems>
</xyz:PurchaseOrder>
```

Similarly, it is valid to serialize a compound value that structurally resembles an arrray but is not of type (or subtype) SOAP-ENC:Array. For example:

```
<PurchaseLineItems>
  <Order>
    <Product>Apple</Product>
    <Price>1.56</Price>
  </Order>
  <Order>
    <Product>Peach</Product>
    <Price>1.48</Price>
  </Order>
</PurchaseLineItems>
```

5.5 Default Values

An omitted accessor element implies either a default value or that no value is known. The specifics depend on the accessor, method, and its context. For example, an omitted accessor typically implies a Null value for polymorphic accessors (with the exact meaning of Null accessor-dependent). Likewise, an omitted Boolean accessor typically implies either a False value or that no value is known, and an omitted numeric accessor typically implies either that the value is zero or that no value is known.

5.6 SOAP root Attribute

The SOAP root attribute can be used to label serialization roots that are not true roots of an object graph so that the object graph can be deserialized. The attribute can have one of two values, either "1" or "0". True roots of an object graph have the implied attribute value of "1". Serialization roots that are not true roots can be labeled as serialization roots with an attribute value of "1" An element can explicitly be labeled as not being a serialization root with a value of "0".

The SOAP root attribute MAY appear on any subelement within the SOAP Header and SOAP Body elements. The attribute does not have a default value.

6. Using SOAP in HTTP

This section describes how to use SOAP within HTTP with or without using the HTTP Extension Framework. Binding SOAP to HTTP provides the advantage of being able to use the formalism and decentralized flexibility of SOAP with the rich feature set of HTTP. Carrying SOAP in HTTP does not mean that SOAP overrides existing semantics of HTTP but rather that the semantics of SOAP over HTTP maps naturally to HTTP semantics.

SOAP naturally follows the HTTP request/response message model providing SOAP request parameters in a HTTP request and SOAP response parameters in a HTTP response. Note, however, that SOAP intermediaries are NOT the same as HTTP intermediaries. That is, an HTTP intermediary addressed with the HTTP Connection header field cannot be expected to inspect or process the SOAP entity body carried in the HTTP request.

HTTP applications MUST use the media type "text/xml" according to RFC 2376 [3] when including SOAP entity bodies in HTTP messages.

6.1 SOAP HTTP Request

Although SOAP might be used in combination with a variety of HTTP request methods, this binding only defines SOAP within HTTP POST requests (see section 7 for how to use SOAP for RPC and section 6.3 for how to use the HTTP Extension Framework).

6.1.1 The SOAPAction HTTP Header Field

The SOAPAction HTTP request header field can be used to indicate the intent of the SOAP HTTP request. The value is a URI identifying the intent. SOAP places no restrictions on the format or specificity of the URI or that it is resolvable. An HTTP client MUST use this header field when issuing a SOAP HTTP Request.

```
soapaction    = "SOAPAction" ":" [ <"> URI-reference <"> ]
URI-reference = <as defined in RFC 2396 [4]>
```

The presence and content of the SOAPAction header field can be used by servers such as firewalls to appropriately filter SOAP request messages in HTTP. The header field value of empty string ("") means that the intent of the SOAP message is provided by the HTTP Request-URI. No value means that there is no indication of the intent of the message.

Examples:

```
SOAPAction:  "http://electrocommerce.org/abc#MyMessage"
SOAPAction:  "myapp.sdl"
SOAPAction:  ""
SOAPAction:
```

6.2 SOAP HTTP Response

SOAP HTTP follows the semantics of the HTTP Status codes for communicating status information in HTTP. For example, a 2xx status code indicates that the client's request including the SOAP component was successfully received, understood, and accepted etc.

In case of a SOAP error while processing the request, the SOAP HTTP server MUST issue an HTTP 500 "Internal Server Error" response and include a SOAP message in the response containing a SOAP Fault element (see section 4.4) indicating the SOAP processing error.

6.3 The HTTP Extension Framework

A SOAP message MAY be used together with the HTTP Extension Framework [6] in order to identify the presence and intent of a SOAP HTTP request.

Whether to use the Extension Framework or plain HTTP is a question of policy and capability of the communicating parties. Clients can force the use of the

HTTP Extension Framework by using a mandatory extension declaration and the "M-" HTTP method name prefix. Servers can force the use of the HTTP Extension Framework by using the 510 "Not Extended" HTTP status code. That is, using one extra round trip, either party can detect the policy of the other party and act accordingly.

The extension identifier used to identify SOAP using the Extension Framework is

```
http://schemas.xmlsoap.org/soap/envelope/
```

6.4 SOAP HTTP Examples

Example 3   SOAP HTTP Using POST

```
POST /StockQuote HTTP/1.1
Content-Type: text/xml; charset="utf-8"
Content-Length: nnnn
SOAPAction: "http://electrocommerce.org/abc#MyMessage"


<SOAP-ENV:Envelope...


HTTP/1.1 200 OK
Content-Type: text/xml; charset="utf-8"
Content-Length: nnnn


<SOAP-ENV:Envelope...
```

Example 4   SOAP Using HTTP Extension Framework

```
M-POST /StockQuote HTTP/1.1
Man: "http://schemas.xmlsoap.org/soap/envelope/"; ns=NNNN
Content-Type: text/xml; charset="utf-8"
Content-Length: nnnn
NNNN-SOAPAction: "http://electrocommerce.org/abc#MyMessage"


<SOAP-ENV:Envelope...


HTTP/1.1 200 OK
Ext:
Content-Type: text/xml; charset="utf-8"
Content-Length: nnnn


<SOAP-ENV:Envelope...
```

7. Using SOAP for RPC

One of the design goals of SOAP is to encapsulate and exchange RPC calls using the extensibility and flexibility of XML. This section defines a uniform representation of remote procedure calls and responses.

Although it is anticipated that this representation is likely to be used in combination with the encoding style defined in <u>section 5</u> other representations are possible. The SOAP encodingStyle attribute (see section <u>4.3.2</u>) can be used to indicate the encoding style of the method call and or the response using the representation described in this section.

Using SOAP for RPC is orthogonal to the SOAP protocol binding (see <u>section 6</u>). In the case of using HTTP as the protocol binding, an RPC call maps naturally to an HTTP request and an RPC response maps to an HTTP response. However, using SOAP for RPC is not limited to the HTTP protocol binding.

To make a method call, the following information is needed:

▼ The URI of the target object

▼ A method name

▼ An optional method signature

▼ The parameters to the method

▼ Optional header data

SOAP relies on the protocol binding to provide a mechanism for carrying the URI. For example, for HTTP the request URI indicates the resource that the invocation is being made against. Other than it be a valid URI, SOAP places no restriction on the form of an address (see [4] for more information on URIs).

7.1 RPC and SOAP Body

RPC method calls and responses are both carried in the SOAP Body element (see section 4.3) using the following representation:

▼ A method invocation is modelled as a struct.

▼ The method invocation is viewed as a single struct containing an accessor for each [in] or [in/out] parameter. The struct is both named and typed identically to the method name.

▼ Each [in] or [in/out] parameter is viewed as an accessor, with a name corresponding to the name of the parameter and type corresponding to the type of the parameter. These appear in the same order as in the method signature.

▼ A method response is modelled as a struct.

▼ The method response is viewed as a single struct containing an accessor for the return value and each [out] or [in/out] parameter. The first accessor is the return value followed by the parameters in the same order as in the method signature.

▼ Each parameter accessor has a name corresponding to the name of the parameter and type corresponding to the type of the parameter. The name of the return value accessor is not significant. Likewise, the name of the struct is not significant. However, a convention is to name it after the method name with the string "Response" appended.

▼ A method fault is encoded using the SOAP Fault element (see section 4.4). If a protocol binding adds additional rules for fault expression, those also MUST be followed.

As noted above, method and response structs can be encoded according to the rules in section 5, or other encodings can be specified using the encodingStyle attribute (see section 4.1.1).

Applications MAY process requests with missing parameters but also MAY return a fault.

Because a result indicates success and a fault indicates failure, it is an error for the method response to contain both a result and a fault.

7.2 RPC and SOAP Header

Additional information relevant to the encoding of a method request but not part of the formal method signature MAY be expressed in the RPC encoding. If so, it MUST be expressed as a subelement of the SOAP Header element.

An example of the use of the header element is the passing of a transaction ID along with a message. Since the transaction ID is not part of the signature and is typically held in an infrastructure component rather than application code, there is no direct way to pass the necessary information with the call. By adding an entry to the headers and giving it a fixed name, the transaction manager on the receiving side can extract the transaction ID and use it without affecting the coding of remote procedure calls.

8. Security Considerations

Not described in this document are methods for integrity and privacy protection. Such issues will be addressed more fully in a future version(s) of this document.

9. References

[1] S. Bradner, "The Internet Standards Process — Revision 3", RFC2026, Harvard University, October 1996

[2] S. Bradner, "Key words for use in RFCs to Indicate Requirement Levels", RFC 2119, Harvard University, March 1997

[3] E. Whitehead, M. Murata, "XML Media Types", RFC2376, UC Irvine, Fuji Xerox Info. Systems, July 1998

[4] T. Berners-Lee, R. Fielding, L. Masinter, "Uniform Resource Identifiers (URI): Generic Syntax", RFC 2396, MIT/LCS, U.C. Irvine, Xerox Corporation, August 1998.

[5] R. Fielding, J. Gettys, J. C. Mogul, H. Frystyk, T. Berners-Lee, "Hypertext Transfer Protocol — HTTP/1.1", RFC 2616, U.C. Irvine, DEC W3C/MIT, DEC, W3C/MIT, W3C/MIT, January 1997

[6] H. Nielsen, P. Leach, S. Lawrence, "An HTTP Extension Framework", RFC 2774, Microsoft, Microsoft, Agranat Systems

[7] W3C Recommendation "The XML Specification"

[8] W3C Recommendation "Namespaces in XML"

[9] W3C Working Draft "XML Linking Language". This is work in progress.

[10] W3C Working Draft "XML Schema Part 1: Structures". This is work in progress.

[11] W3C Working Draft "XML Schema Part 2: Datatypes". This is work in progress.

[12] Transfer Syntax NDR, in "DCE 1.1: Remote Procedure Call"

[13] N. Freed, N. Borenstein, "Multipurpose Internet Mail Extensions (MIME) Part One: Format of Internet Message Bodies", RFC2045, Innosoft, First Virtual, November 1996

A. SOAP Envelope Examples

A.1 Sample Encoding of Call Requests

Example 5   Similar to <u>Example 1</u> but with a Mandatory Header

```
POST /StockQuote HTTP/1.1
Host: www.stockquoteserver.com
Content-Type: text/xml; charset="utf-8"
Content-Length: nnnn
SOAPAction: "Some-URI"

<SOAP-ENV:Envelope
 xmlns:SOAP-ENV="http://schemas.xmlsoap.org/soap/envelope/"
 SOAP-ENV:encodingStyle="http://schemas.xmlsoap.org/soap/
   encoding/"/>
  <SOAP-ENV:Header>
      <t:Transaction
          xmlns:t="some-URI"
          SOAP-ENV:mustUnderstand="1">
              5
      </t:Transaction>
  </SOAP-ENV:Header>
  <SOAP-ENV:Body>
      <m:GetLastTradePrice xmlns:m="Some-URI">
          <symbol>DEF</symbol>
      </m:GetLastTradePrice>
  </SOAP-ENV:Body>
</SOAP-ENV:Envelope>
```

Example 6   Similar to <u>Example 1</u> but with multiple request parameters

```
POST /StockQuote HTTP/1.1
Host: www.stockquoteserver.com
Content-Type: text/xml; charset="utf-8"
Content-Length: nnnn
SOAPAction: "Some-URI"

<SOAP-ENV:Envelope
 xmlns:SOAP-ENV="http://schemas.xmlsoap.org/soap/envelope/"
```

```
  SOAP-ENV:encodingStyle="http://schemas.xmlsoap.org/soap/
    encoding/"/>
   <SOAP-ENV:Body>
       <m:GetLastTradePriceDetailed
         xmlns:m="Some-URI">
           <Symbol>DEF</Symbol>
           <Company>DEF Corp</Company>
           <Price>34.1</Price>
       </m:GetLastTradePriceDetailed>
   </SOAP-ENV:Body>
 </SOAP-ENV:Envelope>
```

A.2 Sample Encoding of Response

Example 7   Similar to <u>Example 2</u> but with a Mandatory Header

```
HTTP/1.1 200 OK
Content-Type: text/xml; charset="utf-8"
Content-Length: nnnn

<SOAP-ENV:Envelope
 xmlns:SOAP-ENV="http://schemas.xmlsoap.org/soap/envelope/"
 SOAP-ENV:encodingStyle="http://schemas.xmlsoap.org/soap/
   encoding/"/>
  <SOAP-ENV:Header>
      <t:Transaction
        xmlns:t="some-URI"
        xsi:type="xsd:int" mustUnderstand="1">
          5
      </t:Transaction>
  </SOAP-ENV:Header>
  <SOAP-ENV:Body>
      <m:GetLastTradePriceResponse
        xmlns:m="Some-URI">
          <Price>34.5</Price>
      </m:GetLastTradePriceResponse>
  </SOAP-ENV:Body>
</SOAP-ENV:Envelope>
```

Example 8   Similar to <u>Example 2</u> but with a Struct

```
HTTP/1.1 200 OK
Content-Type: text/xml; charset="utf-8"
Content-Length: nnnn
```

```
<SOAP-ENV:Envelope
 xmlns:SOAP-ENV="http://schemas.xmlsoap.org/soap/envelope/"
 SOAP-ENV:encodingStyle="http://schemas.xmlsoap.org/soap/
  encoding/"/>
  <SOAP-ENV:Body>
      <m:GetLastTradePriceResponse
        xmlns:m="Some-URI">
          <PriceAndVolume>
              <LastTradePrice>
                34.5
              </LastTradePrice>
              <DayVolume>
                10000
              </DayVolume>
          </PriceAndVolume>
      </m:GetLastTradePriceResponse>
  </SOAP-ENV:Body>
</SOAP-ENV:Envelope>
```

Example 9   Similar to <u>Example 2</u> but Failing to honor Mandatory Header

```
HTTP/1.1 500 Internal Server Error
Content-Type: text/xml; charset="utf-8"
Content-Length: nnnn

<SOAP-ENV:Envelope
 xmlns:SOAP-ENV="http://schemas.xmlsoap.org/soap/envelope/">
  <SOAP-ENV:Body>
      <SOAP-ENV:Fault>
        <faultcode>SOAP-ENV:MustUnderstand</faultcode>
        <faultstring>SOAP Must Understand Error</faultstring>
      </SOAP-ENV:Fault>
  </SOAP-ENV:Body>
</SOAP-ENV:Envelope>
```

Example 10   Similar to <u>Example 2</u> but Failing to handle Body

```
HTTP/1.1 500 Internal Server Error
Content-Type: text/xml; charset="utf-8"
Content-Length: nnnn

<SOAP-ENV:Envelope
 xmlns:SOAP-ENV="http://schemas.xmlsoap.org/soap/envelope/">
  <SOAP-ENV:Body>
      <SOAP-ENV:Fault>
        <faultcode>SOAP-ENV:Server</faultcode>
        <faultstring>Server Error</faultstring>
```

```
      <detail>
        <e:myfaultdetails xmlns:e="Some-URI">
         <message>
          My application didn't work
         </message>
          <errorcode>
           1001
          </errorcode>
        </e:myfaultdetails>
      </detail>
   </SOAP-ENV:Fault>
  </SOAP-ENV:Body>
 </SOAP-ENV:Envelope>
```

CHAPTER
8

SOAP 1.1 External Hyperlinks

The following external hyperlinks appear in the text of the Simple Object Access Protocol (SOAP) 1.1 W3C Note found in the preceding chapter. These hyperlinks appear in the preceding chapter as <u>underlined text</u> and refer to external resources referenced by the SOAP 1.1 specification (such as email addresses and Web pages). The URL corresponding to each of these external links is provided here as a convenience to readers of this book.

Hyperlink Name	Uniform Resource Locator (URL)
Simple Object Access Protocol (SOAP) 1.1	http://www.w3.org/TR/SOAP/
This version	http://www.w3.org/TR/2000/NOTE-SOAP-20000508
Latest version	http://www.w3.org/TR/SOAP
Don Box	mailto:dbox@develop.com
David Ehnebuske	mailto:davide@us.ibm.com
Gopal Kakivaya	mailto:gopalk@microsoft.com
Andrew Layman	mailto:andrewl@microsoft.com
Noah Mendelsohn	mailto:Noah_Mendelsohn@lotus.com
Henrik Frystyk Nielsen	mailto:frystyk@microsoft.com
Satish Thatte	mailto:satisht@microsoft.com
Dave Winer	mailto:dave@userland.com
DevelopMentor	http://www.develop.com/
International Business Machines Corporation	http://www.ibm.com/
Lotus Development Corporation	http://www.lotus.com/
Microsoft	http://www.microsoft.com/
UserLand Software	http://www.userland.com/
World Wide Web Consortium	http://www.w3.org/
Submission Request	http://www.w3.org/Submission/2000/05/
W3C Staff Comment	http://www.w3.org/Submission/2000/05/Comment
Authors	http://www.w3.org/TR/SOAP/#_Toc478383537
W3C's public mailing list	mailto:xml-dist-app@w3.org
Archives	http://lists.w3.org/Archives/Public/xml-dist-app/
Technical Reports page	http://www.w3.org/TR/
RFC2026	http://www.normos.org/ietf/rfc/rfc2026.txt
RFC 2119	http://www.normos.org/ietf/rfc/rfc2119.txt
RFC2376	http://www.normos.org/ietf/rfc/rfc2376.txt

RFC 2396	http://www.normos.org/ietf/rfc/rfc2396.txt
RFC 2616	http://www.normos.org/ietf/rfc/rfc2616.txt
RFC 2774	http://www.normos.org/ietf/rfc/rfc2774.txt
The XML Specification	http://www.w3.org/TR/REC-xml
Namespaces in XML	http://www.w3.org/TR/REC-xml-names/
XML Linking Language	http://www.w3.org/TR/xlink/
XML Schema Part 1: Structures	http://www.w3.org/TR/xmlschema-1/
XML Schema Part 2: Datatypes	http://www.w3.org/TR/xmlschema-2/
DCE 1.1: Remote Procedure Call	http://www.opengroup.org/public/pubs/catalog/c706.htm
RFC2045	http://www.normos.org/ietf/rfc/rfc2045.txt

CHAPTER
9

SOAP 1.1 Envelope Schema

```
<?xml version='1.0' encoding='UTF-8' ?>

<!-- Schema for the SOAP/1.1 envelope

    This schema has been produced using W3C's SOAP Version 1.2
    schema found at:

    http://www.w3.org/2001/06/soap-envelope

    Copyright 2001 Martin Gudgin, Developmentor.

    Changes made are the following:
    - reverted namespace to http://schemas.xmlsoap.org/soap/
      envelope/
    - reverted mustUnderstand to only allow 0 and 1 as lexical
      values

    Original copyright:

    Copyright 2001 W3C (Massachusetts Institute of Technology,
    Institut National de Recherche en Informatique et en
      Automatique,
    Keio University). All Rights Reserved.
    http://www.w3.org/Consortium/Legal/

    This document is governed by the W3C Software License [1] as
    described in the FAQ [2].

    [1] http://www.w3.org/Consortium/Legal/copyright-software-
        19980720
    [2] http://www.w3.org/Consortium/Legal/IPR-FAQ-
        20000620.html#DTD
-->
<xs:schema xmlns:xs="http://www.w3.org/2001/XMLSchema"
           xmlns:tns="http://schemas.xmlsoap.org/soap/envelope/"
           targetNamespace="http://schemas.xmlsoap.org/soap/
             envelope/" >


  <!-- Envelope, header and body -->
  <xs:element name="Envelope" type="tns:Envelope" />
  <xs:complexType name="Envelope" >
    <xs:sequence>
      <xs:element ref="tns:Header" minOccurs="0" />
      <xs:element ref="tns:Body" minOccurs="1" />
      <xs:any namespace="##other" minOccurs="0" maxOccurs=
        "unbounded" processContents="lax" />
```

```
    </xs:sequence>
    <xs:anyAttribute namespace="##other" processContents="lax" />
  </xs:complexType>

  <xs:element name="Header" type="tns:Header" />
  <xs:complexType name="Header" >
    <xs:sequence>
      <xs:any namespace="##other" minOccurs="0" maxOccurs=
        "unbounded" processContents="lax" />
    </xs:sequence>
    <xs:anyAttribute namespace="##other" processContents="lax" />
  </xs:complexType>

  <xs:element name="Body" type="tns:Body" />
  <xs:complexType name="Body" >
    <xs:sequence>
      <xs:any namespace="##any" minOccurs="0" maxOccurs=
        "unbounded" processContents="lax" />
    </xs:sequence>
    <xs:anyAttribute namespace="##any" processContents="lax" >
        <xs:annotation>
          <xs:documentation>
              Prose in the spec does not specify that attributes
                are allowed on the Body element
            </xs:documentation>
        </xs:annotation>
      </xs:anyAttribute>
  </xs:complexType>


  <!-- Global Attributes.  The following attributes are intended
    to be usable via qualified attribute names on any complex type
    referencing them.  -->
  <xs:attribute name="mustUnderstand" default="0" >
    <xs:simpleType>
    <xs:restriction base='xs:boolean'>
        <xs:pattern value='0|1' />
      </xs:restriction>
   </xs:simpleType>
  </xs:attribute>
  <xs:attribute name="actor" type="xs:anyURI" />

  <xs:simpleType name="encodingStyle" >
    <xs:annotation>
       <xs:documentation>
          'encodingStyle' indicates any canonicalization
            conventions followed in the contents of the containing
```

```
       element.  For example, the value 'http://schemas
       .xmlsoap.org/soap/encoding/' indicates the pattern
       described in SOAP specification
     </xs:documentation>
   </xs:annotation>
   <xs:list itemType="xs:anyURI" />
 </xs:simpleType>


 <xs:attributeGroup name="encodingStyle" >
   <xs:attribute name="encodingStyle" type="tns:encodingStyle" />
 </xs:attributeGroup>


 <xs:complexType name="Fault" final="extension" >
   <xs:annotation>
       <xs:documentation>
         Fault reporting structure
       </xs:documentation>
     </xs:annotation>
   <xs:sequence>
     <xs:element name="faultcode" type="xs:QName" />
     <xs:element name="faultstring" type="xs:string" />
     <xs:element name="faultactor" type="xs:anyURI" minOccurs=
       "0" />
     <xs:element name="detail" type="tns:detail" minOccurs="0" />
   </xs:sequence>
 </xs:complexType>


 <xs:complexType name="detail">
   <xs:sequence>
     <xs:any namespace="##any" minOccurs="0" maxOccurs=
     "unbounded" processContents="lax" />
   </xs:sequence>
   <xs:anyAttribute namespace="##any" processContents="lax" />
 </xs:complexType>

</xs:schema>
```

SOAP 1.1 Encoding Schema

```
<?xml version='1.0' encoding='UTF-8' ?>

<!-- Schema for the SOAP/1.1 encoding

    This schema has been produced using W3C's SOAP Version 1.2
    schema found at:

    http://www.w3.org/2001/06/soap-encoding

    Copyright 2001 Martin Gudgin, Developmentor.
      http://www.develop.co.uk

    Changes made are the following:
    - reverted namespace to http://schemas.xmlsoap.org/soap/
      encoding/
    - reverted root to only allow 0 and 1 as lexical values


    Original copyright:

    Copyright 2001 W3C (Massachusetts Institute of Technology,
    Institut National de Recherche en Informatique et en
      Automatique,
    Keio University). All Rights Reserved.
    http://www.w3.org/Consortium/Legal/

    This document is governed by the W3C Software License [1] as
    described in the FAQ [2].

    [1] http://www.w3.org/Consortium/Legal/copyright-software-
        19980720
    [2] http://www.w3.org/Consortium/Legal/IPR-FAQ-
        20000620.html#DTD
-->
<xs:schema xmlns:xs="http://www.w3.org/2001/XMLSchema"
           xmlns:tns="http://schemas.xmlsoap.org/soap/encoding/"
           targetNamespace="http://schemas.xmlsoap.org/soap/
             encoding/" >

  <xs:attribute name="root" default="0" >
    <xs:annotation>
      <xs:documentation>
          'root' can be used to distinguish serialization roots
            from other elements that are present in a serialization
            but are not roots of a serialized value graph
        </xs:documentation>
    </xs:annotation>
```

```
  <xs:simpleType>
    <xs:restriction base='xs:boolean'>
        <xs:pattern value='0|1' />
      </xs:restriction>
  </xs:simpleType>
</xs:attribute>

 <xs:attributeGroup name="commonAttributes" >
   <xs:annotation>
      <xs:documentation>
        Attributes common to all elements that function as
          accessors or represent independent (multi-ref) values.
          The href attribute is intended to be used in a manner
          like CONREF. That is, the element content should be
          empty iff the href attribute appears
      </xs:documentation>
    </xs:annotation>
   <xs:attribute name="id" type="xs:ID" />
   <xs:attribute name="href" type="xs:anyURI" />
   <xs:anyAttribute namespace="##other" processContents="lax" />
 </xs:attributeGroup>

<!-- Global Attributes.  The following attributes are intended
  to be usable via qualified attribute names on any complex type
  referencing them. -->

<!-- Array attributes. Needed to give the type and dimensions of
  an array's contents, and the offset for partially-transmitted
  arrays. -->

<xs:simpleType name="arrayCoordinate" >
  <xs:restriction base="xs:string" />
</xs:simpleType>

<xs:attribute name="arrayType" type="xs:string" />
<xs:attribute name="offset" type="tns:arrayCoordinate" />

<xs:attributeGroup name="arrayAttributes" >
  <xs:attribute ref="tns:arrayType" />
  <xs:attribute ref="tns:offset" />
</xs:attributeGroup>

<xs:attribute name="position" type="tns:arrayCoordinate" />

<xs:attributeGroup name="arrayMemberAttributes" >
  <xs:attribute ref="tns:position" />
</xs:attributeGroup>
```

```
<xs:group name="Array" >
  <xs:sequence>
    <xs:any namespace="##any" minOccurs="0" maxOccurs=
      "unbounded" processContents="lax" />
    </xs:sequence>
</xs:group>

<xs:element name="Array" type="tns:Array" />
<xs:complexType name="Array" >
  <xs:annotation>
      <xs:documentation>
        'Array' is a complex type for accessors identified by
          position
      </xs:documentation>
    </xs:annotation>
  <xs:group ref="tns:Array" minOccurs="0" />
  <xs:attributeGroup ref="tns:arrayAttributes" />
  <xs:attributeGroup ref="tns:commonAttributes" />
</xs:complexType>

<!-- 'Struct' is a complex type for accessors identified by
    name.
      Constraint: No element may be have the same name as any
      other, nor may any element have a maxOccurs > 1. -->

<xs:element name="Struct" type="tns:Struct" />

<xs:group name="Struct" >
  <xs:sequence>
    <xs:any namespace="##any" minOccurs="0" maxOccurs=
      "unbounded" processContents="lax" />
    </xs:sequence>
</xs:group>

<xs:complexType name="Struct" >
  <xs:group ref="tns:Struct" minOccurs="0" />
  <xs:attributeGroup ref="tns:commonAttributes"/>
</xs:complexType>

<!-- 'Base64' can be used to serialize binary data using base64
  encoding as defined in RFC2045 but without the MIME line length
  limitation. -->

<xs:simpleType name="base64" >
  <xs:restriction base="xs:base64Binary" />
</xs:simpleType>
```

```
<!-- Element declarations corresponding to each of the simple
  types in the XML Schemas Specification. -->

<xs:element name="duration" type="tns:duration" />
<xs:complexType name="duration" >
  <xs:simpleContent>
    <xs:extension base="xs:duration" >
      <xs:attributeGroup ref="tns:commonAttributes" />
    </xs:extension>
  </xs:simpleContent>
</xs:complexType>

<xs:element name="dateTime" type="tns:dateTime" />
<xs:complexType name="dateTime" >
  <xs:simpleContent>
    <xs:extension base="xs:dateTime" >
      <xs:attributeGroup ref="tns:commonAttributes" />
    </xs:extension>
  </xs:simpleContent>
</xs:complexType>



<xs:element name="NOTATION" type="tns:NOTATION" />
<xs:complexType name="NOTATION" >
  <xs:simpleContent>
    <xs:extension base="xs:QName" >
      <xs:attributeGroup ref="tns:commonAttributes" />
    </xs:extension>
  </xs:simpleContent>
</xs:complexType>



<xs:element name="time" type="tns:time" />
<xs:complexType name="time" >
  <xs:simpleContent>
    <xs:extension base="xs:time" >
      <xs:attributeGroup ref="tns:commonAttributes" />
    </xs:extension>
  </xs:simpleContent>
</xs:complexType>

<xs:element name="date" type="tns:date" />
<xs:complexType name="date" >
  <xs:simpleContent>
    <xs:extension base="xs:date" >
      <xs:attributeGroup ref="tns:commonAttributes" />
```

```
        </xs:extension>
      </xs:simpleContent>
  </xs:complexType>

  <xs:element name="gYearMonth" type="tns:gYearMonth" />
  <xs:complexType name="gYearMonth" >
    <xs:simpleContent>
      <xs:extension base="xs:gYearMonth" >
        <xs:attributeGroup ref="tns:commonAttributes" />
      </xs:extension>
    </xs:simpleContent>
  </xs:complexType>

  <xs:element name="gYear" type="tns:gYear" />
  <xs:complexType name="gYear" >
    <xs:simpleContent>
      <xs:extension base="xs:gYear" >
        <xs:attributeGroup ref="tns:commonAttributes" />
      </xs:extension>
    </xs:simpleContent>
  </xs:complexType>

  <xs:element name="gMonthDay" type="tns:gMonthDay" />
  <xs:complexType name="gMonthDay" >
    <xs:simpleContent>
      <xs:extension base="xs:gMonthDay" >
        <xs:attributeGroup ref="tns:commonAttributes" />
      </xs:extension>
    </xs:simpleContent>
  </xs:complexType>

  <xs:element name="gDay" type="tns:gDay" />
  <xs:complexType name="gDay" >
    <xs:simpleContent>
      <xs:extension base="xs:gDay" >
        <xs:attributeGroup ref="tns:commonAttributes" />
      </xs:extension>
    </xs:simpleContent>
  </xs:complexType>

  <xs:element name="gMonth" type="tns:gMonth" />
  <xs:complexType name="gMonth" >
    <xs:simpleContent>
      <xs:extension base="xs:gMonth" >
        <xs:attributeGroup ref="tns:commonAttributes" />
      </xs:extension>
    </xs:simpleContent>
```

```
    </xs:complexType>

    <xs:element name="boolean" type="tns:boolean" />
    <xs:complexType name="boolean" >
      <xs:simpleContent>
        <xs:extension base="xs:boolean" >
          <xs:attributeGroup ref="tns:commonAttributes" />
        </xs:extension>
      </xs:simpleContent>
    </xs:complexType>

    <xs:element name="base64Binary" type="tns:base64Binary" />
    <xs:complexType name="base64Binary" >
      <xs:simpleContent>
        <xs:extension base="xs:base64Binary" >
          <xs:attributeGroup ref="tns:commonAttributes" />
        </xs:extension>
      </xs:simpleContent>
    </xs:complexType>

    <xs:element name="hexBinary" type="tns:hexBinary" />
    <xs:complexType name="hexBinary" >
      <xs:simpleContent>
       <xs:extension base="xs:hexBinary" >
         <xs:attributeGroup ref="tns:commonAttributes" />
       </xs:extension>
      </xs:simpleContent>
    </xs:complexType>

    <xs:element name="float" type="tns:float" />
    <xs:complexType name="float" >
      <xs:simpleContent>
        <xs:extension base="xs:float" >
          <xs:attributeGroup ref="tns:commonAttributes" />
        </xs:extension>
      </xs:simpleContent>
    </xs:complexType>

    <xs:element name="double" type="tns:double" />
    <xs:complexType name="double" >
      <xs:simpleContent>
        <xs:extension base="xs:double" >
          <xs:attributeGroup ref="tns:commonAttributes" />
        </xs:extension>
      </xs:simpleContent>
    </xs:complexType>
```

```
<xs:element name="anyURI" type="tns:anyURI" />
<xs:complexType name="anyURI" >
  <xs:simpleContent>
    <xs:extension base="xs:anyURI" >
      <xs:attributeGroup ref="tns:commonAttributes" />
    </xs:extension>
  </xs:simpleContent>
</xs:complexType>

<xs:element name="QName" type="tns:QName" />
<xs:complexType name="QName" >
  <xs:simpleContent>
    <xs:extension base="xs:QName" >
      <xs:attributeGroup ref="tns:commonAttributes" />
    </xs:extension>
  </xs:simpleContent>
</xs:complexType>


<xs:element name="string" type="tns:string" />
<xs:complexType name="string" >
  <xs:simpleContent>
    <xs:extension base="xs:string" >
      <xs:attributeGroup ref="tns:commonAttributes" />
    </xs:extension>
  </xs:simpleContent>
</xs:complexType>

<xs:element name="normalizedString" type="tns:normalized-
  String" />
<xs:complexType name="normalizedString" >
  <xs:simpleContent>
    <xs:extension base="xs:normalizedString" >
      <xs:attributeGroup ref="tns:commonAttributes" />
    </xs:extension>
  </xs:simpleContent>
</xs:complexType>

<xs:element name="token" type="tns:token" />
<xs:complexType name="token" >
  <xs:simpleContent>
    <xs:extension base="xs:token" >
      <xs:attributeGroup ref="tns:commonAttributes" />
    </xs:extension>
  </xs:simpleContent>
</xs:complexType>
```

```
<xs:element name="language" type="tns:language" />
<xs:complexType name="language" >
  <xs:simpleContent>
    <xs:extension base="xs:language" >
      <xs:attributeGroup ref="tns:commonAttributes" />
    </xs:extension>
  </xs:simpleContent>
</xs:complexType>

<xs:element name="Name" type="tns:Name" />
<xs:complexType name="Name" >
  <xs:simpleContent>
    <xs:extension base="xs:Name" >
      <xs:attributeGroup ref="tns:commonAttributes" />
    </xs:extension>
  </xs:simpleContent>
</xs:complexType>

<xs:element name="NMTOKEN" type="tns:NMTOKEN" />
<xs:complexType name="NMTOKEN" >
  <xs:simpleContent>
    <xs:extension base="xs:NMTOKEN" >
      <xs:attributeGroup ref="tns:commonAttributes" />
    </xs:extension>
  </xs:simpleContent>
</xs:complexType>

<xs:element name="NCName" type="tns:NCName" />
<xs:complexType name="NCName" >
  <xs:simpleContent>
    <xs:extension base="xs:NCName" >
      <xs:attributeGroup ref="tns:commonAttributes" />
    </xs:extension>
  </xs:simpleContent>
</xs:complexType>

<xs:element name="NMTOKENS" type="tns:NMTOKENS" />
<xs:complexType name="NMTOKENS" >
  <xs:simpleContent>
    <xs:extension base="xs:NMTOKENS" >
      <xs:attributeGroup ref="tns:commonAttributes" />
    </xs:extension>
  </xs:simpleContent>
</xs:complexType>

<xs:element name="ID" type="tns:ID" />
```

```
<xs:complexType name="ID" >
  <xs:simpleContent>
    <xs:extension base="xs:ID" >
      <xs:attributeGroup ref="tns:commonAttributes" />
    </xs:extension>
  </xs:simpleContent>
</xs:complexType>

<xs:element name="IDREF" type="tns:IDREF" />
<xs:complexType name="IDREF" >
  <xs:simpleContent>
    <xs:extension base="xs:IDREF" >
      <xs:attributeGroup ref="tns:commonAttributes" />
    </xs:extension>
  </xs:simpleContent>
</xs:complexType>

<xs:element name="ENTITY" type="tns:ENTITY" />
<xs:complexType name="ENTITY" >
  <xs:simpleContent>
    <xs:extension base="xs:ENTITY" >
      <xs:attributeGroup ref="tns:commonAttributes" />
    </xs:extension>
  </xs:simpleContent>
</xs:complexType>

<xs:element name="IDREFS" type="tns:IDREFS" />
<xs:complexType name="IDREFS" >
  <xs:simpleContent>
    <xs:extension base="xs:IDREFS" >
      <xs:attributeGroup ref="tns:commonAttributes" />
    </xs:extension>
  </xs:simpleContent>
</xs:complexType>

<xs:element name="ENTITIES" type="tns:ENTITIES" />
<xs:complexType name="ENTITIES" >
  <xs:simpleContent>
    <xs:extension base="xs:ENTITIES" >
      <xs:attributeGroup ref="tns:commonAttributes" />
    </xs:extension>
  </xs:simpleContent>
</xs:complexType>

<xs:element name="decimal" type="tns:decimal" />
<xs:complexType name="decimal" >
  <xs:simpleContent>
```

```xml
      <xs:extension base="xs:decimal" >
        <xs:attributeGroup ref="tns:commonAttributes" />
      </xs:extension>
    </xs:simpleContent>
  </xs:complexType>

  <xs:element name="integer" type="tns:integer" />
  <xs:complexType name="integer" >
    <xs:simpleContent>
      <xs:extension base="xs:integer" >
        <xs:attributeGroup ref="tns:commonAttributes" />
      </xs:extension>
    </xs:simpleContent>
  </xs:complexType>

  <xs:element name="nonPositiveInteger" type="tns:nonPositive-
Integer" />
  <xs:complexType name="nonPositiveInteger" >
    <xs:simpleContent>
      <xs:extension base="xs:nonPositiveInteger" >
        <xs:attributeGroup ref="tns:commonAttributes" />
      </xs:extension>
    </xs:simpleContent>
  </xs:complexType>

  <xs:element name="negativeInteger" type="tns:negativeInteger" />
  <xs:complexType name="negativeInteger" >
    <xs:simpleContent>
      <xs:extension base="xs:negativeInteger" >
        <xs:attributeGroup ref="tns:commonAttributes" />
      </xs:extension>
    </xs:simpleContent>
  </xs:complexType>

  <xs:element name="long" type="tns:long" />
  <xs:complexType name="long" >
    <xs:simpleContent>
      <xs:extension base="xs:long" >
        <xs:attributeGroup ref="tns:commonAttributes" />
      </xs:extension>
    </xs:simpleContent>
  </xs:complexType>

  <xs:element name="int" type="tns:int" />
  <xs:complexType name="int" >
    <xs:simpleContent>
      <xs:extension base="xs:int" >
```

```
        <xs:attributeGroup ref="tns:commonAttributes" />
      </xs:extension>
    </xs:simpleContent>
</xs:complexType>

<xs:element name="short" type="tns:short" />
<xs:complexType name="short" >
  <xs:simpleContent>
    <xs:extension base="xs:short" >
      <xs:attributeGroup ref="tns:commonAttributes" />
    </xs:extension>
  </xs:simpleContent>
</xs:complexType>

<xs:element name="byte" type="tns:byte" />
<xs:complexType name="byte" >
  <xs:simpleContent>
    <xs:extension base="xs:byte" >
      <xs:attributeGroup ref="tns:commonAttributes" />
    </xs:extension>
  </xs:simpleContent>
</xs:complexType>

<xs:element name="nonNegativeInteger" type="tns:nonNegative-
  Integer" />
<xs:complexType name="nonNegativeInteger" >
  <xs:simpleContent>
    <xs:extension base="xs:nonNegativeInteger" >
      <xs:attributeGroup ref="tns:commonAttributes" />
    </xs:extension>
  </xs:simpleContent>
</xs:complexType>

<xs:element name="unsignedLong" type="tns:unsignedLong" />
<xs:complexType name="unsignedLong" >
  <xs:simpleContent>
    <xs:extension base="xs:unsignedLong" >
      <xs:attributeGroup ref="tns:commonAttributes" />
    </xs:extension>
  </xs:simpleContent>
</xs:complexType>

<xs:element name="unsignedInt" type="tns:unsignedInt" />
<xs:complexType name="unsignedInt" >
  <xs:simpleContent>
    <xs:extension base="xs:unsignedInt" >
      <xs:attributeGroup ref="tns:commonAttributes" />
```

```
          </xs:extension>
       </xs:simpleContent>
    </xs:complexType>

    <xs:element name="unsignedShort" type="tns:unsignedShort" />
    <xs:complexType name="unsignedShort" >
      <xs:simpleContent>
        <xs:extension base="xs:unsignedShort" >
          <xs:attributeGroup ref="tns:commonAttributes" />
        </xs:extension>
      </xs:simpleContent>
    </xs:complexType>

    <xs:element name="unsignedByte" type="tns:unsignedByte" />
    <xs:complexType name="unsignedByte" >
      <xs:simpleContent>
        <xs:extension base="xs:unsignedByte" >
          <xs:attributeGroup ref="tns:commonAttributes" />
        </xs:extension>
      </xs:simpleContent>
    </xs:complexType>

    <xs:element name="positiveInteger" type="tns:positiveInteger" />
    <xs:complexType name="positiveInteger" >
      <xs:simpleContent>
        <xs:extension base="xs:positiveInteger" >
          <xs:attributeGroup ref="tns:commonAttributes" />
        </xs:extension>
      </xs:simpleContent>
    </xs:complexType>

    <xs:element name="anyType" />
</xs:schema>
```

PART
3

Web Services Description Language (WSDL) 1.1

CHAPTER
11

W3C Web Services Description Language (WSDL) 1.1

W3C Note 15 March 2001

This version:

http://www.w3.org/TR/2001/NOTE-wsdl-20010315

Latest version:

http://www.w3.org/TR/wsdl

Authors (alphabetically):

Erik Christensen, Microsoft

Francisco Curbera, IBM Research

Greg Meredith, Microsoft

Sanjiva Weerawarana, IBM Research

Abstract

WSDL is an XML format for describing network services as a set of endpoints operating on messages containing either document-oriented or procedure-oriented information. The operations and messages are described abstractly, and then bound to a concrete network protocol and message format to define an endpoint. Related concrete endpoints are combined into abstract endpoints (services). WSDL is extensible to allow description of endpoints and their messages regardless of what message formats or network protocols are used to communicate, however, the only bindings described in this document describe how to use WSDL in conjunction with SOAP 1.1, HTTP GET/POST, and MIME.

Status

This document is a submission to the World Wide Web Consortium (see Submission Request, W3C Staff Comment) as a suggestion for describing services for the W3C XML Activity on XML Protocols. For a full list of all acknowledged Submissions, please see Acknowledged Submissions to W3C.

This draft represents the current thinking with regard to descriptions of services within Ariba, IBM and Microsoft. It consolidates concepts found in NASSL, SCL, and SDL (earlier proposals in this space).

This document is a NOTE made available by the W3C for discussion only. Publication of this Note by W3C indicates no endorsement by W3C or the W3C Team, or any W3C Members. W3C has had no editorial control over the preparation of this Note. This document is a work in progress and may be updated, replaced, or rendered obsolete by other documents at any time.

A list of current W3C technical documents can be found at the <u>Technical Reports</u> page.

TABLE OF CONTENTS

1. Introduction

As communications protocols and message formats are standardized in the web community, it becomes increasingly possible and important to be able to describe the communications in some structured way. WSDL addresses this need by defining an XML grammar for describing network services as collections of communication endpoints capable of exchanging messages. WSDL service definitions provide documentation for distributed systems and serve as a recipe for automating the details involved in applications communication.

A WSDL document defines **services** as collections of network endpoints, or **ports.** In WSDL, the abstract definition of endpoints and messages is separated from their concrete network deployment or data format bindings. This allows the reuse of abstract definitions: **messages,** which are abstract descriptions of the data being exchanged, and **port types** which are abstract collections of **operations.** The concrete protocol and data format specifications for a particular port type constitutes a reusable **binding.** A port is defined by associating a network address with a reusable binding, and a collection of ports define a service. Hence, a WSDL document uses the following elements in the definition of network services:

▼ **Types**– a container for data type definitions using some type system (such as XSD).

▼ **Message**– an abstract, typed definition of the data being communicated.

▼ **Operation**– an abstract description of an action supported by the service.

▼ **Port Type**–an abstract set of operations supported by one or more endpoints.

▼ **Binding**– a concrete protocol and data format specification for a particular port type.

▼ **Port**– a single endpoint defined as a combination of a binding and a network address.

▼ **Service**– a collection of related endpoints.

These elements are described in detail in Section 2. It is important to observe that WSDL does not introduce a new type definition language. WSDL recognizes the need for rich type systems for describing message formats, and supports the XML Schemas specification (XSD) [11] as its canonical type system. However, since it is unreasonable to expect a single type system grammar to be used to describe all message formats present and future, WSDL allows using other type definition languages via extensibility.

In addition, WSDL defines a common **binding** mechanism. This is used to attach a specific protocol or data format or structure to an abstract message, operation, or endpoint. It allows the reuse of abstract definitions.

In addition to the core service definition framework, this specification introduces specific **binding extensions** for the following protocols and message formats:

▼ SOAP 1.1 (<u>see Section 3</u>)

▼ HTTP GET / POST (<u>see Section 4</u>)

▼ MIME (<u>see Section 5</u>)

Although defined within this document, the above language extensions are layered on top of the core <u>service definition framework</u>. Nothing precludes the use of other binding extensions with WSDL.

1.2 WSDL Document Example

The following example shows the WSDL definition of a simple service providing stock quotes. The service supports a single operation called GetLastTradePrice, which is deployed using the SOAP 1.1 protocol over HTTP. The request takes a ticker symbol of type string, and returns the price as a float. A detailed description of the elements used in this definition can be found in Section 2 (core language) and Section 3 (SOAP binding).

This example uses a fixed XML format instead of the SOAP encoding (for an example using the SOAP encoding, see <u>Example 4</u>).

Example 1   SOAP 1.1 Request/Response via HTTP

```xml
<?xml version="1.0"?>
<definitions name="StockQuote"
targetNamespace="http://example.com/stockquote.wsdl"
          xmlns:tns="http://example.com/stockquote.wsdl"
          xmlns:xsd1="http://example.com/stockquote.xsd"
          xmlns:soap="http://schemas.xmlsoap.org/wsdl/soap/"
          xmlns="http://schemas.xmlsoap.org/wsdl/">
    <types>
      <schema targetNamespace="http://example.com/stockquote.xsd"
            xmlns="http://www.w3.org/2000/10/XMLSchema">
        <element name="TradePriceRequest">
          <complexType>
            <all>
              <element name="tickerSymbol" type="string"/>
            </all>
```

```
                    </complexType>
                </element>
                <element name="TradePrice">
                    <complexType>
                        <all>
                            <element name="price" type="float"/>
                        </all>
                    </complexType>
                </element>
            </schema>
        </types>
        <message name="GetLastTradePriceInput">
            <part name="body" element="xsd1:TradePriceRequest"/>
        </message>
        <message name="GetLastTradePriceOutput">
            <part name="body" element="xsd1:TradePrice"/>
        </message>
        <portType name="StockQuotePortType">
            <operation name="GetLastTradePrice">
                <input message="tns:GetLastTradePriceInput"/>
                <output message="tns:GetLastTradePriceOutput"/>
            </operation>
        </portType>
        <binding name="StockQuoteSoapBinding" type="tns:StockQuote-
          PortType">
            <soap:binding style="document" transport="http://schemas
              .xmlsoap.org/soap/http"/>
            <operation name="GetLastTradePrice">
                <soap:operation soapAction="http://example.com/GetLast-
                  TradePrice"/>
                <input>
                    <soap:body use="literal"/>
                </input>
                <output>
                    <soap:body use="literal"/>
                </output>
            </operation>
        </binding>
        <service name="StockQuoteService">
            <documentation>My first service</documentation>
            <port name="StockQuotePort" binding="tns:StockQuote-
              Binding">
                <soap:address location="http://example.com/stockquote"/>
            </port>
        </service>
    </definitions>
```

1.2 Notational Conventions

1. The keywords "MUST", "MUST NOT", "REQUIRED", "SHALL", "SHALL NOT", "SHOULD", "SHOULD NOT", "RECOMMENDED", "MAY", and "OPTIONAL" in this document are to be interpreted as described in RFC-2119 [2].

2. The following namespace prefixes are used throughout this document:

prefix	namespace URI	definition
wsdl	http://schemas.xmlsoap.org/wsdl/	WSDL namespace for WSDL framework.
soap	http://schemas.xmlsoap.org/wsdl/soap/	WSDL namespace for WSDL SOAP binding.
http	http://schemas.xmlsoap.org/wsdl/http/	WSDL namespace for WSDL HTTP GET & POST binding.
mime	http://schemas.xmlsoap.org/wsdl/mime/	WSDL namespace for WSDL MIME binding.
soapenc	http://schemas.xmlsoap.org/soap/encoding/	Encoding namespace as defined by SOAP 1.1 [8].
soapenv	http://schemas.xmlsoap.org/soap/envelope/	Envelope namespace as defined by SOAP 1.1 [8].
xsi	http://www.w3.org/2000/10/XML Schema-instance	Instance namespace as defined by XSD [10].
xsd	http://www.w3.org/2000/10/XML Schema	Schema namespace as defined by XSD [10].
tns	(various)	The "this namespace" (tns) prefix is used as a convention to refer to the current document.
(other)	(various)	All other namespace prefixes are samples only. In particular, URIs starting with "http://example.com" represent some application-dependent or context-dependent URI [4].

3. This specification uses an **informal syntax** to describe the XML grammar of a WSDL document:

▼ The syntax appears as an XML instance, but the values indicate the data types instead of values.

▼ Characters are appended to elements and attributes as follows: "?" (0 or 1), "*" (0 or more), "+" (1 or more).

▼ Elements names ending in "..." (such as <element.../> or <element...>) indicate that elements/attributes irrelevant to the context are being omitted.

▼ Grammar in bold has not been introduced earlier in the document, or is of particular interest in an example.

▼ <-- extensibility element --> is a placeholder for elements from some "other" namespace (like ##other in XSD).

▼ The XML namespace prefixes (defined above) are used to indicate the namespace of the element being defined.

▼ Examples starting with <?xml contain enough information to conform to this specification; others examples are fragments and require additional information to be specified in order to conform.

XSD schemas are provided as a formal definition of WSDL grammar (see section A4).

2. Service Definition

This section describes the core elements of the WSDL language. Binding extensions for SOAP, HTTP and MIME are included in Sections 3, 4 and 5.

2.1 WSDL Document Structure

A WSDL document is simply a **set of definitions.** There is a **definitions** element at the root, and definitions inside. The grammar is as follows:

```
<wsdl:definitions name="nmtoken"? targetNamespace="uri"?>
    <import namespace="uri" location="uri"/>*
    <wsdl:documentation .... /> ?
    <wsdl:types> ?
        <wsdl:documentation .... />?
        <xsd:schema .... />*
        <-- extensibility element --> *
    </wsdl:types>
    <wsdl:message name="nmtoken"> *
        <wsdl:documentation .... />?
```

```
        <part name="nmtoken" element="qname"? type="qname"?/> *
    </wsdl:message>
    <wsdl:portType name="nmtoken">*
        <wsdl:documentation .... />?
        <wsdl:operation name="nmtoken">*
            <wsdl:documentation .... /> ?
            <wsdl:input name="nmtoken"? message="qname">?
                <wsdl:documentation .... /> ?
            </wsdl:input>
            <wsdl:output name="nmtoken"? message="qname">?
                <wsdl:documentation .... /> ?
            </wsdl:output>
            <wsdl:fault name="nmtoken" message="qname"> *
                <wsdl:documentation .... /> ?
            </wsdl:fault>
        </wsdl:operation>
    </wsdl:portType>
    <wsdl:binding name="nmtoken" type="qname">*
        <wsdl:documentation .... />?
        <-- extensibility element --> *
        <wsdl:operation name="nmtoken">*
            <wsdl:documentation .... /> ?
            <-- extensibility element --> *
            <wsdl:input> ?
                <wsdl:documentation .... /> ?
                <-- extensibility element -->
            </wsdl:input>
            <wsdl:output> ?
                <wsdl:documentation .... /> ?
                <-- extensibility element --> *
            </wsdl:output>
            <wsdl:fault name="nmtoken"> *
                <wsdl:documentation .... /> ?
                <-- extensibility element --> *
            </wsdl:fault>
        </wsdl:operation>
    </wsdl:binding>
    <wsdl:service name="nmtoken"> *
        <wsdl:documentation .... />?
        <wsdl:port name="nmtoken" binding="qname"> *
            <wsdl:documentation .... /> ?
            <-- extensibility element -->
        </wsdl:port>
        <-- extensibility element -->
    </wsdl:service>
    <-- extensibility element --> *
</wsdl:definitions>
```

Services are defined using six major elements:

▼ **types,** which provides data type definitions used to describe the messages exchanged.

▼ **message,** which represents an abstract definition of the data being transmitted. A message consists of logical parts, each of which is associated with a definition within some type system.

▼ **portType,** which is a set of abstract operations. Each operation refers to an input message and output messages.

▼ **binding,** which specifies concrete protocol and data format specifications for the operations and messages defined by a particular portType.

▼ **port,** which specifies an address for a binding, thus defining a single communication endpoint.

▼ **service,** which is used to aggregate a set of related ports.

These elements will be described in detail in Sections 2.2 to 2.7. In the rest of this section we describe the rules introduced by WSDL for naming documents, referencing document definitions, using language extensions and adding contextual documentation.

2.1.1 Document Naming and Linking

WSDL documents can be assigned an optional **name** attribute of type NCNAME that serves as a lightweight form of documentation. Optionally, a **targetNamespace** attribute of type URI may be specified. The URI MUST NOT be a relative URI.

WSDL allows associating a **namespace** with a document **location** using an **import** statement:

```
<definitions .... >
   <import namespace="uri" location="uri"/> *
</definitions>
```

A reference to a WSDL definition is made using a QName. The following types of definitions contained in a WSDL document may be referenced:

▼ WSDL definitions: service, port, message, bindings, and portType

▼ Other definitions: if additional definitions are added via extensibility, they SHOULD use QName linking.

Each WSDL definition type listed above has its own **name scope** (i.e. port names and message names never conflict). Names within a name scope MUST be unique within the WSDL document.

The resolution of QNames in WSDL is similar to the resolution of QNames described by the XML Schemas specification [11].

2.1.2 Authoring Style

The use of the **import** element allows the separation of the different elements of a service definition into independent documents, which can then be imported as needed. This technique helps writing clearer service definitions, by separating the definitions according to their level of abstraction. It also maximizes the ability to reuse service definitions of all kinds. As a result, WSDL documents structured in this way are easier to use and maintain. Example 2 below shows how to use this authoring style to define the service presented in Example 1. Here we separate the definitions in three documents: data type definitions, abstract definitions, and specific service bindings. The use of this mechanism is of course not limited to the definitions explicitly presented in the example, which uses only language elements defined in this specification. Other types of definitions based on additional language extensions can be encoded and reused in a similar fashion.

Example 2.   Alternative authoring style for the service in Example 1.

```
http://example.com/stockquote/stockquote.xsd
<?xml version="1.0"?>
<schema targetNamespace="http://example.com/stockquote/schemas"
     xmlns="http://www.w3.org/2000/10/XMLSchema">
         <element name="TradePriceRequest">
       <complexType>
          <all>
              <element name="tickerSymbol" type="string"/>
          </all>
       </complexType>
   </element>
   <element name="TradePrice">
       <complexType>
          <all>
              <element name="price" type="float"/>
          </all>
       </complexType>
   </element>
</schema>
http://example.com/stockquote/stockquote.wsdl
  <?xml version="1.0"?>
<definitions name="StockQuote"
targetNamespace="http://example.com/stockquote/definitions"
         xmlns:tns="http://example.com/stockquote/definitions"
         xmlns:xsd1="http://example.com/stockquote/schemas"
```

```
            xmlns:soap="http://schemas.xmlsoap.org/wsdl/soap/"
            xmlns="http://schemas.xmlsoap.org/wsdl/">
    <import namespace="http://example.com/stockquote/schemas"
            location="http://example.com/stockquote/stockquote
               .xsd"/>
   <message name="GetLastTradePriceInput">
       <part name="body" element="xsd1:TradePriceRequest"/>
   </message>
   <message name="GetLastTradePriceOutput">
       <part name="body" element="xsd1:TradePrice"/>
   </message>
   <portType name="StockQuotePortType">
       <operation name="GetLastTradePrice">
          <input message="tns:GetLastTradePriceInput"/>
          <output message="tns:GetLastTradePriceOutput"/>
       </operation>
   </portType>
</definitions>
http://example.com/stockquote/stockquoteservice.wsdl
 <?xml version="1.0"?>
<definitions name="StockQuote"
targetNamespace="http://example.com/stockquote/service"
        xmlns:tns="http://example.com/stockquote/service"
        xmlns:soap="http://schemas.xmlsoap.org/wsdl/soap/"
        xmlns:defs="http://example.com/stockquote/definitions"
        xmlns="http://schemas.xmlsoap.org/wsdl/">
   <import namespace="http://example.com/stockquote/definitions"
            location="http://example.com/stockquote/stockquote
               .wsdl"/>
    <binding name="StockQuoteSoapBinding"
type="defs:StockQuotePortType">
       <soap:binding style="document"
transport="http://schemas.xmlsoap.org/soap/http"/>
       <operation name="GetLastTradePrice">
          <soap:operation
soapAction="http://example.com/GetLastTradePrice"/>
          <input>
             <soap:body use="literal"/>
          </input>
          <output>
             <soap:body use="literal"/>
          </output>
       </operation>
    </binding>
    <service name="StockQuoteService">
       <documentation>My first service</documentation>
       <port name="StockQuotePort" binding="tns:StockQuote-
         Binding">
```

```
            <soap:address location="http://example.com/stockquote"/>
        </port>
    </service>
</definitions>
```

2.1.3 *Language Extensibility and Binding*

In WSDL the term binding refers to the process associating protocol or data format information with an abstract entity like a message, operation, or portType. WSDL allows elements representing a specific technology (referred to here as **extensibility elements**) under various elements defined by WSDL. These points of extensibility are typically used to specify binding information for a particular protocol or message format, but are not limited to such use. Extensibility elements MUST use an XML namespace different from that of WSDL. The specific locations in the document where extensibility elements can appear are described in detail in <u>section A3</u>.

Extensibility elements are commonly used to specify some technology specific binding. To distinguish whether the semantic of the technology specific binding is required for communication or optional, extensibility elements MAY place a **wsdl:required** attribute of type boolean on the element. The default value for required is false. The required attribute is defined in the namespace "http:// schemas.xmlsoap.org/wsdl/".

Extensibility elements allow innovation in the area of network and message protocols without having to revise the base WSDL specification. WSDL recommends that specifications defining such protocols also define any necessary WSDL extensions used to describe those protocols or formats.

See Sections 3, 4, and 5 for examples of extensibility elements defined as part of the base WSDL specification.

2.1.4 *Documentation*

WSDL uses the optional **wsdl:document** element as a container for human readable documentation. The content of the element is arbitrary text and elements ("mixed" in XSD). The documentation element is allowed inside any WSDL language element.

2.2 Types

The **types** element encloses data type definitions that are relevant for the exchanged messages. For maximum interoperability and platform neutrality, WSDL prefers the use of XSD as the canonical type system, and treats it as the intrinsic type system.

```
<definitions .... >
   <types>
       <xsd:schema .... />*
   </types>
</definitions>
```

The XSD type system can be used to define the types in a message regardless of whether or not the resulting wire format is actually XML, or whether the resulting XSD schema validates the particular wire format. This is especially interesting if there will be multiple bindings for the same message, or if there is only one binding but that binding type does not already have a type system in widespread use. In these cases, the recommended approach for encoding abstract types using XSD is as follows:

▼ Use element form (not attribute).

▼ Don't include attributes or elements that are peculiar to the wire encoding (e.g. have nothing to do with the abstract content of the message). Some examples are soap:root, soap:encodingStyle, xmi:id, xmi:name.

▼ Array types should extend the Array type defined in the SOAP v1.1 encoding schema (http://schemas.xmlsoap.org/soap/encoding/) (regardless of whether the resulting form actually uses the encoding specified in Section 5 of the SOAP v1.1 document). Use the name ArrayOfXXX for array types (where XXX is the type of the items in the array). The type of the items in the array and the array dimensions are specified by using a default value for the soapenc:arrayType attribute. At the time of this writing, the XSD specification does not have a mechanism for specifying the default value of an attribute which contains a QName value. To overcome this limitation, WSDL introduces the **arrayType** attribute (from namespace http://schemas.xmlsoap.org/wsdl/) which has the semantic of providing the default value. If XSD is revised to support this functionality, the revised mechanism SHOULD be used in favor of the arrayType attribute defined by WSDL.

▼ Use the xsd:anyType type to represent a field/parameter which can have any type.

However, since it is unreasonable to expect a single type system grammar can be used to describe all abstract types present and future, WSDL allows type systems to be added via extensibility elements. An extensibility element may appear under the **types** element to identify the type definition system being used and to provide an XML container element for the type definitions. The role of this element can be compared to that of the **schema** element of the XML Schema language.

```
<definitions .... >
   <types>
       <-- type-system extensibility element --> *
   </types>
</definitions>
```

2.3 Messages

Messages consist of one or more logical **parts**. Each part is associated with a type from some type system using a message-typing attribute. The set of message-typing attributes is extensible. WSDL defines several such message-typing attributes for use with XSD:

▼ **element**. Refers to an XSD element using a QName.

▼ **type**. Refers to an XSD simpleType or complexType using a QName.

Other message-typing attributes may be defined as long as they use a namespace different from that of WSDL. Binding extensibility elements may also use message-typing attributes.

The syntax for defining a message is as follows. The message-typing attributes (which may vary depending on the type system used) are shown in **bold**.

```
<definitions .... >
   <message name="nmtoken"> *
       <part name="nmtoken" element="qname"? type="qname"?/> *
   </message>
</definitions>
```

The message **name** attribute provides a unique name among all messages defined within the enclosing WSDL document.

The part **name** attribute provides a unique name among all the parts of the enclosing message.

2.3.1 Message Parts

Parts are a flexible mechanism for describing the logical abstract content of a message. A binding may reference the name of a part in order to specify binding-specific information about the part. For example, if defining a message for use with RPC, a part MAY represent a parameter in the message. However, the bindings must be inspected in order to determine the actual meaning of the part.

Multiple part elements are used if the message has multiple logical units. For example, the following message consists of a Purchase Order and an Invoice.

```
<definitions .... >
    <types>
        <schema .... >
            <element name="PO" type="tns:POType"/>
            <complexType name="POType">
                <all>
                    <element name="id" type="string/>
                    <element name="name" type="string"/>
                    <element name="items">
                        <complexType>
                            <all>
                                <element name="item" type="tns:Item"
minOccurs="0" maxOccurs="unbounded"/>
                            </all>
                        </complexType>
                    </element>
                </all>
            </complexType>
            <complexType name="Item">
                <all>
                    <element name="quantity" type="int"/>
                    <element name="product" type="string"/>
                </all>
            </complexType>
            <element name="Invoice" type="tns:InvoiceType"/>
            <complexType name="InvoiceType">
                <all>
                    <element name="id" type="string"/>
                </all>
            </complexType>
        </schema>
    </types>
    <message name="PO">
        <part name="po" element="tns:PO"/>
        <part name="invoice" element="tns:Invoice"/>
    </message>
</definitions>
```

However, if the message contents are sufficiently complex, then an alternative syntax may be used to specify the composite structure of the message using the type system directly. In this usage, only one part may be specified. In the following example, the body is either a purchase order, or a set of invoices.

```
<definitions .... >
    <types>
        <schema .... >
```

```
                <complexType name="POType">
                    <all>
                        <element name="id" type="string"/>
                        <element name="name" type="string"/>
                        <element name="items">
                            <complexType>
                                <all>
                                    <element name="item" type="tns:Item"
minOccurs="0" maxOccurs="unbounded"/>
                                </all>
                            </complexType>
                        </element>
                    </all>
                </complexType>
                <complexType name="Item">
                    <all>
                        <element name="quantity" type="int"/>
                        <element name="product" type="string"/>
                    </all>
                </complexType>
                <complexType name="InvoiceType">
                    <all>
                        <element name="id" type="string"/>
                    </all>
                </complexType>
                <complexType name="Composite">
                    <choice>
                        <element name="PO" minOccurs="1" maxOccurs="1"
type="tns:POType"/>
                        <element name="Invoice" minOccurs="0"
maxOccurs="unbounded" type="tns:InvoiceType"/>
                    </choice>
                </complexType>
            </schema>
        </types>
        <message name="PO">
            <part name="composite" type="tns:Composite"/>
        </message>
</definitions>
```

2.3.2 *Abstract vs. Concrete Messages*

Message definitions are always considered to be an abstract definition of the
message content. A message binding describes how the abstract content is
mapped into a concrete format. However, in some cases, the abstract definition
may match the concrete representation very closely or exactly for one or more

bindings, so those binding(s) will supply little or no mapping information. However, another binding of the same message definition may require extensive mapping information. For this reason, it is not until the binding is inspected that one can determine "how abstract" the message really is.

2.4 Port Types

A port type is a named set of abstract operations and the abstract messages involved.

```
<wsdl:definitions .... >
    <wsdl:portType name="nmtoken">
        <wsdl:operation name="nmtoken" .... /> *
    </wsdl:portType>
</wsdl:definitions>
```

The port type **name** attribute provides a unique name among all port types defined within in the enclosing WSDL document.

An operation is named via the **name** attribute.

WSDL has four transmission primitives that an endpoint can support:

▼ **One-way.** The endpoint receives a message.

▼ **Request-response.** The endpoint receives a message, and sends a correlated message.

▼ **Solicit-response.** The endpoint sends a message, and receives a correlated message.

▼ **Notification.** The endpoint sends a message.

WSDL refers to these primitives as **operations.** Although request/response or solicit/response can be modeled abstractly using two one-way messages, it is useful to model these as primitive operation types because:

▼ They are very common.

▼ The sequence can be correlated without having to introduce more complex flow information.

▼ Some endpoints can only receive messages if they are the result of a synchronous request response.

▼ A simple flow can algorithmically be derived from these primitives at the point when flow definition is desired.

Although request/response or solicit/response are logically correlated in the WSDL document, a given binding describes the concrete correlation information.

For example, the request and response messages may be exchanged as part of one or two actual network communications.

Although the base WSDL structure supports bindings for these four transmission primitives, WSDL only defines bindings for the One-way and Request-response primitives. It is expected that specifications that define the protocols for Solicit-response or Notification would also include WSDL binding extensions that allow use of these primitives.

Operations refer to the messages involved using the **message** attribute of type QName. This attribute follows the rules defined by WSDL for linking (see section 2.1.2).

2.4.1 One-way Operation

The grammar for a one-way operation is:

```
<wsdl:definitions .... > <wsdl:portType .... > *
        <wsdl:operation name="nmtoken">
           <wsdl:input name="nmtoken"? message="qname"/>
        </wsdl:operation>
   </wsdl:portType >
</wsdl:definitions>
```

The **input** element specifies the abstract message format for the one-way operation.

2.4.2 Request-response Operation

The grammar for a request-response operation is:

```
<wsdl:definitions .... >
   <wsdl:portType .... > *
        <wsdl:operation name="nmtoken" parameterOrder="nmtokens">
           <wsdl:input name="nmtoken"? message="qname"/>
           <wsdl:output name="nmtoken"? message="qname"/>
           <wsdl:fault name="nmtoken" message="qname"/>*
        </wsdl:operation>
   </wsdl:portType >
</wsdl:definitions>
```

The input and output elements specify the abstract message format for the request and response, respectively. The optional fault elements specify the abstract message format for any error messages that may be output as the result of the operation (beyond those specific to the protocol).

Note that a request-response operation is an abstract notion; a particular binding must be consulted to determine how the messages are actually sent: within a single communication (such as a HTTP request/response), or as two independent communications (such as two HTTP requests).

2.4.3   *Solicit-response Operation*

The grammar for a solicit-response operation is:

```
<wsdl:definitions .... >
    <wsdl:portType .... > *
        <wsdl:operation name="nmtoken" parameterOrder="nmtokens">
            <wsdl:output name="nmtoken"? message="qname"/>
            <wsdl:input name="nmtoken"? message="qname"/>
            <wsdl:fault name="nmtoken" message="qname"/>*
        </wsdl:operation>
    </wsdl:portType >
</wsdl:definitions>
```

The output and input elements specify the abstract message format for the solicited request and response, respectively. The optional fault elements specify the abstract message format for any error messages that may be output as the result of the operation (beyond those specific to the protocol).

Note that a solicit-response operation is an abstract notion; a particular binding must be consulted to determine how the messages are actually sent: within a single communication (such as a HTTP request/response), or as two independent communications (such as two HTTP requests).

2.4.4   *Notification Operation*

The grammar for a notification operation is:

```
<wsdl:definitions .... >
    <wsdl:portType .... > *
        <wsdl:operation name="nmtoken">
            <wsdl:output name="nmtoken"? message="qname"/>
        </wsdl:operation>
    </wsdl:portType >
</wsdl:definitions>
```

The **output** element specifies the abstract message format for the notification operation.

2.4.5   *Names of Elements within an Operation*

The **name** attribute of the input and output elements provides a unique name among all input and output elements within the enclosing port type.

In order to avoid having to name each input and output element within an operation, WSDL provides some default values based on the operation name. If the name attribute is not specified on a one-way or notification message, it defaults to the name of the operation. If the name attribute is not specified on the input or output messages of a request-response or solicit-response operation, the name defaults to the name of the operation with "Request"/"Solicit" or "Response" appended, respectively.

Each fault element must be named to allow a binding to specify the concrete format of the fault message. The name of the fault element is unique within the set of faults defined for the operation.

2.4.6   Parameter Order within an Operation

Operations do not specify whether they are to be used with RPC-like bindings or not. However, when using an operation with an RPC-binding, it is useful to be able to capture the original RPC function signature. For this reason, a request-response or solicit-response operation MAY specify a list of parameter names via the **parameterOrder** attribute (of type nmtokens). The value of the attribute is a list of message part names separated by a single space. The value of the parameterOrder attribute MUST follow the following rules:

▼ The part name order reflects the order of the parameters in the RPC signature

▼ The **return** value part is not present in the list

▼ If a part name appears in both the input and output message, it is an **in/out** parameter

▼ If a part name appears in only the input message, it is an **in** parameter

▼ If a part name appears in only the output message, it is an **out** parameter

Note that this information serves as a "hint" and may safely be ignored by those not concerned with RPC signatures. Also, it is not required to be present, even if the operation is to be used with an RPC-like binding.

2.5   Bindings

A binding defines message format and protocol details for operations and messages defined by a particular portType. There may be any number of bindings for a given portType. The grammar for a binding is as follows:

```
<wsdl:definitions .... >
    <wsdl:binding name="nmtoken" type="qname"> *
        <-- extensibility element (1) --> *
```

```
        <wsdl:operation name="nmtoken"> *
           <-- extensibility element (2) --> *
           <wsdl:input name="nmtoken"? > ?
               <-- extensibility element (3) -->
           </wsdl:input>
           <wsdl:output name="nmtoken"? > ?
               <-- extensibility element (4) --> *
           </wsdl:output>
           <wsdl:fault name="nmtoken"> *
               <-- extensibility element (5) --> *
           </wsdl:fault>
        </wsdl:operation>
     </wsdl:binding>
</wsdl:definitions>
```

The **name** attribute provides a unique name among all bindings defined within in the enclosing WSDL document.

A binding references the portType that it binds using the **type** attribute. This QName value follows the linking rules defined by WSDL (see <u>section 2.1.2</u>).

Binding extensibility elements are used to specify the concrete grammar for the input (3), output (4), and fault messages (5). Per-operation binding information (2) as well as per-binding information (1) may also be specified.

An operation element within a binding specifies binding information for the operation with the same name within the binding's portType. Since operation names are not required to be unique (for example, in the case of overloading of method names), the name attribute in the operation binding element might not be enough to uniquely identify an operation. In that case, the correct operation should be identified by providing the **name** attributes of the corresponding wsdl:input and wsdl:output elements.

A binding MUST specify exactly one protocol.

A binding MUST NOT specify address information.

2.6   Ports

A port defines an individual endpoint by specifying a single address for a binding.

```
<wsdl:definitions .... >
   <wsdl:service .... > *
       <wsdl:port name="nmtoken" binding="qname"> *
          <-- extensibility element (1) -->
       </wsdl:port>
   </wsdl:service>
```

```
</wsdl:definitions>
```

The **name** attribute provides a unique name among all ports defined within in the enclosing WSDL document.

The **binding** attribute (of type QName) refers to the binding using the linking rules defined by WSDL (see <u>Section 2.1.2</u>).

Binding extensibility elements (1) are used to specify the address information for the port.

> A port MUST NOT specify more than one address.

> A port MUST NOT specify any binding information other than address information.

2.7   Services

A service groups a set of related ports together:

```
<wsdl:definitions .... >
    <wsdl:service name="nmtoken"> *
        <wsdl:port .... />*
    </wsdl:service>
</wsdl:definitions>
```

The **name** attribute provides a unique name among all services defined within in the enclosing WSDL document.

Ports within a service have the following relationship:

▼ None of the ports communicate with each other (e.g. the output of one port is not the input of another).

▼ If a service has several ports that share a port type, but employ different bindings or addresses, the ports are alternatives. Each port provides semantically equivalent behavior (within the transport and message format limitations imposed by each binding). This allows a consumer of a WSDL document to choose particular port(s) to communicate with based on some criteria (protocol, distance, etc.).

▼ By examining it's ports, we can determine a service's port types. This allows a consumer of a WSDL document to determine if it wishes to communicate to a particular service based whether or not it supports several port types. This is useful if there is some implied relationship between the operations of the port types, and that the entire set of port types must be present in order to accomplish a particular task.

3. SOAP Binding

WSDL includes a binding for SOAP 1.1 endpoints, which supports the specification of the following protocol specific information:

▼ An indication that a binding is bound to the SOAP 1.1 protocol

▼ A way of specifying an address for a SOAP endpoint.

▼ The URI for the SOAPAction HTTP header for the HTTP binding of SOAP

▼ A list of definitions for Headers that are transmitted as part of the SOAP Envelope

This binding grammar it is not an exhaustive specification since the set of SOAP bindings is evolving. Nothing precludes additional SOAP bindings to be derived from portions of this grammar. For example:

▼ SOAP bindings that do not employ a URI addressing scheme may substitute another addressing scheme by replacing the soap:address element defined in <u>section 3.8</u>.

▼ SOAP bindings that do not require a SOAPAction omit the soapAction attribute defined in <u>section 3.4</u>.

3.1 SOAP Examples

In the following example, a SubscribeToQuotes SOAP 1.1 one-way message is sent to a StockQuote service via a SMTP binding. The request takes a ticker symbol of type string, and includes a header defining the subscription URI.

Example 3.   SOAP binding of one-way operation over SMTP using a SOAP Header

```
 <?xml version="1.0"?>
<definitions name="StockQuote"
        targetNamespace="http://example.com/stockquote.wsdl"
        xmlns:tns="http://example.com/stockquote.wsdl"
        xmlns:xsd1="http://example.com/stockquote.xsd"
        xmlns:soap="http://schemas.xmlsoap.org/wsdl/soap/"
        xmlns="http://schemas.xmlsoap.org/wsdl/">
   <message name="SubscribeToQuotes">
      <part name="body" element="xsd1:SubscribeToQuotes"/>
      <part name="subscribeheader" element="xsd1:Subscription
       Header"/>
```

```
    </message>
    <portType name="StockQuotePortType">
        <operation name="SubscribeToQuotes">
            <input message="tns:SubscribeToQuotes"/>
        </operation>
    </portType>
    <binding name="StockQuoteSoap" type="tns:StockQuotePortType">
        <soap:binding style="document"
transport="http://example.com/smtp"/>
        <operation name="SubscribeToQuotes">
            <input message="tns:SubscribeToQuotes">
                <soap:body parts="body" use="literal"/>
                <soap:header message="tns:SubscribeToQuotes"
part="subscribeheader" use="literal"/>
            </input>
        </operation>
    </binding>
    <service name="StockQuoteService">
        <port name="StockQuotePort" binding="tns:StockQuoteSoap">
            <soap:address location="mailto:subscribe@example.com"/>
        </port>
    </service>
    <types>
        <schema targetNamespace="http://example.com/stockquote.xsd"
                xmlns="http://www.w3.org/2000/10/XMLSchema">
        <element name="SubscribeToQuotes">
            <complexType>
                <all>
                    <element name="tickerSymbol" type="string"/>
                </all>
            </complexType>
        </element>
        <element name="SubscriptionHeader" type="uriReference"/>
        </schema>
    </types>
</definitions>
```

This example describes that a GetTradePrice SOAP 1.1 request may be sent to a StockQuote service via the SOAP 1.1 HTTP binding. The request takes a ticker symbol of type string, a time of type timeInstant, and returns the price as a float in the SOAP response.

Example 4.   SOAP binding of request-response RPC operation over HTTP

```
 <?xml version="1.0"?>
<definitions name="StockQuote"
```

```
                    targetNamespace="http://example.com/stockquote.wsdl"
                    xmlns:tns="http://example.com/stockquote.wsdl"
                    xmlns:xsd="http://www.w3.org/2000/10/XMLSchema"
                    xmlns:xsd1="http://example.com/stockquote.xsd"
                    xmlns:soap="http://schemas.xmlsoap.org/wsdl/soap/"
                    xmlns="http://schemas.xmlsoap.org/wsdl/">
        <message name="GetTradePriceInput">
            <part name="tickerSymbol" element="xsd:string"/>
            <part name="time" element="xsd:timeInstant"/>
        </message>
        <message name="GetTradePriceOutput">
            <part name="result" type="xsd:float"/>
        </message>
        <portType name="StockQuotePortType">
            <operation name="GetTradePrice">
                <input message="tns:GetTradePriceInput"/>
                <output message="tns:GetTradePriceOutput"/>
            </operation>
        </portType>
        <binding name="StockQuoteSoapBinding" type="tns:StockQuote
          PortType">
            <soap:binding style="rpc"
transport="http://schemas.xmlsoap.org/soap/http"/>
            <operation name="GetTradePrice">
                <soap:operation
soapAction="http://example.com/GetTradePrice"/>
                <input>
                    <soap:body use="encoded"
namespace="http://example.com/stockquote"
encodingStyle= "http://schemas.xmlsoap .org/soap/encoding/"/>
                </input>
                <output>
                    <soap:body use="encoded"
namespace="http://example .com/stockquote" encodingStyle=
"http://schemas.xmlsoap .org/soap/encoding/"/>
                </output>
            </operation>>
        </binding>
        <service name="StockQuoteService">
            <documentation>My first service</documentation>
            <port name="StockQuotePort" binding="tns:StockQuote
              Binding">
                <soap:address location="http://example.com/stockquote"/>
            </port>
        </service>
</definitions>
```

This example describes that a GetTradePrices SOAP 1.1 request may be sent to a StockQuote service via the SOAP 1.1 HTTP binding. The request takes a stock quote symbol string, an application defined TimePeriod structure containing a start and end time and returns an array of stock prices recorded by the service within that period of time, as well as the frequency at which they were recorded as the SOAP response. The RPC signature that corresponds to this service has in parameters tickerSymbol and timePeriod followed by the output parameter frequency, and returns an array of floats.

Example 5.   SOAP binding of request-response RPC operation over HTTP

```xml
<?xml version="1.0"?>
<definitions name="StockQuote"
targetNamespace="http://example.com/stockquote.wsdl"
          xmlns:tns="http://example.com/stockquote.wsdl"
          xmlns:xsd="http://www.w3.org/2000/10/XMLSchema"
          xmlns:xsd1="http://example.com/stockquote/schema"
          xmlns:soap="http://schemas.xmlsoap.org/wsdl/soap/"
          xmlns:soapenc="http://schemas.xmlsoap.org/soap/
            encoding/"
          xmlns="http://schemas.xmlsoap.org/wsdl/">
   <types>
     <schema targetNamespace="http://example.com/stockquote/
       schema"
             xmlns="http://www.w3.org/2000/10/XMLSchema">
       <complexType name="TimePeriod">
          <all>
              <element name="startTime" type="xsd:time
                Instant"/>
              <element name="endTime" type="xsd:timeInstant"/>
          </all>
       </complexType>
       <complexType name="ArrayOfFloat">
          <complexContent>
              <restriction base="soapenc:Array">
                  <attribute ref="soapenc:arrayType"
wsdl:arrayType="xsd:float[]"/>
              </restriction>
          </complexContent>
       </complexType>
     </schema>
   </types>
   <message name="GetTradePricesInput">
       <part name="tickerSymbol" element="xsd:string"/>
       <part name="timePeriod" element="xsd1:TimePeriod"/>
   </message>
```

```
<message name="GetTradePricesOutput">
    <part name="result" type="xsd1:ArrayOfFloat"/>
    <part name="frequency" type="xsd:float"/>
</message>
<portType name="StockQuotePortType">
    <operation name="GetLastTradePrice" parameterOrder=
      "tickerSymbol timePeriod frequency">
        <input message="tns:GetTradePricesInput"/>
        <output message="tns:GetTradePricesOutput"/>
    </operation>
</portType>
<binding name="StockQuoteSoapBinding"
type="tns:StockQuotePortType">
    <soap:binding style="rpc"
transport="http://schemas.xmlsoap.org/soap/http"/>
    <operation name="GetTradePrices">
        <soap:operation
soapAction="http://example.com/GetTradePrices"/>
        <input>
            <soap:body use="encoded"
namespace="http://example.com/stockquote"
encodingStyle="http://schemas.xmlsoap.org/soap/encoding/"/>
        </input>
        <output>
            <soap:body use="encoded"
namespace="http://example.com/stockquote"
encodingStyle="http://schemas.xmlsoap.org/soap/encoding/"/>
        </output>
    </operation>>
</binding>
<service name="StockQuoteService">
    <documentation>My first service</documentation>
    <port name="StockQuotePort" binding="tns:StockQuote-
      Binding">
        <soap:address location="http://example.com/stockquote"/>
    </port>
</service>
</definitions>
```

3.2   How the SOAP Binding Extends WSDL

The SOAP Binding extends WSDL with the following extension elements:

```
<definitions .... >
   <binding .... >
```

```
<soap:binding style="rpc|document" transport="uri">
<operation .... >
    <soap:operation soapAction="uri"? style="rpc|
      document"?>?
    <input>
        <soap:body parts="nmtokens"? use="literal|encoded"
                    encodingStyle="uri-list"? namespace =
                      "uri"?>
        <soap:header message="qname" part="nmtoken"
use="literal|encoded"
                              encodingStyle="uri-list"? namespace=
                                "uri"?>*
            <soap:headerfault message="qname" part="nmtoken"
use="literal|encoded"
                                        encodingStyle="uri-list"?
namespace="uri"?/>*
        <soap:header>
    </input>
    <output>
        <soap:body parts="nmtokens"? use="literal|encoded"
                    encodingStyle="uri-list"? namespace=
                      "uri"?>
        <soap:header message="qname" part="nmtoken"
use="literal|encoded"
                              encodingStyle="uri-list"? namespace=
                                "uri"?>*
            <soap:headerfault message="qname" part="nmtoken"
use="literal|encoded"
                                        encodingStyle="uri-list"?
namespace="uri"?/>*
        <soap:header>
    </output>
    <fault>*
        <soap:fault name="nmtoken" use="literal|encoded"
                    encodingStyle="uri-list"? namespace=
                      "uri"?>
    </fault>
</operation>
</binding>
<port .... >
    <soap:address location="uri"/>
</port>
</definitions>
```

Each extension element of the SOAP binding is covered in subsequent sections.

3.3   soap:binding

The purpose of the SOAP binding element is to signify that the binding is bound to the SOAP protocol format: Envelope, Header and Body. This element makes no claims as to the encoding or format of the message (e.g. that it necessarily follows section 5 of the SOAP 1.1 specification).

The soap:binding element MUST be present when using the SOAP binding.

```
<definitions .... >
   <binding .... >
       <soap:binding transport="uri"? style="rpc|document"?>
   </binding>
</definitions>
```

The value of the **style** attribute is the default for the style attribute for each contained operation. If the style attribute is omitted, it is assumed to be "document". See section 3.4 for more information on the semantics of style.

The value of the required **transport** attribute indicates which transport of SOAP this binding corresponds to. The URI value **http://schemas.xmlsoap.org/ soap/http** corresponds to the HTTP binding in the SOAP specification. Other URIs may be used here to indicate other transports (such as SMTP, FTP, etc.).

3.4   soap:operation

The soap:operation element provides information for the operation as a whole.

```
<definitions .... >
   <binding .... >
       <operation .... >
           <soap:operation soapAction="uri"? style="rpc|
             document"?>?
       </operation>
   </binding>
</definitions>
```

The **style** attribute indicates whether the operation is RPC-oriented (messages containing parameters and return values) or document-oriented (message containing document(s)). This information may be used to select an appropriate programming model. The value of this attribute also affects the way in which the Body of the SOAP message is constructed, as explained in Section 3.5 below. If the attribute is not specified, it defaults to the value specified in the soap:binding element. If the soap:binding element does not specify a style, it is assumed to be "document".

The **soapAction** attribute specifies the value of the SOAPAction header for this operation. This URI value should be used directly as the value for the SOAP-Action header; no attempt should be made to make a relative URI value absolute when making the request. For the HTTP protocol binding of SOAP, this is value required (it has no default value). For other SOAP protocol bindings, it MUST NOT be specified, and the soap:operation element MAY be omitted.

3.5   soap:body

The soap:body element specifies how the message parts appear inside the SOAP Body element.

The parts of a message may either be abstract type definitions, or concrete schema definitions. If abstract definitions, the types are serialized according to some set of rules defined by an encoding style. Each encoding style is identified using a list of URIs, as in the SOAP specification. Since some encoding styles such as the SOAP Encoding (http://schemas.xmlsoap.org/soap/encoding/) allow variation in the message format for a given set of abstract types, it is up to the reader of the message to understand all the format variations: "reader makes right". To avoid having to support all variations, a message may be defined concretely and then indicate it's original encoding style (if any) as a hint. In this case, the writer of the message must conform exactly to the specified schema: "writer makes right".

The soap:body binding element provides information on how to assemble the different message parts inside the Body element of the SOAP message. The soap:body element is used in both RPC-oriented and document-oriented messages, but the style of the enclosing operation has important effects on how the Body section is structured:

▼ If the operation style is rpc each part is a parameter or a return value and appears inside a wrapper element within the body (following Section 7.1 of the SOAP specification). The wrapper element is named identically to the operation name and its namespace is the value of the namespace attribute. Each message part (parameter) appears under the wrapper, represented by an accessor named identically to the corresponding parameter of the call. Parts are arranged in the same order as the parameters of the call.

▼ If the operation style is document there are no additional wrappers, and the message parts appear directly under the SOAP Body element.

The same mechanisms are used to define the content of the Body and parameter accessor elements.

```
<definitions .... >
    <binding .... >
        <operation .... >
            <input>
                <soap:body parts="nmtokens"? use="literal|encoded"?
                            encodingStyle="uri-list"? namespace=
                            "uri"?>
            </input>
            <output>
                <soap:body parts="nmtokens"? use="literal|encoded"?
                            encodingStyle="uri-list"? namespace
                            ="uri"?>
            </output>
        </operation>
    </binding>
</definitions>
```

The optional **parts** attribute of type nmtokens indicates which parts appear somewhere within the SOAP Body portion of the message (other parts of a message may appear in other portions of the message such as when SOAP is used in conjunction with the multipart/related MIME binding). If the parts attribute is omitted, then all parts defined by the message are assumed to be included in the SOAP Body portion.

The required **use** attribute indicates whether the message parts are encoded using some encoding rules, or whether the parts define the concrete schema of the message.

If use is **encoded,** then each message part references an abstract type using the **type** attribute. These abstract types are used to produce a concrete message by applying an encoding specified by the **encodingStyle** attribute. The part **names, types** and value of the **namespace** attribute are all inputs to the encoding, although the namespace attribute only applies to content not explicitly defined by the abstract types. If the referenced encoding style allows variations in it's format (such as the SOAP encoding does), then all variations MUST be supported ("reader makes right").

If use is **literal,** then each part references a concrete schema definition using either the **element** or **type** attribute. In the first case, the element referenced by the part will appear directly under the Body element (for document style bindings) or under an accessor element named after the message part (in rpc style). In the second, the type referenced by the part becomes the schema type of the enclosing element (Body for document style or part accessor element for rpc style).

For an example that illustrates defining the contents of a composite Body using a type, see section 2.3.1. The value of the **encodingStyle** attribute MAY be used when the use is literal to indicate that the concrete format was derived using a particular encoding (such as the SOAP encoding), but that only the specified variation is supported ("writer makes right").

The value of the **encodingStyle** attribute is a list of URIs, each separated by a single space. The URI's represent encodings used within the message, in order from most restrictive to least restrictive (exactly like the encodingStyle attribute defined in the SOAP specification).

3.6   soap:fault

The soap:fault element specifies the contents of the contents of the SOAP Fault Details element. It is patterned after the soap:body element (see section 3.5).

```
<definitions .... >
   <binding .... >
       <operation .... >
          <fault>*
             <soap:fault name="nmtoken" use="literal|encoded"
                         encodingStyle="uri-list"?
namespace="uri"?>
          </fault>
       </operation>
   </binding>
</definitions>
```

The **name** attribute relates the soap:fault to the wsdl:fault defined for the operation.

The fault message MUST have a single part. The **use, encodingStyle** and **namespace** attributes are all used in the same way as with soap:body (see section 3.5), only style="document" is assumed since faults do not contain parameters.

3.7   soap:header and soap:headerfault

The soap:header and soap:headerfault elements allows header to be defined that are transmitted inside the Header element of the SOAP Envelope. It is patterned after the soap:body element (see section 3.5).

It is not necessary to exhaustively list all headers that appear in the SOAP Envelope using soap:header. For example, extensions (see section 2.1.3) to WSDL may imply specific headers should be added to the actual payload and it is not required to list those headers here.

```
<definitions .... >
   <binding .... >
       <operation .... >
          <input>
             <soap:header message="qname" part="nmtoken"
use="literal|encoded"
                          encodingStyle="uri-list"? namespace=
                          "uri"?>*
             <soap:headerfault message="qname" part="nmtoken"
use="literal|encoded"
                                 encodingStyle="uri-list"?
namespace="uri"?/>*
             <soap:header>
          </input>
          <output>
             <soap:header message="qname" part="nmtoken"
use="literal|encoded"
                          encodingStyle="uri-list"? namespace=
                          "uri"?>*
             <soap:headerfault message="qname" part="nmtoken"
use="literal|encoded"
                                  encodingStyle="uri-list"?
namespace="uri"?/>*
             <soap:header>
          </output>
       </operation>
   </binding>
</definitions>
```

The **use**, **encodingStyle** and **namespace** attributes are all used in the same way as with soap:body (see section 3.5), only style="document" is assumed since headers do not contain parameters.

Together, the **message** attribute (of type QName) and the **part** attribute (of type nmtoken) reference the message part that defines the header type. The schema referenced by the part MAY include definitions for the soap:actor and soap:mustUnderstand attributes if use="literal", but MUST NOT if use=" encoded". The referenced message need not be the same as the message that defines the SOAP Body.

The optional **headerfault** elements which appear inside soap:header and have the same syntax as soap:header) allows specification of the header type(s) that are used to transmit error information pertaining to the header defined by the soap:header. The SOAP specification states that errors pertaining to headers must be returned in headers, and this mechanism allows specification of the format of such headers.

3.8 soap:address

The SOAP address binding is used to give a port an address (a URI). A port using the SOAP binding MUST specify exactly one address. The URI scheme specified for the address must correspond to the transport specified by the soap:binding.

```
<definitions .... >
   <port .... >
      <binding .... >
         <soap:address location="uri"/>
      </binding>
   </port>
</definitions>
```

4. HTTP GET & POST Binding

WSDL includes a binding for HTTP 1.1's GET and POST verbs in order to describe the interaction between a Web Browser and a web site. This allows applications other than Web Browsers to interact with the site. The following protocol specific information may be specified:

▼ An indication that a binding uses HTTP GET or POST

▼ An address for the port

▼ A relative address for each operation (relative to the base address defined by the port)

4.1 HTTP GET/POST Examples

The following example shows three ports that are bound differently for a given port type.

If the values being passed are part1=1, part2=2, part3=3, the request format would be as follows for each port:

```
 port1: GET, URL="http://example.com/o1/A1B2/3"
port2: GET, URL="http://example.com/o1?p1=1&p2=2&p3=3"
port3: POST, URL="http://example.com/o1", PAYLOAD="p1=1&p2=2&p3=3"
```

For each port, the response is either a GIF or a JPEG image.

Example 6.   GET and FORM POST returning GIF or JPG

```
<definitions .... >
    <message name="m1">
        <part name="part1" type="xsd:string"/>
        <part name="part2" type="xsd:int"/>
        <part name="part3" type="xsd:string"/>
    </message>
    <message name="m2">
        <part name="image" type="xsd:binary"/>
    </message>
    <portType name="pt1">
        <operation name="o1">
            <input message="tns:m1"/>
            <output message="tns:m2"/>
        </operation>
    </portType>
    <service name="service1">
        <port name="port1" binding="tns:b1">
            <http:address location="http://example.com/"/>
        </port>
        <port name="port2" binding="tns:b2">
            <http:address location="http://example.com/"/>
        </port>
        <port name="port3" binding="tns:b3">
            <http:address location="http://example.com/"/>
        </port>
    </service>
    <binding name="b1" type="pt1">
        <http:binding verb="GET"/>
        <operation name="o1">
            <http:operation location="o1/A(part1)B(part2)/(part3)"/>
            <input>
                <http:urlReplacement/>
            </input>
            <output>
                <mime:content type="image/gif"/>
                <mime:content type="image/jpeg"/>
            </output>
        </operation>
    </binding>
    <binding name="b2" type="pt1">
        <http:binding verb="GET"/>
        <operation name="o1">
            <http:operation location="o1"/>
            <input>
```

```
                <http:urlEncoded/>
            </input>
            <output>
                <mime:content type="image/gif"/>
                <mime:content type="image/jpeg"/>
            </output>
        </operation>
    </binding>
    <binding name="b3" type="pt1">
        <http:binding verb="POST"/>
        <operation name="o1">
            <http:operation location="o1"/>
            <input>
                <mime:content type="application/x-www-form-
                    urlencoded"/>
            </input>
            <output>
                <mime:content type="image/gif"/>
                <mime:content type="image/jpeg"/>
            </output>
        </operation>
    </binding>
</definitions>
```

4.2 How the HTTP GET/POST Binding Extends WSDL

The HTTP GET/POST Binding extends WSDL with the following extension elements:

```
<definitions .... >
    <binding .... >
        <http:binding verb="nmtoken"/>
        <operation .... >
            <http:operation location="uri"/>
            <input .... >
                <-- mime elements -->
            </input>
            <output .... >
                <-- mime elements -->
            </output>
        </operation>
    </binding>
    <port .... >
        <http:address location="uri"/>
    </port>
</definitions>
```

These elements are covered in the subsequent sections.

4.3   http:address

The **location** attribute specifies the base URI for the port. The value of the attribute is combined with the values of the location attribute of the http:operation binding element. See <u>section 4.5</u> for more details.

4.4   http:binding

The **http:binding** element indicates that this binding uses the HTTP protocol.

```
<definitions .... >
   <binding .... >
       <http:binding verb="nmtoken"/>
   </binding>
</definitions>
```

The value of the required **verb** attribute indicates the HTTP verb. Common values are GET or POST, but others may be used. Note that HTTP verbs are case sensitive.

4.5   http:operation

The **location** attribute specifies a relative URI for the operation. This URI is combined with the URI specified in the http:address element to form the full URI for the HTTP request. The URI value MUST be a relative URI.

```
<definitions .... >
   <binding .... >
       <operation .... >
           <http:operation location="uri"/>
       </operation>
   </binding>
</definitions>
```

4.6   http:urlEncoded

The urlEncoded element indicates that all the message parts are encoded into the HTTP request URI using the standard URI-encoding rules (name1=value&name2 =value...). The names of the parameters correspond to the names of the message parts. Each value contributed by the part is encoded using a name=value pair.

This may be used with GET to specify URL encoding, or with POST to specify a FORM-POST. For GET, the "?" character is automatically appended as necessary.

```
<http:urlEncoded/>
```

For more information on the rules for URI-encoding parameters, see [5], [6], and [7].

4.7   http:urlReplacement

The **http:urlReplacement** element indicates that all the message parts are encoded into the HTTP request URI using a replacement algorithm:

▼ The relative URI value of http:operation is searched for a set of search patterns.

▼ The search occurs before the value of the http:operation is combined with the value of the location attribute from http:address.

▼ There is one search pattern for each message part. The search pattern string is the name of the message part surrounded with parenthesis "(" and ")".

▼ For each match, the value of the corresponding message part is substituted for the match at the location of the match.

▼ Matches are performed before any values are replaced (replaced values do not trigger additional matches).

Message parts MUST NOT have repeating values.

```
<http:urlReplacement/>
```

5.   MIME Binding

WSDL includes a way to bind abstract types to concrete messages in some MIME format. Bindings for the following MIME types are defined:

▼ multipart/related

▼ text/xml

▼ application/x-www-form-urlencoded (the format used to submit a form in HTML)

▼ Others (by specifying the MIME type string)

The set of defined MIME types is both large and evolving, so it is not a goal for WSDL to exhaustively define XML grammar for each MIME type. Nothing precludes additional grammar to be added to define additional MIME types as necessary. If a MIME type string is sufficient to describe the content, the mime element defined below can be used.

5.11   MIME Binding example

Example 7.   Using multipart/related with SOAP

This example describes that a GetCompanyInfo SOAP 1.1 request may be sent to a StockQuote service via the SOAP 1.1 HTTP binding. The request takes a ticker symbol of type string. The response contains multiple parts encoded in the MIME format multipart/related: a SOAP Envelope containing the current stock price as a float, zero or more marketing literature documents in HTML format, and an optional company logo in either GIF or JPEG format.

```
<definitions .... >
   <types>
       <schema .... >
          <element name="GetCompanyInfo">
              <complexType>
                 <all>
                     <element name="tickerSymbol "
                        type="string"/>
                 </all>
              </complexType>
          </element>
          <element name="GetCompanyInfoResult">
              <complexType>
                 <all>
                     <element name="result" type="float"/>
                 </all>
              </complexType>
          </element>
          <complexType name="ArrayOfBinary">
              <complexContent>
                  <restriction base="soapenc:Array">
                     <attribute ref="soapenc:arrayType"
wsdl:arrayType="xsd:binary[]"/>
                  </restriction>
              <complexContent>
```

```
            </complexType>
        </schema>
    </types>
    <message name="m1">
        <part name="body" element="tns:GetCompanyInfo"/>
    </message>
    <message name="m2">
        <part name="body" element="tns:GetCompanyInfoResult"/>
        <part name="docs" type="xsd:string"/>
        <part name="logo" type="tns:ArrayOfBinary"/>
    </message>
    <portType name="pt1">
        <operation name="GetCompanyInfo">
            <input message="m1"/>
            <output message="m2"/>
        </operation>
    </portType>
    <binding name="b1" type="tns:pt1">
        <operation name="GetCompanyInfo">
            <soap:operation
soapAction="http://example.com/Get-CompanyInfo"/>
            <input>
                <soap:body use="literal"/>
            </input>
            <output>
                <mime:multipartRelated>
                    <mime:part>
                        <soap:body parts="body" use="literal"/>
                    </mime:part>
                    <mime:part>
                        <mime:content part="docs" type="text/html"/>
                    </mime:part>
                    <mime:part>
                        <mime:content part="logo" type="image/gif"/>
                        <mime:content part="logo" type="image/
                          jpeg"/>
                    </mime:part>
                </mime:multipartRelated>
            </output>
        </operation>
    </binding>
    <service name="CompanyInfoService">
        <port name="CompanyInfoPort"binding="tns:b1">
            <soap:address location="http://example.com/company
              info"/>
        </port>
    </service>
</definitions>
```

5.2 How the MIME Binding extends WSDL

The MIME Binding extends WSDL with the following extension elements:

```
 <mime:content part="nmtoken"? type="string"?/>
<mime:multipartRelated>
    <mime:part> *
        <-- mime element -->
    </mime:part>
</mime:multipartRelated>

<mime:mimeXml part="nmtoken"?/>
```

They are used at the following locations in WSDL:

```
<definitions .... >
    <binding .... >
        <operation .... >
            <input .... >
                <-- mime elements -->
            </input>
            <output .... >
                <-- mime elements -->
            </output>
        </operation>
    </binding>
</definitions>
```

MIME elements appear under input and output to specify the MIME format. If multiple appear, they are considered to be alternatives.

5.3 mime:content

To avoid having to define a new element for every MIME format, the **mime:content** element may be used if there is no additional information to convey about the format other than its MIME type string.

```
<mime:content part="nmtoken"? type="string"?/>
```

The **part** attribute is used to specify the name of the message part. If the message has a single part, then the part attribute is optional. The **type** attribute contains the MIME type string. A type value has two portions, separated by a slash (/), either of which may be a wildcard (*). Not specifying the type attribute indicates that all MIME types are acceptable.

If the return format is XML, but the schema is not known ahead of time, the generic mime element can be used indicating text/xml:

```
<mime:content type="text/xml"/>
```

A wildcard (*) can be used to specify a family of mime types, for example all text types.

```
<mime:content type="text/*"/>
```

The following two examples both specify all mime types:

```
<mime:content type="*/*"/>
<mime:content/>
```

5.4   mime:multipartRelated

The multipart/related MIME type aggregates an arbitrary set of MIME format-ted parts into one message using the MIME type "multipart/related". The **mime:-multipartRelated** element describes the concrete format of such a message:

```
<mime:multipartRelated>
    <mime:part> *
        <-- mime element -->
    </mime:part>
</mime:multipartRelated>
```

The **mime:part** element describes each part of a multipart/related message. MIME elements appear within **mime:part** to specify the concrete MIME type for the part. If more than one MIME element appears inside a mime:part, they are alternatives.

5.5   soap:body

When using the MIME binding with SOAP requests, it is legal to use the soap: body element as a MIME element. It indicates the content type is "text/xml", and there is an enclosing SOAP Envelope.

5.6   mime:mimeXml

To specify XML payloads that are not SOAP compliant (do not have a SOAP En-velope), but do have a particular schema, the **mime:mimeXml** element may be used to specify that concrete schema. The **part** attribute refers to a message part defining the concrete schema of the root XML element. The part attribute MAY be omitted if the message has only a single part. The part references a concrete schema using the **element** attribute for simple parts or **type** attribute for composite parts (see section 2.3.1).

```
<mime:mimeXml part="nmtoken"?/>
```

6. References

[2] S. Bradner, "Key words for use in RFCs to Indicate Requirement Levels", RFC 2119, Harvard University, March 1997

[4] T. Berners-Lee, R. Fielding, L. Masinter, "Uniform Resource Identifiers (URI): Generic Syntax", RFC 2396, MIT/LCS, U.C. Irvine, Xerox Corporation, August 1998.

[5] http://www.w3.org/TR/html401/interact/forms.html - submit-format

[6] http://www.w3.org/TR/html401/appendix/notes.html - ampersands-in-uris

[7] http://www.w3.org/TR/html401/interact/forms.html - h-17.13.4

[8] Simple Object Access Protocol (SOAP) 1.1 "http://www.w3.org/TR/2000/NOTE-SOAP-20000508/"

[10] W3C Working Draft "XML Schema Part 1: Structures". This is work in progress.

[11] W3C Working Draft "XML Schema Part 2: Datatypes". This is work in progress.

A 1. Notes on URIs

This section does not directly contribute to the specification, but provide background that may be useful when implementing the specification.

A 1.1   XML namespaces & schema locations

It is a common misperception to equate the targetNamespace of an XML schema or the value of the *xmlns* attribute in XML instances with the location of the corresponding schema. Since namespaces are in fact URIs, and URIs may be locations, and you may be able to retrieve a schema from that location, it does not mean that is the only schema that is associated with that namespace. There can be multiple schemas associated with a particular namespace, and it is up to a processor of XML to determine which one to use in a particular processing context. The WSDL specification provides the processing context here via the *<import>* mechanism, which is based on the XML schemas grammar for the similar concept.

A 1.2   Relative URIs

Throughout this document you see fully qualified URIs used in WSDL and XSD documents. The use of a fully qualified URI is simply to illustrate the referencing concepts. The use of relative URIs is completely allowed and is warranted in many cases. For information on processing relative URIs, see http://www. normos.org/ietf/rfc/rfc2396.txt.

A 1.3   Generating URIs

When working with WSDL, it is sometimes desirable to make up a URI for an entity, but not make the URI globally unique for all time and have it "mean" that version of the entity (schema, WSDL document, etc.). There is a particular URI base reserved for use for this type of behavior. The base URI "http:// tempuri.org/" can be used to construct a URI without any unique association to an entity. For example, two people or programs could choose to simultaneously use the URI "http://tempuri.org/myschema" for two completely different schemas, and as long as the scope of the use of the URIs does not intersect, then they are considered unique enough. This has the further benefit that the entity referred to by the URI can be versioned without having to generate a new URI, as long as it makes sense within the processing context. It is not recommended that "http://tempuri.org/" be used as a base for stable, fixed entities.

A 2. Wire format for WSDL examples

A 2.1. Example 1

SOAP Message Embedded in HTTP Request

```
POST /StockQuote HTTP/1.1
Host: www.stockquoteserver.com
Content-Type: text/xml; charset="utf-8"
Content-Length: nnnn
SOAPAction: "Some-URI"
<soapenv:Envelope
xmlns:soapenv="http://schemas.xmlsoap.org/soap/envelope/">
    <soapenv:Body>
        <m:GetLastTradePrice xmlns:m="Some-URI">
            <m:tickerSymbol>DIS</m:tickerSymbol>
        </m:GetLastTradePrice>
    </soapenv:Body>
</soapenv:Envelope>
```

SOAP Message Embedded in HTTP Response

```
HTTP/1.1 200 OK
Content-Type: text/xml; charset="utf-8"
Content-Length: nnnn
<soapenv:Envelope
xmlns:soapenv="http://schemas.xmlsoap.org/soap/envelope/">
    <soapenv:Body>
        <m:GetLastTradePriceResponse xmlns:m="Some-URI">
            <m:price>34.5</m:price>
        </m:GetLastTradePriceResponse>
    </soapenv:Body>
</soapenv:Envelope>
```

A 3.   Location of Extensibility Elements

Extensibility elements can appear at the following locations in a WSDL document:

Location	Meaning	Possible usage
definitions	The extensibility element applies to the WSDL document as a whole.	• Introduce additional information or definitions to a WSDLdocument as a whole.
definitions/types	The extensibility element is a type system.	• Specify the format of the message in a type system other than XSD.
definitions/service	The extensibility element applies to the service.	• Introduce additional information or definitions for the service.
definitions/service/ port	The extensibility element applies to the port.	• Specify an address for the port.
definitions/binding	The extensibility element applies to the binding as a whole.	• Provide protocol specific information that applies to all the operations in the port type being bound.
definitions/binding/ operation	The extensibility element applies to the operation as a whole.	• Provide protocol specific information that applies to both the input message and the output message.
definitions/binding/ operation/input	The extensibility element applies to the input message for the operation.	• Provide details on how abstract message parts map into the concrete protocol and data formats of the binding. • Provide additional protocol specific information for the input message.

| definitions/binding/ operation/output | The extensibility element applies to the output message of the operation. | • Provide details on how abstract message parts map into the concrete protocol and data formats of the binding.
• Provide additional protocol specific information for the output message. |
| definitions/binding/ operation/fault | The extensibility element applies to a fault message of the operation. | • Provide details on how ab stract message parts map into the concrete protocol and data formats of the binding.
• Provide additional protocol specific information for the fault message. |

A 4.   Schemas

A 4.1   WSDL Schema

```
<schema xmlns="http://www.w3.org/2000/10/XMLSchema"
        xmlns:wsdl="http://schemas.xmlsoap.org/wsdl/"
        targetNamespace="http://schemas.xmlsoap.org/wsdl/"
        elementFormDefault="qualified">
   <element name="documentation">
      <complexType mixed="true">
         <choice minOccurs="0" maxOccurs="unbounded">
            <any minOccurs="0" maxOccurs="unbounded"/>
         </choice>
         <anyAttribute/>
      </complexType>
   </element>
   <complexType name="documented" abstract="true">
      <sequence>
         <element ref="wsdl:documentation" minOccurs="0"/>
      </sequence>
   </complexType>
   <complexType name="openAtts" abstract="true">
      <annotation>
         <documentation>
         This type is extended by  component types
         to allow attributes from other namespaces to be added.
         </documentation>
```

```
    </annotation>
    <sequence>
       <element ref="wsdl:documentation" minOccurs="0"/>
    </sequence>
    <anyAttribute namespace="##other"/>
 </complexType>
 <element name="definitions" type="wsdl:definitionsType">
    <key name="message">
       <selector xpath="message"/>
       <field xpath="@name"/>
    </key>
    <key name="portType">
       <selector xpath="portType"/>
       <field xpath="@name"/>
    </key>
    <key name="binding">
       <selector xpath="binding"/>
       <field xpath="@name"/>
    </key>
    <key name="service">
       <selector xpath="service"/>
       <field xpath="@name"/>
    </key>
    <key name="import">
          <selector xpath="import"/>
          <field xpath="@namespace"/>
       </key>
    <key name="port">
       <selector xpath="service/port"/>
       <field xpath="@name"/>
    </key>
 </element>
 <complexType name="definitionsType">
    <complexContent>
       <extension base="wsdl:documented">
          <sequence>
             <element ref="wsdl:import"
minOccurs="0"maxOccurs="unbounded"/>
             <element ref="wsdl:types" minOccurs="0"/>
             <element ref="wsdl:message" minOccurs="0"
maxOccurs="unbounded"/>
             <element ref="wsdl:portType" minOccurs="0"
maxOccurs="unbounded"/>
             <element ref="wsdl:binding" minOccurs="0"
maxOccurs="unbounded"/>
             <element ref="wsdl:service" minOccurs="0"
maxOccurs="unbounded"/>
```

```
                        <any namespace="##other" minOccurs="0"
maxOccurs="unbounded">
                            <annotation>
                                <documentation>to support extensibility
                                    elements
</documentation>
                            </annotation>
                        </any>
                    </sequence>
                    <attribute name="targetNamespace" type="uriReference"
use="optional"/>
                        <attribute name="name" type="NMTOKEN" use="optional"/>
                    </extension>
                </complexContent>
            </complexType>
            <element name="import" type="wsdl:importType"/>
            <complexType name="importType">
                <complexContent>
            <extension base="wsdl:documented">
            <attribute name="namespace" type="uriReference" use="required"/>
                <attribute name="location" type="uriReference" use=
                    "required"/>
            </extension>
        </complexContent>
        </complexType>
            <element name="types" type="wsdl:typesType"/>
            <complexType name="typesType">
                <complexContent>
            <extension base="wsdl:documented">
            <sequence>
            <any namespace="##other" minOccurs="0" maxOccurs="unbounded"/>
        </sequence>
            </extension>
        </complexContent>
        </complexType>
            <element name="message" type="wsdl:messageType">
                <unique name="part">
                    <selector xpath="part"/>
                    <field xpath="@name"/>
                </unique>
            </element>
            <complexType name="messageType">
                <complexContent>
            <extension base="wsdl:documented">
            <sequence>
            <element ref="wsdl:part" minOccurs="0" maxOccurs="unbounded"/>
        </sequence>
                <attribute name="name" type="NCName" use="required"/>
```

```
  </extension>
 </complexContent>
</complexType>
 <element name="part" type="wsdl:partType"/>
 <complexType name="partType">
    <complexContent>
 <extension base="wsdl:openAtts">
 <attribute name="name" type="NMTOKEN" use="optional"/>
    <attribute name="type" type="QName" use="optional"/>
    <attribute name="element" type="QName" use="optional"/>
 </extension>
</complexContent>
</complexType>
 <element name="portType" type="wsdl:portTypeType"/>
 <complexType name="portTypeType">
    <complexContent>
 <extension base="wsdl:documented">
 <sequence>
 <element ref="wsdl:operation" minOccurs="0" maxOccurs=
   "unbounded"/>
</sequence>
    <attribute name="name" type="NCName" use="required"/>
 </extension>
</complexContent>
</complexType>
 <element name="operation" type="wsdl:operationType"/>
 <complexType name="operationType">
    <complexContent>
 <extension base="wsdl:documented">
    <choice>
       <group ref="wsdl:one-way-operation"/>
       <group ref="wsdl:request-response-operation"/>
       <group ref="wsdl:solicit-response-operation"/>
       <group ref="wsdl:notification-operation"/>
    </choice>
    <attribute name="name" type="NCName" use="required"/>
 </extension>
</complexContent>
</complexType>
 <group name="one-way-operation">
    <sequence>
       <element ref="wsdl:input"/>
    </sequence>
 </group>
 <group name="request-response-operation">
    <sequence>
       <element ref="wsdl:input"/>
```

```
         <element ref="wsdl:output"/>
         <element ref="wsdl:fault" minOccurs="0" maxOccurs=
           "unbounded"/>
     </sequence>
 </group>
 <group name="solicit-response-operation">
     <sequence>
         <element ref="wsdl:output"/>
         <element ref="wsdl:input"/>
         <element ref="wsdl:fault" minOccurs="0" maxOccurs=
           "unbounded"/>
     </sequence>
 </group>
 <group name="notification-operation">
     <sequence>
         <element ref="wsdl:output"/>
     </sequence>
 </group>
 <element name="input" type="wsdl:paramType"/>
 <element name="output" type="wsdl:paramType"/>
 <element name="fault" type="wsdl:faultType"/>
 <complexType name="paramType">
     <complexContent>
 <extension base="wsdl:documented">
 <attribute name="name" type="NMTOKEN" use="optional"/>
     <attribute name="message" type="QName" use="required"/>
 </extension>
 </complexContent>
 </complexType>
 <complexType name="faultType">
     <complexContent>
 <extension base="wsdl:documented">
 <attribute name="name" type="NMTOKEN" use="required"/>
     <attribute name="message" type="QName" use="required"/>
 </extension>
 </complexContent>
 </complexType>
 <complexType name="startWithExtensionsType" abstract="true">
     <complexContent>
 <extension base="wsdl:documented">
 <sequence>
 <any namespace="##other" minOccurs="0" maxOccurs="unbounded"/>
 </sequence>
 </extension>
 </complexContent>
 </complexType>
 <element name="binding" type="wsdl:bindingType"/>
```

```
<complexType name="bindingType">
    <complexContent>
<extension base="wsdl:startWithExtensionsType">
<sequence>
<element name="operation" type="wsdl:binding_operationType"
minOccurs="0" maxOccurs="unbounded"/>
 </sequence>
    <attribute name="name" type="NCName" use="required"/>
    <attribute name="type" type="QName" use="required"/>
 </extension>
</complexContent>
</complexType>
 <complexType name="binding_operationType">
    <complexContent>
<extension base="wsdl:startWithExtensionsType">
<sequence>
<element name="input" type="wsdl:startWithExtensionsType"
minOccurs="0"/>
    <element name="output" type="wsdl:startWithExtensionsType"
minOccurs="0"/>
    <element name="fault" minOccurs="0" maxOccurs="unbounded">
        <complexType>
            <complexContent>
<extension base="wsdl:startWithExtensionsType">
<attribute name="name" type="NMTOKEN" use="required"/>
        </extension>
 </complexContent>
</complexType>
    </element>
 </sequence>
    <attribute name="name" type="NCName" use="required"/>
 </extension>
</complexContent>
</complexType>
 <element name="service" type="wsdl:serviceType"/>
 <complexType name="serviceType">
    <complexContent>
<extension base="wsdl:documented">
<sequence>
<element ref="wsdl:port" minOccurs="0" maxOccurs="unbounded"/>
    <any namespace="##other" minOccurs="0"/>
 </sequence>
    <attribute name="name" type="NCName" use="required"/>
 </extension>
</complexContent>
</complexType>
 <element name="port" type="wsdl:portType"/>
```

```
<complexType name="portType">
   <complexContent>
<extension base="wsdl:documented">
<sequence>
<any namespace="##other" minOccurs="0"/>
</sequence>
      <attribute name="name" type="NCName" use="required"/>
      <attribute name="binding" type="QName" use="required"/>
   </extension>
</complexContent>
</complexType>
<attribute name="arrayType" type="string"/>
</schema>
```

A 4.2   SOAP Binding Schema

```
<schema xmlns="http://www.w3.org/2000/10/XMLSchema"
        xmlns:soap="http://schemas.xmlsoap.org/wsdl/soap/"
        targetNamespace="http://schemas.xmlsoap.org/wsdl/soap/">
   <element name="binding" type="soap:bindingType"/>
   <complexType name="bindingType">
      <attribute name="transport" type="uriReference" use=
        "optional"/>
      <attribute name="style" type="soap:styleChoice" use=
        "optional"/>
   </complexType>
   <simpleType name="styleChoice">
      <restriction base="string">
   <enumeration value="rpc"/>
      <enumeration value="document"/>
 </restriction>
   </simpleType>
   <element name="operation" type="soap:operationType"/>
   <complexType name="operationType">
      <attribute name="soapAction" type="uriReference" use=
        "optional"/>
      <attribute name="style" type="soap:styleChoice" use=
        "optional"/>
   </complexType>
   <element name="body" type="soap:bodyType"/>
   <complexType name="bodyType">
     <attribute name="encodingStyle" type="uriReference"
use="optional"/>
     <attribute name="parts" type="NMTOKENS" use="optional"/>
     <attribute name="use" type="soap:useChoice" use="optional"/>
```

```
        <attribute name="namespace" type="uriReference" use=
          "optional"/>
  </complexType>
  <simpleType name="useChoice">
      <restriction base="string">
  <enumeration value="literal"/>
      <enumeration value="encoded"/>
 </restriction>
  </simpleType>
  <element name="fault" type="soap:faultType"/>
  <complexType name="faultType">
      <complexContent>
  <restriction base="soap:bodyType">
  <attribute name="parts" type="NMTOKENS" use="prohibited"/>
  </restriction>
 </complexContent>
 </complexType>
  <element name="header" type="soap:headerType"/>
  <complexType name="headerType">
      <all>
          <element ref="soap:headerfault">
      </all>
      <attribute name="message" type="QName" use="required"/>
      <attribute name="parts" type="NMTOKENS" use="required"/>
      <attribute name="use" type="soap:useChoice" use="required"/>
        <attribute name="encodingStyle" type="uriReference"
use="optional"/>
      <attribute name="namespace" type="uriReference" use=
          "optional"/>
  </complexType>
  <element name="headerfault" type="soap:headerfaultType"/>
  <complexType name="headerfaultType">
      <attribute name="message" type="QName" use="required"/>
      <attribute name="parts" type="NMTOKENS" use="required"/>
      <attribute name="use" type="soap:useChoice" use="required"/>
      <attribute name="encodingStyle" type="uriReference"
use="optional"/>
      <attribute name="namespace" type="uriReference" use=
          "optional"/>
  </complexType>
  <element name="address" type="soap:addressType"/>
  <complexType name="addressType">
      <attribute name="location" type="uriReference" use=
          "required"/>
  </complexType>
</schema>
```

A 4.3 HTTP Binding Schema

```
<schema xmlns="http://www.w3.org/2000/10/XMLSchema"
        xmlns:http="http://schemas.xmlsoap.org/wsdl/http/"
        targetNamespace="http://schemas.xmlsoap.org/wsdl/http/">
   <element name="address" type="http:addressType"/>
   <complexType name="addressType">
     <attribute name="location" type="uriReference" use=
       "required"/>
   </complexType>
   <element name="binding" type="http:bindingType"/>
   <complexType name="bindingType">
      <attribute name="verb" type="NMTOKEN" use="required"/>
   </complexType>
   <element name="operation" type="http:operationType"/>
   <complexType name="operationType">
      <attribute name="location" type="uriReference" use=
        "required"/>
   </complexType>
   <element name="urlEncoded">
      <complexType>
  </complexType>
   </element>
   <element name="urlReplacement">
      <complexType>
 </complexType>
   </element>
</schema>
```

A 4.4 MIME Binding Schema

```
<schema   targetNamespace="http://schemas.xmlsoap.org/
  wsdl/mime/"
        xmlns:mime="http://schemas.xmlsoap.org/wsdl/mime/"
        xmlns="http://www.w3.org/2000/10/XMLSchema">
   <element name="content" type="mime:contentType"/>
   <complexType name="contentType" content="empty">
     <attribute name="type" type="string" use="optional"/>
     <attribute name="part" type="NMTOKEN" use="optional"/>
   </complexType>
   <element name="multipartRelated" type="mime:multipartRelated
   Type"/>
   <complexType name="multipartRelatedType" content="elementOnly">
     <element ref="mime:part" minOccurs="0" maxOccurs=
       "unbounded"/>
```

```
  </complexType>
  <element name="part" type="mime:partType"/>
  <complexType name="partType" content="elementOnly">
      <any namespace="targetNamespace" minOccurs="0"
maxOccurs="unbounded"/>
      <attribute name="name" type="NMTOKEN" use="required"/>
  </complexType>
  <element name="mimeXml" type="mime:mimeXmlType"/>
  <complexType name="mimeXmlType" content="empty">
      <attribute name="part" type="NMTOKEN" use="optional"/>
  </complexType>
</schema>
```

CHAPTER
12

WSDL 1.1   External Hyperlinks

The following external hyperlinks appear in the text of the Web Service Definition Language (WSDL) 1.1 W3C Note found in the preceding chapter. These hyperlinks appear in the preceding chapter as <u>underlined text</u> and refer to external resources referenced by the WSDL 1.1 specification (such as email addresses and Web pages). The URL corresponding to each of these external links is provided here as a convenience to readers of this book.

Hyperlink Name	Uniform Resource Locator (URL)
Web Service Definition Language (WSDL)	http://www.w3.org/TR/wsdl
Web Service Definition Language (WSDL)	http://www.w3.org/TR/2001/NOTE-wsdl-20010315
Erik Christensen	mailto:erikc@microsoft.com
Francisco Curbera	mailto:curbera@us.ibm.com
Greg Meredith	mailto:gregmer@microsoft.com
Sanjiva Weerawarana	mailto:sanjiva@us.ibm.com
Ariba	http://www.ariba.com/
International Business Machines Corporation	http://www.ibm.com/
World Wide Web Consortium	http://www.w3.org/
Microsoft	http://www.microsoft.com/
World Wide Web Consortium	http://www.w3.org/
Submission Request	http://www.w3.org/Submission/2001/07/
W3C Staff Comment	http://www.w3.org/Submission/2001/07/Comment
W3C XML Activity on XML Protocols	http://www.w3.org/2000/xp/
Acknowledged Submissions to W3C	http://www.w3.org/Submission/
W3C Technical Reports and Publications	http://www.w3.org/TR/
QName	http://www.w3.org/TR/xmlschema-2/#QName
RFC 2119	http://www.normos.org/ietf/rfc/rfc2119.txt
RFC 2396	http://www.normos.org/ietf/rfc/rfc2396.txt
Forms in HTML documents	http://www.w3.org/TR/html401/interact/forms.html#submit-format
Performance, Implementation, and Design Notes	http://www.w3.org/TR/html401/appendix/notes.html#ampersands-in-uris
Form content types	http://www.w3.org/TR/html401/interact/forms.html#h-17.13.4

Simple Object Access Protocol (SOAP) 1.1	http://www.w3.org/TR/2000/NOTE-SOAP-20000508/
XML Schema Part 1: Structures	http://www.w3.org/TR/xmlschema-1/
XML Schema Part 2: Datatypes	http://www.w3.org/TR/xmlschema-2/
Uniform Resource Identifiers (URI): Generic Syntax	http://www.normos.org/ietf/rfc/rfc2396.txt.

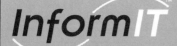

Solutions from experts you know and trust.

| Articles | Free Library | eBooks | Expert Q & A | Training | Career Center | Downloads | MyInformIT |

Login   Register   About InformIT

Topics
Operating Systems
Web Development
Programming
Networking
Certification
and more...

Expert Access

Free Content

www.informit.com

✓ Free, in-depth articles and supplements

✓ Master the skills you need, when you need them

✓ Choose from industry leading books, ebooks, and training products

✓ Get answers when you need them - from live experts or InformIT's comprehensive library

✓ Achieve industry certification and advance your career

Visit *InformIT* today and get great content from PH PTR

Prentice Hall and InformIT are trademarks of Pearson plc /
Copyright © 2000 Pearson

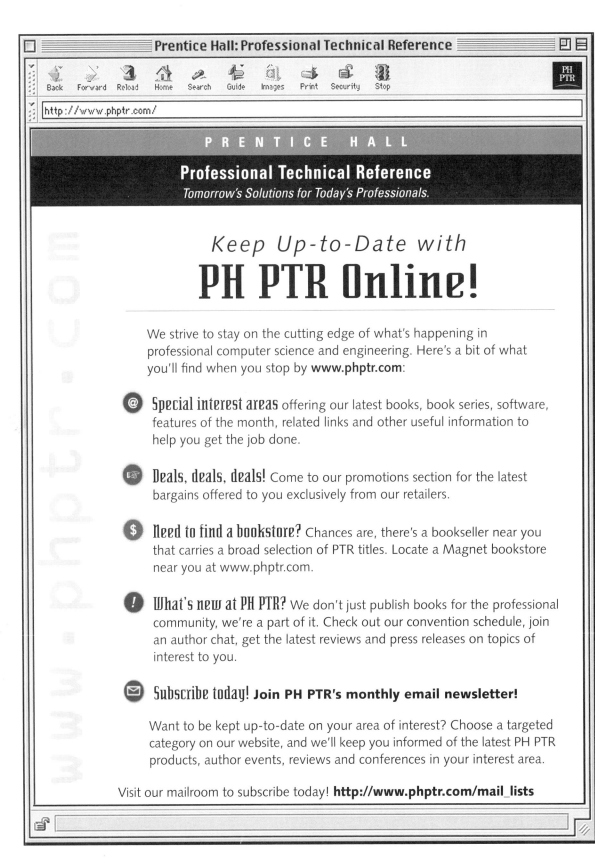

Prentice Hall: Professional Technical Reference

http://www.phptr.com/

PRENTICE HALL

Professional Technical Reference
Tomorrow's Solutions for Today's Professionals.

Keep Up-to-Date with
PH PTR Online!

We strive to stay on the cutting edge of what's happening in professional computer science and engineering. Here's a bit of what you'll find when you stop by **www.phptr.com**:

Special interest areas offering our latest books, book series, software, features of the month, related links and other useful information to help you get the job done.

Deals, deals, deals! Come to our promotions section for the latest bargains offered to you exclusively from our retailers.

Need to find a bookstore? Chances are, there's a bookseller near you that carries a broad selection of PTR titles. Locate a Magnet bookstore near you at www.phptr.com.

What's new at PH PTR? We don't just publish books for the professional community, we're a part of it. Check out our convention schedule, join an author chat, get the latest reviews and press releases on topics of interest to you.

Subscribe today! **Join PH PTR's monthly email newsletter!**

Want to be kept up-to-date on your area of interest? Choose a targeted category on our website, and we'll keep you informed of the latest PH PTR products, author events, reviews and conferences in your interest area.

Visit our mailroom to subscribe today! **http://www.phptr.com/mail_lists**